The Evolution of Canadian Literature in English 1945-1970

The Evolution of Canadian Literature in English 1945-1970

Edited by
Paul Denham

Holt, Rinehart and Winston of Canada, Limited
Toronto   Montreal

Distributed in the United States of America by Winston Press, Minneapolis

Other Titles in the Series

The Evolution of Canadian Literature in English: Beginnings to 1867
Edited by Mary Jane Edwards, Carleton University, Ottawa

The Evolution of Canadian Literature in English 1867-1914
Edited by Mary Jane Edwards, Paul Denham, University of Saskatchewan, and
George L. Parker, Royal Military College of Canada, Kingston, Ontario

The Evolution of Canadian Literature in English 1914-1945
Edited by George L. Parker

General Editor:

Mary Jane Edwards
Assistant Professor,
Department of English,
Carleton University,
Ottawa.

Printed in Canada
1 2 3 4 5   77 76 75 74 73

Preface

Two years ago I agreed to be general editor of a series of anthologies designed to show the development of Canadian literature in English from its beginnings to the present. At that point I asked Paul Denham to prepare the volume on contemporary Canadian literature. *Evolution of Canadian Literature in English 1945-1970* is the result of his response to my request. Certain aspects of this anthology, however, have been shaped by our joint editorial decisions; others, as the saying goes, by circumstances beyond our control.

We agreed, for example, to select for this anthology only works which could be published in their entirety. This means that we have confined our choices of fiction to short stories. It also means that we have used selections which are non-fiction for some novelists who have written few or no short stories but whom we wished to include in this anthology. Thus, Hugh MacLennan, probably the most widely-read Canadian novelist since 1945, and Mordecai Richler, possibly the most exciting Canadian novelist since the fifties, are each represented by an essay.

These essays, however, reveal another editorial decision. We wished to show what significant Canadian writers have been thinking about important issues in contemporary Canadian society. MacLennan's essay about the de-Canadianization of Canadian universities and Richler's about Quebec in the sixties are, therefore, here for the positive reason that each considers a problem worrying many Canadians today. George Grant's essay is included for the same reason.

A third editorial decision concerned the organization of this anthology. With its lengthy general introduction and its short introduction to each of the authors, it follows a pattern established for all four volumes in the *Evolution of Canadian Literature* series. In each the "Introduction" attempts to trace and interpret the history of Canadian literature in English in a specific period and to justify to some extent the choice of authors and works in the volume itself. The short introduction for each author aims to fill in details about the writer's life and works.

To interpret a body of literature and to select representative authors and works are probably the most complex problems which an anthologist has to solve. It is particularly difficult to offer a coherent interpretation of contemporary literature, writing which by its very nature is still in the making. Thus, while I think that Paul Denham's reading of contemporary Canadian literature in the "Introduction" to this volume is both wise and just, each reader must decide for himself about it and the literature that it discusses.

Criticisms, too, can always be levelled at the anthologist for his selection of authors and works. We have tried to be as eclectic as possible in our choice of both, but personal preferences have swayed us. I, for example, demanded that a short story by Ethel Wilson be included. Paul Denham was equally adamant that Milton Acorn be in. I pushed strongly for Irving Layton's "A Tall Man Executes a Jig"; Paul, equally firmly for Layton's "Confederation Ode." The selections, in fact, are the result of many lists of "absolute necessities," "strong probabilities," and "weak possibilities."

These, then, are some editorial decisions which we made both while the *Evolution of Canadian Literature in English 1945-1970* was being planned and while it was being prepared. Other decisions were made for us. One author refused to allow his work to be published by a company with American connections. Very high permission fees restricted our choice of other authors and works. Limitations of space had us jigging occasionally as craftily as Layton's "tall man." But, on the whole, we have included the selections we wished, and when we changed dancers, we did not break the patterns of the dance. And the dance of Canadian literature in English from 1945 to 1970 is, after all, the subject of this anthology.

Ottawa,   Mary Jane Edwards
June, 1972

Contents

Preface   v

Introduction   1

Ethel Wilson   13

       Mrs. Golightly and Other Stories (1961)
       The Window   14

Earle Birney   24

       Selected Poems (1966)
       David   25
       Anglosaxon Street   31
       The Road to Nijmégen   33
       From the Hazel Bough   34
       Canada: Case History   35
       Bushed   36
       The Bear on the Delhi Road   37
       El Greco: *Espolio*   38

       Rag and Bone Shop (1971)
       Like an Eddy   39

       The Creative Writer (1966)
       Experimentation Today   40

Hugh MacLennan   49

       The Struggle for Canadian Universities (1969)
       Address to the Montreal Symposium on De-Canadianization   50

Irving Layton   57

> *Collected Poems* (1965)
> The Birth of Tragedy   58
> Song for Naomi   59
> The Bull Calf   60
> On Seeing the Statuettes of Ezekiel and Jeremiah in the Church of
>   Notre Dame   61
> Whatever Else Poetry is Freedom   62
> Keine Lazarovitch, 1870-1959   64
> A Tall Man Executes a Jig   64
>
> *Periods of the Moon* (1967)
> Confederation Ode   67
> Above All, Avoid Halitosis   68
>
> *A Red Carpet for the Sun* (1959)
> Foreword   69

Hugh Garner   72

> *Hugh Garner's Best Stories* (1963)
> One-Two-Three Little Indians   73

W. O. Mitchell   81

> *Jake and the Kid* (1961)
> Two Kinds of Sinner   82

Margaret Avison   88

> *The Book of Canadian Poetry* (1957)
> Neverness, or, The One Ship Beached on One Far Distant Shore   89
> The Butterfly   91
>
> *Winter Sun* (1960)
> New Year's Poem   92
> Butterfly Bones; or, Sonnet against Sonnets   93
> Snow   93
> Apocalyptic?   94
> Grammarian on a Lakefront Parkbench   95
> The Swimmer's Moment   95

Origin, No. 4 (January, 1962)
Waking Up   96

The Dumbfounding (1966)
First   96
The Dumbfounding   97

George Grant   99

Technology and Empire (1969)
Canadian Fate and Imperialism   100

Al Purdy   110

Poems for All the Annettes (1962; 1968)
Mind Process re a Faucet   111

The Cariboo Horses (1965)
The Country North of Belleville   112
The Cariboo Horses   114
Hockey Players   115

North of Summer (1967)
Innuit   117

Wild Grape Wine (1968)
Wilderness Gothic   119
Lament for the Dorsets   120

Raymond Souster   122

The Colour of the Times (1964)
The Hunter   123
Dominion Square   124
Lagoons, Hanlan's Point   124
Downtown Corner News Stand   125
The Flight of the Roller-Coaster   126
The Six-Quart Basket   126

Ten Elephants on Yonge Street (1965)
This Lizard of Summer   127
Maryrose Visits the Stock Exchange   127
Walking River Ice   128

As Is (1967)
So Easy to Explain   128
The Cry   129

Lost and Found (1968)
The Pouring   129
Killing a Bat   130

So Far So Good (1969)
Weeping Willow in Winter   131
Pomegranates in Studio One   131

Mavis Gallant   133

My Heart is Broken (1964)
My Heart is Broken   134

Eli Mandel   139

Trio (1954)
Estevan Saskatchewan   140
IV (from Minotaur Poems)   140

Fuseli Poems (1960)
A Castle and Two Inhabitants   141
Notes from the Underground   143

Black and Secret Man (1964)
Black and Secret Man   144
Day of Atonement, Standing   144

An Idiot Joy (1967)
Houdini   145
Pictures in an Institution   146

Milton Acorn   148

I've Tasted My Blood (1969)
Charlottetown Harbor   149
Lyric   149
I've Tasted My Blood   150
Poem with Fat Cats in the Background   151
Sky's Poem for Christmas   151

Knowing I Live in a Dark Age   153
I Shout Love   154

Margaret Laurence   159

The Tomorrow-Tamer (1963)
The Drummer of All the World   160

James Reaney   171

Twelve Letters to a Small Town (1962)
First Letter: to the Avon River above Stratford, Canada   172

The Killdeer and Other Plays (1962)
One-Man Masque   173

Alphabet, No. 4 (June, 1962)
Editorial   190

Hugh Hood   191

Flying a Red Kite (1962)
Flying a Red Kite   192

Alice Munro   200

Dance of the Happy Shades (1968)
A Trip to the Coast   201

Mordecai Richler   212

Tamarack Review, No. 34 (Winter, 1965)
"Quebec Oui, Ottawa Non!"   213

Alden Nowlan   227

Wind in a Rocky Country (1960)
God Sour the Milk of the Knacking Wench   228

The Things Which Are (1962)
The Bull Moose   228
Canadian Love Song   229

Bread, Wine, and Salt (1967)
And He Wept Aloud, so that the Egyptians Heard It   230
Daughter of Zion   231
For Jean Vincent d'Abbadie, Baron St. Castin   232

The Mysterious Naked Man (1969)
Greatness   233
The Mysterious Naked Man   233
The People Who Are Gone   234

Leonard Cohen   235

Let Us Compare Mythologies (1956)
For Wilf and his House   236
Warning   237

The Spice-Box of Earth (1961)
A Kite is a Victim   238
You Have the Lovers   239
For Anne   240

Flowers for Hitler (1964)
The Only Tourist in Havana Turns his Thoughts Homeward   240
All There is to Know about Adolph Eichmann   242

Parasites of Heaven (1966)
Suzanne Takes You Down   242

Songs of Leonard Cohen (1967)
The Stranger Song   244

Songs from a Room (1969)
Story of Isaac   246

John Newlove   248

Moving in Alone (1965)
Kamsack   249
Vancouver   249
By the Church Wall   249

Black Night Window (1968)
The Hitchhiker   251
The Pride   252

xii

The Cave (1970)
The Flower   258

Margaret Atwood   259

The Circle Game (1966)
This is a Photograph of Me   260
The City Planners   261

The Animals in that Country (1968)
Provisions   262
The Animals in that Country   263
Backdrop Addresses Cowboy   264

The Journals of Susanna Moodie (1970)
Further Arrivals   265
The Two Fires   266
Thoughts from Underground   268

Procedures for Underground (1970)
Two Gardens   269

Power Politics (1971)
You Fit into Me   270

b p Nichol   271

Journeyings and the Returns (1967)
Turnips   272
To a Loved One   273
1335 Comox Avenue   274

Gordon to Watkins to You (1970)
Inquiry of Ministry/Demande de Renseignements au Gouvernement   275

Concrete Poetry (1968)
Love   282

The Cosmic Chef (1970)
Untitled   283

Bibliography   285

Acknowledgments

Ethel Wilson. "The Window," from *Mrs. Golightly and Other Stories* by Ethel Wilson. Reprinted by permission of The Macmillan Company of Canada Limited and Macmillan, London and Basingstoke.

Earle Birney. "David," "The Road to Nijmégen," "From the Hazel Bough," "Canada: Case History," "Anglosaxon Street," "Bushed," "El Greco: *Espolio*," "The Bear on the Delhi Road," from *Selected Poems* by Earle Birney. "Like an Eddy," from *Rag and Bone Shop* by Earle Birney. Reprinted by permission of The Canadian Publishers, McClelland and Stewart Limited, Toronto. "Experimentation Today," from *The Creative Writer* by Earle Birney. Copyright © by Canadian Broadcasting Corporation, 1966. CBC Learning Systems, Toronto.

Hugh MacLennan. "Address to the Montreal Symposium on De-Canadianization," from *The Struggle for Canadian Universities* edited by Robin Mathews and James Steele. Toronto: new press, 1970. Reprinted by permission of the author.

Irving Layton. "The Birth of Tragedy," "The Bull Calf," "Song for Naomi," "Keine Lazarovitch, 1870-1959," "A Tall Man Executes a Jig," "On Seeing the Statuettes of Ezekiel and Jeremiah in the Church of Notre Dame," "Whatever Else Poetry is Freedom," from *Collected Poems* by Irving Layton. "Confederation Ode," "Above All, Avoid Halitosis," from *Periods of the Moon* by Irving Layton. "Foreword" to *A Red Carpet for the Sun* by Irving Layton. Reprinted by permission of The Canadian Publishers, McClelland and Stewart Limited, Toronto.

Hugh Garner. "One-Two-Three Little Indians," from *Hugh Garner's Best Stories* by Hugh Garner. Toronto: Ryerson Press. Reprinted by permission of the author.

W. O. Mitchell. "Two Kinds of Sinner," from *Jake and the Kid* by W. O. Mitchell. Reprinted by permission of The Macmillan Company of Canada Limited and Collins-Knowlton-Wing Inc. Copyright © 1961 W. O. Mitchell.

Margaret Avison. "Neverness, or, the One Ship Beached on One Far Distant Shore," "The Butterfly," from *The Book of Canadian Poetry*, edited by A.J.M. Smith. Toronto: Gage Educational Publishing Limited. Reprinted by permission of the author. "New Year's Poem," "Butterfly Bones; or, Sonnet against Sonnets," "Snow," "Apocalyptic?" "Grammarian on a Lakefront Parkbench," "The Swimmer's Moment," from *Winter Sun* by Margaret Avison. Toronto: University of Toronto Press. Reprinted by permission of the author. "Waking Up" from *Thirteen Poems, Origin*, No. 4, January, 1962. Reprinted by permission of the author. "First," "The Dumbfounding," reprinted from *The Dumbfounding*, poems by Margaret Avison. By permission of W. W. Norton and Company, Inc. Copyright © 1966 by Margaret Avison.

George Grant. "Canadian Fate and Imperialism," from *Technology and Empire: Perspectives on North America* by George Grant. Reprinted by permission of House of Anansi Press Limited, Toronto.

Introduction

Although the fixing of limits to historical periods is an arbitrary business at best, the period since 1945 may conveniently be considered as a unit in the history of Canadian society and literature. Since the end of World War II, Canada has found herself, to an unprecedented extent, dominated by American mass media and progressively drawn into the sphere of influence of the United States in military and economic matters. The country is no longer primarily agrarian and rural; the basis of the economy has become increasingly industrial, and the population increasingly urban. In literature, writers who had established reputations in the nineteen-twenties and thirties — Morley Callaghan, F. R. Scott, Dorothy Livesay, E. J. Pratt, for example — continued to publish, but the immediate postwar years were also marked by the emergence of a significant number of new voices. Earle Birney's first book of poetry had been published in 1942; P. K. Page, Irving Layton, Raymond Souster, and James Reaney, among others, published their first books of poetry in the years immediately after 1945. At the same time, Ethel Wilson, W. O. Mitchell, and Hugh Garner appeared as important new writers of fiction. Since both Canadian poetry and Canadian fiction in English have been subject to many different influences since 1945, tracing the development of this literature is a complex task. A discussion of the social background of this postwar period, however, will be a useful preliminary to a treatment of the literature.

The extent of American influence in Canada has provided an important subject for debate since the end of World War II. Donald Creighton argues, in fact, that the two major influences on Canadian life have always been the United States and Great Britain and that the first real test of where Canada's allegiance would lie in the postwar period was over the issue of the recognition of the People's Republic of China, proclaimed in 1949.[1] Great Britain and most members of the British Commonwealth recognized the new Communist government in Peking as the legitimate government. Canada, however, followed the lead of the United States Department of State in denying recognition. Although she has now recognized China, Canada has mostly continued to support, though sometimes with reservations, the American crusade against Communism. The nineteen-fifties were prosperous as industry expanded, but during the nineteen-sixties it became increasingly clear that industrialization depended on foreign, principally American, capital, and that, as a result, Americans

1

were assuming control of an increasing proportion of the Canadian economy. This first became a serious political issue in the Pipeline Debate of 1956; in the late nineteen-sixties it became once more a hot political subject. There is still, however, no agreement in Canada on "de-Canadianization." George Grant's essay, "Canadian Fate and Imperialism," reflects one viewpoint. Grant attempts to see Canada's present in the light of modern technology and the whole history of Western civilization.

During this period too, industrialization led to demands for more and better educational facilities. The problem of raising postsecondary educational standards also contributed to the debate about Canadian-American relations. Because of previous underdevelopment of Canadian graduate schools, it was not always possible to staff new or expanded institutions with Canadian teachers; consequently a number of non-Canadian teachers, many of them Americans, were hired. Some people, while recognizing the obvious advantages of this development for Canadian colleges and universities, worried that the high proportion of American teachers might result in the Americanizing of the values of a whole generation. Hugh MacLennan's "Address to the Montreal Symposium on De-Canadianization" reflects both the nationalist side of the argument and some objections to be made to it. Relations between the United States and Canada thus form a continuing theme in Canadian writing. They have provided material not only for essayists but also for poets. Margaret Atwood's "Backdrop addresses cowboy" and b p Nichol's "Inquiry of Ministry . . . " show that this theme is capable of poetic treatment.

An equally important issue during the present period, as throughout Canadian history, has been the role of French-speaking Canadians within Confederation. During World War II, this question was raised in the form of the Conscription Crisis, but between 1945 and 1960, under Duplessis and the Union Nationale government in Quebec, it remained ostensibly dormant. Beneath the surface, however, were developing social tensions which were released by the electoral victory of the Lesage government in 1960 and by its reform program. The history of Quebec nationalism in the nineteen-sixties is a complicated one and cannot be told here.[2] Viewpoints on it are legion; one, that of Mordecai Richler, is represented in "Quebec Oui, Ottawa Non." Richler, having come from a working-class Jewish area in Montreal, can in his essay view with some scepticism the claims of both English and French Quebeckers. Among English-speaking writers of fiction, there has been a growing interest in exploring this aspect of Canadian society; Hugh MacLennan's two books, *Two Solitudes* (1945) and *Return of the Sphinx* (1967), Ellis Portal's *Killing Ground* (1968), and James Bacque's *The Lonely Ones* (1969) are obvious examples of fictional treatments of this theme. In poetry there has been little of importance on this subject since Klein's experiments with "bilingual" poetry and F. R. Scott's "Bonne Entente." Irving Layton, however, has dealt with the collision of Catholic and Jewish cultures in Montreal in his poem "On Seeing the Statuettes of Ezekiel and Jeremiah in the Church of Notre Dame."

Both these themes — Quebec's role in Confederation and Canada's relations with the United States — indicate the continuing interest of Canadian writers in discussing the kind of society Canada should have. Much of the fictional and nonfictional prose writing about Canadian social problems reflects considerable pessimism and a continuing sense of crisis. Scott and Layton, however, show that these same problems can be treated in comic or satirical terms. Earle Birney's "Canada: Case History" is a classic example of a satirical anatomizing of Canadian society; Leonard Cohen's "The Only Tourist in Havana" is in this same tradition.

Public issues may be used as subject matter for literature, but literature also deals with private and individual matters. Thus, other influences besides those of Canadian society have helped shape recent Canadian literature in English. In poetry, especially, these influences have been complex and diversified. They have resulted in a poetry which exhibits much variety and which has been marked by controversies among poets about the nature of poetry itself. A discussion of "schools" of poetry is always of limited value in explaining the literary history of a period. It involves categorizing poets, and many poets do not belong in categories. Still, a discussion of controversies can cast some light on the literary ideas which have helped to shape contemporary Canadian poetry.

Ralph Gustafson says that the poetry of the nineteen-sixties is divided between "the Yeats/Eliot axis [and] the Pound/Williams axis."[3] To some extent this division can be traced through the whole history of modern Canadian poetry. In the nineteen-forties it took the form of a rivalry between two groups of poets in Montreal, a rivalry chronicled by Wynne Francis in "Montreal Poets of the Forties."[4] Associated with Patrick Anderson's little magazine *Preview* (1942-1945) were such established poets as F. R. Scott and A. M. Klein, as well as younger ones like P. K. Page. These poets tended to be intellectuals and professional people, politically left-wing; their poetry, influenced by Eliot, Spender, and Auden, was complex, metaphysical, and sometimes propagandist. P. K. Page's poem "The Stenographers,"[5] possibly her best-known work, illustrates a complex metaphorical style and an interest in social pressures on the individual:

> After the brief bivouac of Sunday,
> their eyes, in the forced march of Monday to Saturday,
> hoist the white flag, flutter in the snow-storm of paper,
> haul it down and crack in the mid-sun of temper.
>
> In the pause between the first draft and the carbon
> they glimpse the smooth hours when they were children —
> the ride in the ice-cart, the ice-man's name,
> the end of the route and the long walk home;
>
> remember the sea where floats at high tide
> were sea marrows growing on the scatter-green vine
> or spools of grey toffee, or wasps' nests on water;
> remember the sand and the leaves of the country.
>
> Bell rings and they go and the voice draws their pencil
> like a sled across snow; when its runners are frozen

3

rope snaps and the voice then is pulling no burden
but runs like a dog on the winter of paper.

Their climates are winter and summer — no wind
for the kites of their hearts — no wind for a flight;
a breeze at the most, to tumble them over
and leave them like rubbish — the boy-friends of blood.

In the inch of the noon as they move they are stagnant.
The terrible calm of the noon is their anguish;
the lip of the counter, the shapes of the straws
like icicles breaking their tongues, are invaders.

Their beds are their oceans — salt water of weeping
the waves that they know — the tide before sleep;
and fighting to drown they assemble their sheep
in columns and watch them leap desks for their fences
and stare at them with their own mirror-worn faces.

In the felt of the morning the calico-minded,
sufficiently starched, insert papers, hit keys,
efficient and sure as their adding machines;
yet they weep in the vault, they are taut as net curtains
stretched upon frames. In their eyes I have seen
the pin men of madness in marathon trim
race round the track of the stadium pupil.

Critical of the wit and sophistication of these poets and distrustful of their acknowledged dependence on British models, John Sutherland, Irving Layton, and Louis Dudek, editors of a rival magazine *First Statement* (1942-1945), preferred direct and passionate statements of experience more in the tradition of American poets such as Walt Whitman, Hart Crane, and Ezra Pound. Though the rivalry between the poets of *Preview* and those of *First Statement* had its origin during the war years, it continued after 1945, even when the two magazines were merged to form *Northern Review* (1945-1956).

The career of Irving Layton is especially instructive about this whole period in the development of Canadian poetry. His interest in American poetry is indicated by the fact that he was a contributing editor for the short-lived but influential American poetry magazine *Black Mountain Review* (1954-1957), the mouthpiece for the "Black Mountain" poets who were to have an important influence on Canadian poetry. Also, he can be considered partly responsible for the change in the audience for poetry in Canada. In 1945 poetry was still a coterie activity. Layton, however, conceiving of a prophetic role for the poet, attacked not only the poetry of intellect and wit, but also what he considered to be the arid intellectualism of Canadian literary criticism and the philistinism and puritanism of Anglo-Saxon society in Canada. His own poetry was often as complex and as metaphysical as that of his rivals, but he refused to consider poetry as the preserve of an intellectual elite. His running quarrels with the academic world and with his fellow poets were in some respects attention-getting devices, but to many he represented a liberating voice. In 1959 his volume of poetry, *A Red Carpet for the Sun*, became something of a Canadian best seller; since then the audience for poetry in Canada has steadily widened.[6]

Raymond Souster was another poet published in *First Statement*. Although his personal and poetic styles were somewhat more understated than Layton's, he too argued for a poetry of direct experience. His little magazine *Contact* (1952-1954) represented a further attempt to reduce Canadian poets' dependence on British models by publishing poems by Canadians alongside work by Americans and translations of European poets. Notable among the American writers were Cid Corman, Robert Creeley, and Charles Olson, who were associated with the Black Mountain poets.

A quite different kind of poetry has been produced by a group of poets who were influenced by the teaching and criticism of Northrop Frye at the University of Toronto in the nineteen-fifties. Usually referred to as "mythopoeic," their most notable members are James Reaney, Jay Macpherson, and Eli Mandel. Their wit, allusiveness, and interest in the formal principles of poetry produced precisely the kind of poetry to which Layton and Souster objected. For these poets myths are not only ways of making man's surroundings comprehensible to him; they are also structural patterns underlying all literature and inherent in the nature of poetic language. In an article on Jay Macpherson, Reaney discusses this idea:

> ...the very process of being interested in metaphor evidently must lead to an interest in giant and mythical figures. Once you start saying that "my love is like a red, red rose", you might as well start saying that she is like a great many other beautiful things as well, and then of course if she really is a goddess she is like everything, because a goddess isn't a goddess unless she can control both beautiful and ugly things, even things indifferent. So she is everything and contains all the things she is like. If anything is like anything (metaphor), it eventually is everything (myth)....[7]

Thus, for example, Mandel's Minotaur poems use classical myth to provide a framework for comments on contemporary life.

Because her major work, *The Boatman* (1957), is a book of carefully related lyrics which suffer when removed from their context, Jay Macpherson has, with regret, been omitted from this collection.

> Show pity, Reader, for my plight:
> Let be, or else consume me quite,[8]

she pleads. "The Beauty of Job's Daughters,"[9] however, is a later poem, not part of the original *Boatman* sequence:

The old, the mad, the blind have fairest daughters.
Take Job: the beasts the accuser sends at evening
Shoulder his house and shake it; he's not there,
Attained in age to inwardness of daughters,
In all the land no women found so fair.

Angels and sons of God are nearest neighbours,
And even the accuser may repair
To walk with Job in pleasures of his daughters:
Wide shining rooms more warmly lit at evening,
Gardens beyond whose secrets scent the air.

Not wiles of men nor envy of the neighbours,
Riches of earth, nor what heaven holds more rare,
Can take from Job the beauty of his daughters,
The gardens in the rock, music at evening,
And cup so full that all who come must share.

Perhaps we passed them? it was late, or evening,
And surely those were desert stumps, not
    daughters,
In fact we doubt that they were ever there.
The old, the mad, the blind have fairest daughters.
In all the land no women found so fair.

After 1960, Vancouver, which had long provided a home for Earle Birney, became an important creative centre for many younger poets. Warren Tallman has explained how the visits of the American poets Robert Duncan and Robert Creeley to the University of British Columbia in the early sixties stimulated students Frank Davey, George Bowering, Fred Wah, James Reid, and Dave Dawson to found a little mimeographed magazine *Tish* (1961-   ), in which the theory and practice of the Black Mountain poets — Duncan, Creeley, and Charles Olson, among others — were enthusiastically discussed and served as a kind of catalyst for new poetry.[10] These poets had already, of course, influenced Canadian poetry through Layton and Souster.

One of the principal tenets of the Black Mountain creed is expressed in the term "organic form." This means that poetic form does not exist independent of experience (as the criticism of Northrop Frye might be thought to imply), but that experience creates its own form. Experience must be treated directly, without complicated reinforcement by myth or religion; the "image" is all important. Also, poetic rhythm depends primarily on speech rhythms, and poetry must return to its origins as a spoken art. Charles Olson writes that

> [the poet] is not free to be a part of, or to be any sect; . . . there are no symbols to him, there are only his own composed forms, and each one solely the issue of the time of the moment of its creation, not any ultimate except what he in his heart and that instant in its solidity yield.[11]

6

This aesthetic is exemplified by George Bowering's poem "A Sudden Measure":[12]

> This sudden snow:
>   immediately
> the prairie is!
>
> Those houses are:
>   dark
> under roofs of snow —
>
> That hill up to the cloud is:
>   marked
> by snow creeks down to town —
>
> This footpath is:
>   a bare line
> across white field —
>
>   This woman appears
>   thru drift of snow:
>
> a red coat.

Here Bowering implies that the prairie's importance for the poet does not reside in its symbolic value or its place in a mythological framework; rather, what matters is the existential presence of the prairie at that particular moment.

The Black Mountain movement has had far-ranging effects, some of which Earle Birney traces in his essay "Experimentation Today." John Newlove's poetry shows its influence, although Newlove himself was never actually part of the *Tish* group. Not surprisingly, this movement has generated a certain amount of theoretical controversy, especially about the practice of the mythopoeic poets whose concept of poetry is quite different from that of the Black Mountain poets. Raymond Souster's anthology, *New Wave Canada* (1966), indicates his own sympathy with the poets in this tradition, his belief that the Black Mountain poets and their precursors, Pound and Williams, are the most fruitful influences on modern Canadian poetry, and his scepticism about the accomplishments of mythopoeic writing. In a prefatory note, he states that

> the most important fact for Canadian poetry has been that Canada is situated on the northern border of the United States of America. But until the early 1940's, no one would have been remotely aware of this given the poetry written before that time. In that decade two or three Canadian poets began to read and be influenced by the work of certain modern American poets, most notably Ezra Pound and William Carlos Williams, and several others to a lesser degree. This forward progress was negated almost entirely by developments in our literary situation in the 1950's, but by the end of this largely reactionary period had begun slowly to recover its initial impetus. Since then it has never looked back.[13]

Although his dedication of *New Wave Canada* "to W. W. E. Ross, the first modern Canadian poet," indicates a desire to trace a Canadian ancestry for this type of poetry, the preface to Souster's *Made in Canada* (1970), his recent anthology of Canadian poetry, stresses once again the debt which Canadian poets owe to modern American poets.

Still, it is not possible to divide all the poets into two groups, as this discussion may have implied. Earle Birney, for example, has in his recent poetry shown some of the Black Mountain interest in speech rhythms and "breath," but he has also assimilated many other influences as well — an interest in the narrative form, the stress patterns of Old English poetry, and the visual possibilities of concrete poetry. Similarly, while Margaret Avison has been called a mythopoeic poet by Desmond Pacey[14] and a metaphysical by George Woodcock, [15] she has been associated with the Black Mountain group by her American publishers. [16] Irving Layton, as has been indicated, is an equally complicated case. The classification of these and many other poets according to "schools" of poetry is difficult and not particularly useful; they are interesting precisely because their work combines a number of influences to create a unique voice.

While the poets of central and western Canada have diverged and converged in various ways in the last twenty-five years, most poets in the Maritimes, especially those associated with the magazine *Fiddlehead* (1945-   ), have shown little inclination to engage in theoretical controversy. They have written, however, some graphically regional poetry. Alden Nowlan, who represents these poets in this collection, presents vignettes of rural life that examine the effects of both economic and spiritual poverty on individuals. Milton Acorn, another Maritimer who has been somewhat neglected, also comments on society, but from a viewpoint of idealistic revolutionary proletarianism unique among English-speaking Canadian poets.

Alfred Purdy, whose roots are in Ontario, might also be called a regionalist in his Ameliasburg poems. He is also, however, the only modern Canadian poet to make an extended attempt to deal with the Canadian north. Margaret Atwood too stands somewhat apart. Her laconic and restrained manner looks rather as if she has been influenced by the West Coast poets. But her surrealistic images of private experience make her poetry quite different from that of most of her contemporaries.

Leonard Cohen, a complex figure, is easily the most popular contemporary Canadian poet, although at times he seems more respected as a culture hero than as a poet. He illustrates an important contemporary phenomenon — the poetic use of the folk song for which Bob Dylan's work is the prototype. Some critics, both musical and literary, doubt that the contemporary folk song is really a proper vehicle for poetry since the words tend to be subordinated to the music.[17] But "Suzanne" was published as a poem, and considered as such, before Cohen recorded it as a song which was received as an important document of the youth culture. Frank Davey is, of course, quite right to insist that the poetry of the folk song be evaluated according to the same standards used in judging any poetry; [18] but if such analysis can be sustained, it means that poetry and song are being reunited to an extent which has not been seen since the death of Ben Jonson. For this trend, significant for both poetry and music, is an important international phenomenon. One might point to several other Canadians, such as Bruce Cockburn, Joni Mitchell, and Gordon Lightfoot, who are part of this development and who have achieved expression in idioms which are very different from, or even antithetical to, Cohen's. Whether the popularization of poetry which is represented by this trend is a positive gain for the cause of poetry may be open to question; Louis Dudek recently complained of "the degeneration of poetry to a teeny-bopper fad."[19] One can also argue, or at least hope, that this trend will result in a greater public sensitivity to poetic language, as it has already resulted in raising the level of popular music.

Another aspect of experimental poetry which has become important in Canada is "concrete" poetry, one of the few poetic movements that is genuinely international in scope. As a movement, its origin was a meeting which took place in Ulm, Germany, in 1955 between the Swiss poet Eugen Gomringer and the Brazilian poet Decio Pignitari. Pignitari had already been associated with Augusto and Haraldo da Campos in the "Noigandres" group of poets in Brazil, but although they and Gomringer had both used the term "concrete" to describe what they were doing, they had previously been unaware of each other's existence.[20] But concrete poetry as a movement began in Germany in 1955; since then, poets in many countries have experimented with it. b p Nichol's recent anthology *The Cosmic Chef* (1970) shows that a wide variety of Canadian poets — Margaret Avison, Earle Birney, and Phyllis Webb, among others — have written concrete poetry. Somewhat difficult to define because of the multiplicity of its manifestations, concrete poetry, like many other new poetic movements, implies a getting rid of worn-out syntax and rhetorical forms. It involves "a concentration upon the physical materials from which the poem is made."[21] Either the visual effect of the letters and words on the page or the sound of words can become an important aspect of the poem's meaning. In Canada, leading concretists have been b p Nichol in Toronto and Bill Bissett in Vancouver. Bissett's sound poetry and some of his visual effects are difficult to reproduce in a conventional anthology, so b p Nichol has been chosen to represent this movement.

Since 1945 Canadian poetry has attracted much critical attention. Canadian fiction, particularly the short story, on the whole, has not. One reason for this critical neglect of the short story is that its writing is often regarded as an apprenticeship for the writing of longer works of fiction. From this point of view, then, a short story is interesting chiefly for the part it plays in the development of the techniques and themes of its author. Another reason for its neglect is that generally the short story is a less controversial form of literature than either poetry or longer fiction. This has its advantages, of course; Dave Godfrey remarks that "the novel and poetry are marked, year by year, with battles between new school and newer school, with changing styles and the influence of theory and of foreign advances, with high sales and critical acclaim. Terrible distractions. Working in the short narrative form I can project, write, and publish a series of ten to fifteen narratives almost entirely on my own. Fertility is all."[22]

There has been a good deal of formal experimentation in fiction in Canada, especially in the nineteen-sixties; a list of the more notable achievements in the area of the experimental novel might include Sheila Watson's *The Double Hook* (1959), Leonard Cohen's *Beautiful Losers* (1966), Graeme Gibson's *Five Legs* (1969), and Dave Godfrey's *The New Ancestors* (1970). In these cases the major experimentation has been in the primacy accorded to language, myth, and symbol over the realistic demands of plot and character. In other words, experimental poetry tends to assimilate elements from music and the visual arts; experimental fiction tends to move closer to poetry. In the short story, there has not been quite the same interest in formal experimentation as in poetry and the novel. There are, of course, exceptions to this statement, such as some of the stories in Godfrey's *Death Goes Better with Coca-Cola* (1967), and Ray Smith's *Cape Breton is the Thought Control Centre of Canada* (1969). But if the short story has been, on the whole, less experimental, less *avant-garde*, and less controversial than other forms, it nevertheless exhibits considerable variety and vitality, and it remains a popular form. Writers like Ethel Wilson, Hugh Garner, and W. O. Mitchell, all of whom began publishing in the years immediately after 1945, wrote short stories as well as longer works of fiction. In the past two decades Mavis Gallant, Hugh Hood, Alice Munro, Mordecai Richler, Margaret Laurence, and many others have continued to explore the possibilities of the short story.

Regionalism, the depiction of a particular physical and social environment and the illustration of its effects, has remained a strongly marked characteristic of the short story. In the work of Mitchell, of Alice Munro, and in Margaret Laurence's *A Bird in the House* (1969), this regionalism is rural, as it has often been in earlier periods. But the continuing urbanization of Canadian society has meant that contemporary rural regional writing is frequently dominated by a nostalgic tone and is often cast in the form of childhood reminiscences. Urbanization has, however, also led to an increased interest in cities as human and fictional environments, and to a kind of urban regionalism in fiction in which the specific social milieu of a particular city or section of a city is rendered. Morley Callaghan's city tends to be anonymous; it could be any one of a number of North American cities. But Ethel Wilson's Vancouver, Garner's Cabbagetown, Richler's St. Urbain Street, and Hugh Hood's Montreal are clearly identifiable.

Canadian fiction in English, however, has not been restricted to Canadian settings. Just as Earle Birney's travels have provided him with poetic material, so Margaret Laurence, Dave Godfrey, and David Knight have, in the sixties, found fictional material in the emerging nations of Africa. It might be argued that the problems of these societies — the conflicting values of different cultural backgrounds and the efforts required to gain and preserve cultural independence and identity — are of special interest to Canadian writers because they are paralleled by similar problems in Canadian society. Also, many talented Canadians have gone to live and work abroad with programs like CUSO and CEDA. It is too soon to tell, but there is enough material to suggest that "fiction about Africa" may be emerging as a significant aspect of Canadian writing. At any rate, one of Margaret Laurence's African stories has been included here to demonstrate how Canadians writing fiction have assimilated non-Canadian material.

Fiction writers in Canada have, in fact, in some ways shown themselves more capable of working in a truly international context than have Canadian poets. Birney's poems inspired by his travels remain, in a sense, the poems of a tourist who looks at an alien set of values from the outside. The writers just mentioned, however, have lived in foreign countries long enough to permit them to approach their values from the inside

— even if, as in the case of Mrs. Laurence's Matthew, the result is a painful knowledge that one is forever "outside" anyway. To this list of temporary expatriates must be added the names of two more permanent expatriates, Mordecai Richler and Mavis Gallant, who still remain identifiably Canadian. Richler's long residence in England, although it may have taught him little about the Canadian scene, has at least permitted him to achieve some aesthetic distance from his own Montreal background. Mrs. Gallant, although she lives in Paris and writes primarily for publication in the United States, continues to make fictional use of her Canadian background.

Donald Stephens has noted the increasing dominance of character over plot in recent short stories.[23] Ethel Wilson's stories are good examples of this trend. Her stories are not neatly plotted, and their incidents often seem trivial, but they reveal her deep interest in human character and psychological states and their manifestations in the ordinary course of life. The stories of Hugh Hood, Alice Munro, and others reveal similar human interests. In fact, this interest is itself a significant area of experimentation in the short story form; it has resulted in a number of stories in which the focus is an internal one, on the thoughts, emotions, and point of view of a single character.

The vigour of the Canadian short story is, on the whole, remarkable in view of the decline in the number of periodical outlets for fiction. Mass-circulation magazines like *Maclean's* and *Saturday Night* stopped publishing fiction in the late nineteen-fifties; thus, among these magazines only *Chatelaine* now publishes short stories. Specialized journals like *Queen's Quarterly*, the *Dalhousie Review*, and the *Canadian Forum* only occasionally publish fiction. Probably the most available outlet now for short stories in Canada is the CBC. Certainly Robert Weaver, through his work on the CBC, his connection with *Tamarack Review*, and his anthologies of short stories, has done much to encourage the writing of short fiction in Canada.

It is still difficult to see the period since 1945 in a clear historical perspective. In many ways Canadian society remains immature and uncertain of its direction. The perennial question "What is a Canadian" which dominated so many conversations about Canada in the fifties and early sixties led Earle Birney to remark that "It's only by our lack of ghosts we're haunted." The nationalism of Centennial year seemed to some people superficial and contrived, and led to such satirical comments as Layton's "Confederation Ode." If, in the last few years, questions about Canadian identity have been heard less often, they have been replaced by a more deeply-rooted uncertainty about whether Canada can long survive in its present form as a united and independent nation.

At the same time, however, it has frequently been suggested that this period marks a maturing of Canadian literature.[24] The most remarkable development, perhaps, has been the increased interest in poetry. In 1945, *Northern Review, Canadian Forum*, and *Contemporary Verse* were almost the only periodicals publishing good Canadian poetry; in 1970 there were poetry magazines (some of them, it must be admitted, of uneven quality and short life) in almost every major urban centre and many of the minor ones. New ones are still springing up all over. If periodical outlets for the short story have not kept pace, there is still no shortage of talented writers interested in working in this form. The Canada Council, established in 1957 to foster scholarship and the arts in Canada, has made money available for writers and little magazines. Universities employ writers and teach Canadian literature to an extent unimagined in 1945. The establishment of the critical quarterly *Canadian Literature* in 1959, and the publication of the *Literary History of Canada* in 1965, indicated that there was not only a substantial body of literature but also a number of competent critics interested in writing about it. And the list of publishing houses issuing books about Canadian literature, history, and society has expanded as well; most notable has been the growth of the "little" presses like Contact, Hurtig, House of Anansi, and new press.

Perhaps the taking over of our writers by public institutions — the universities, the Canada Council, and the CBC — indicates, as George Woodcock suggested in 1964, that we do not yet have a wholly mature literary world in the sense that England or France has.[25] But patronage of the arts by public institutions is a pattern which has become an important aspect of Canadian literary life and one which has done much to encourage the variety of literary expression in recent years. Perhaps the parallel development of commercial outlets for Canadian literature indicates that the future of our literature lies with a typically Canadian mixture of public and private enterprise.

Footnotes

1. Donald Creighton, *Canada's First Century: 1867-1967* (Toronto: 1970), p. 273.
2. See Kenneth McNaught, *The Pelican History of Canada* (London: 1969), pp. 305-315.
3. Ralph Gustafson, "New Wave in Canadian Poetry," *Canadian Literature*, 32 (Spring, 1967), 7-8.
4. Wynne Francis, "Montreal Poets of the Forties," *Canadian Literature*, 14 (Autumn, 1962), 21-24.
5. P. K. Page, *Cry Ararat!* (Toronto: 1967), p. 71.
6. Eli Mandel, *Irving Layton* (Toronto: 1969), pp. 13-16.
7. James Reaney, "The Third Eye: Jay Macpherson's *The Boatman*," *Canadian Literature*, 3 (Winter, 1960), 26-27.
8. Jay Macpherson, "Egg," *The Boatman and other Poems* (Toronto: 1968), p. 64.
9. *The Boatman and Other Poems, op. cit.*, p. 75.
10. Warren Tallman, "Poet in Progress: Notes on Frank Davey," *Canadian Literature*, 24 (Spring, 1965), 23-27.
11. Charles Olson, "Against Wisdom as Such," *Black Mountain Review*, 1 (Spring, 1954), 35.
12. George Bowering, *Rocky Mountain Foot* (Toronto: 1969), p. 50.
13. Raymond Souster, "About this Book," *New Wave Canada* (Toronto: 1966), p. [v].
14. Desmond Pacey, *Creative Writing in Canada* (Toronto: 1961), pp. 240-41.
15. George Woodcock, *Odysseus Ever Returning: Essays on Canadian Writers and Writings* (Toronto: 1970), p. 10.
16. "About the Author," in Margaret Avison, *The Dumbfounding* (New York: 1966), p. 101.
17. John Gabree, *The World of Rock* (Greenwich, Conn: 1968), pp. 50-51; Woodcock, *op. cit.*, p. 109.
18. Frank Davey, "Leonard Cohen and Bob Dylan: Poetry and the Popular Song," *Alphabet*, 17 (December, 1969), 12.
19. Louis Dudek, "Poetry in English," *Canadian Literature*, 41 (Summer, 1969), 115.
20. Stephen Bann, "Introduction," *Concrete Poetry: An International Anthology* (London: 1967), p. 7.
21. Mary Ellen Solt, "Introduction," *Concrete Poetry: A World View* (Bloomington: 1968), p. 7.
22. Dave Godfrey, *New Canadian Writing 1968* (Toronto: 1968), p. 137.
23. Donald Stephens, "The Short Story in English," *Canadian Literature*, 41 (Summer, 1969), 126-27.
24. Woodcock, *op. cit.*, p. 3; Pacey, *op. cit.*, pp. 230-35.
25. Woodcock, *op. cit.*, p. 2.

Ethel Wilson

Ethel David Bryant was born in 1888 in Port Elizabeth, South Africa, the daughter of a Methodist missionary. She spent much of her early childhood in England, but after the deaths of her parents she was brought to live with relatives in Vancouver in 1898. She was educated there and at a girls' school in Southport, England. After she graduated, she returned to Vancouver and became a teacher. In 1921 she married Dr. Wallace Wilson, a physician. At various times they travelled extensively in Canada, Europe, and the Near East. Mrs. Wilson still lives in Vancouver.

During the Second World War Mrs. Wilson edited a Red Cross magazine. Her first story, "I just love dogs," was published in the New Statesman and Nation *in 1937, but it was not until after the war that she devoted herself seriously to the writing of fiction. Since then she has published a number of short stories, several of which are collected in* Mrs. Golightly and Other Stories *(1961), and longer works of fiction. One of these,* The Innocent Traveller *(1949), is partly based on events and people of Mrs. Wilson's own childhood. Its chief character, Topaz Edgeworth, begins her literary career as a young girl crawling under the dining-room table while her family entertains Matthew Arnold at a polite luncheon in their staunchly Victorian home in England and ends it, almost a century later, in Vancouver where she has found her own "sweetness and light."*

Her best novel is probably Swamp Angel *(1954), in which, as Desmond Pacey points out, Mrs. Wilson subordinates the potential melodrama of her plot to complexities of character and symbol.[1] This statement suggests some strengths of her short stories as well. She is not an "experimental" writer; her tone is quiet and matter-of-fact, and she usually deals with apparently ordinary, middle-class characters. Yet the economical delineation of subtleties of character and point of view, her capacity for an unobtrusive handling of symbolism, and the way in which she strives for clarity of perception while leaving the reader to make whatever moral judgments are necessary place her short stories within the tradition of those of Morley Callaghan. These characteristics are evident in "The Window," taken from* Mrs. Golightly and Other Stories. *The regional setting, with its splendid description of Vancouver, evokes Mr. Willy's feeling that he has found an idyllic place to live; the huge empty window through which he views it is a highly complex symbol, suggesting both his self-satisfaction and the ultimate sterility and irresponsibility of the life he has chosen.*

13

Footnotes

[1] *Desmond Pacey, "Introduction," Swamp Angel (Toronto: 1962), p. 5.*

The Window

The great big window must have been at least twenty-five feet wide and ten feet high. It was constructed in sections divided by segments of something that did not interfere with the view; in fact the eye by-passed these divisions and looked only at the entrancing scenes beyond. The window, together with a glass door at the western end, composed a bland shallow curve and formed the entire transparent north-west (but chiefly north) wall of Mr. Willy's living-room.

Upon his arrival from England Mr. Willy had surveyed the various prospects of living in the quickly growing city of Vancouver with the selective and discarding characteristics which had enabled him to make a fortune and retire all of a sudden from business and his country in his advanced middle age. He settled immediately upon the very house. It was a small old house overlooking the sea between Spanish Banks and English Bay. He knocked out the north wall and made the window. There was nothing particular to commend the house except that it faced immediately on the sea-shore and the view. Mr. Willy had left his wife and her three sisters to play bridge together until death should overtake them in England. He now paced from end to end of his living-room, that is to say from east to west, with his hands in his pockets, admiring the northern view. Sometimes he stood with his hands behind him looking through the great glass window, seeing the wrinkled or placid sea and the ships almost at his feet and beyond the sea the mountains, and seeing sometimes his emancipation. His emancipation drove him into a dream, and sea sky mountains swam before him, vanished, and he saw with immense release his wife in still another more repulsive hat. He did not know, nor would he have cared, that much discussion went on in her world, chiefly in the afternoons, and that he was there alleged to have deserted her. So he had, after providing well for her physical needs which were all the needs of which she was capable. Mrs. Willy went on saying " . . . and he would come home my dear and never speak a word I can't tell you my dear how *frightful* it was night after night I might say for *years* I simply can't tell you . . . " No, she could not tell but she did, by day and night. Here he was at peace, seeing out of the window the crimped and wrinkled sea and the ships which passed and passed each other, the seabirds and the dream-inducing sky.

At the extreme left curve of the window an island appeared to slope into the sea. Behind this island and to the north, the mountains rose very high. In the summer time the mountains were soft, deceptive in their innocency, full of crags and crevasses and

14

arêtes and danger. In the winter they lay magnificent, white and much higher, it seemed, than in the summer time. They tossed, static, in almost visible motion against the sky, inhabited only by eagles and — so a man had told Mr. Willy, but he didn't believe the man — by mountain sheep and some cougars, bears, wild cats and, certainly, on the lower slopes, deer, and now a ski camp far out of sight. Mr. Willy looked at the mountains and regretted his past youth and his present wealth. How could he endure to be old and rich and able only to look at these mountains which in his youth he had not known and did not climb. Nothing, now, no remnant of his youth would come and enable him to climb these mountains. This he found hard to believe, as old people do. He was shocked at the newly realized decline of his physical powers which had proved good enough on the whole for his years of success, and by the fact that now he had, at last, time and could not swim (heart), climb mountains (heart and legs), row a boat in a rough enticing sea (call that old age). These things have happened to other people, thought Mr. Willy, but not to us, now, who have been so young, and yet it will happen to those who now are young.

Immediately across the water were less spectacular mountains, pleasant slopes which in winter time were covered with invisible skiers. Up the dark mountain at night sprang the lights of the ski-lift, and ceased. The shores of these mountains were strung with lights, littered with lights, spangled with lights, necklaces, bracelets, constellations, far more beautiful as seen through this window across the dark water than if Mr. Willy had driven his car across the Lions' Gate Bridge and westwards among those constellations which would have disclosed only a shopping centre, people walking in the streets, street lights, innumerable cars and car lights like anywhere else and, up the slopes, peoples' houses. Then, looking back to the south across the dark water towards his own home and the great lighted window which he would not have been able to distinguish so far away, Mr. Willy would have seen lights again, a carpet of glitter thrown over the slopes of the city.

Fly from one shore to the other, fly and fly back again, fly to a continent or to an island, but you are no better off than if you stayed all day at your own window (and such a window), thought Mr. Willy pacing back and forth, then into the kitchen to put the kettle on for a cup of tea which he will drink beside the window, back for a glass of whisky, returning in time to see a cormorant flying level with the water, not an inch too high not an inch too low, flying out of sight. See the small ducks lying on the water, one behind the other, like beads on a string. In the mornings Mr. Willy drove into town to see his investment broker and perhaps to the bank or round the park. He lunched, but not at a club. He then drove home. On certain days a woman called Mrs. Ogden came in to "do" for him. This was his daily life, very simple, and a routine was formed whose pattern could at last be discerned by an interested observer outside the window.

One night Mr. Willy beheld a vast glow arise behind the mountains. The Arctic world was obviously on fire — but no, the glow was not fire glow, flame glow. The great invasion of colour that spread up and up the sky was not red, was not rose, but of a synthetic cyclamen colour. This cyclamen glow remained steady from mountain to zenith and caused Mr. Willy, who had never seen the Northern Lights, to believe that these were not Northern Lights but that something had occurred for which one must be prepared. After about an hour, flanges of green as of putrefaction, and a melodious yellow arose and spread. An hour later the Northern Lights faded, leaving Mr. Willy small and alone.

Sometimes as, sitting beside the window, he drank his tea, Mr. Willy thought that nevertheless it is given to few people to be as happy (or contented, he would say), as he was, at his age, too. In his life of decisions, men, pressures, more men, antagonisms, fusions, fissions and Mrs. Willy, in his life of hard success, that is, he had sometimes looked forward but so vaguely and rarely to a time when he would not only put this life down; he would leave it. Now he had left it and here he was by his window. As time went on, though, he had to make an effort to summon this happiness, for it seemed to elude him. Sometimes a thought or a shape (was it?), gray, like wood ash that falls in pieces when it is touched, seemed to be behind his chair, and this shape teased him and communicated to him that he had left humanity behind, that a man needs humanity and that if he ceases to be in touch with man and is not in touch with God, he does not matter. "You do not matter any more," said the spectre like wood ash before it fell to pieces, "because you are no longer in touch with any one and so you do not exist. You are in a vacuum and so you are nothing." Then Mr. Willy, at first uneasy, became satisfied again for a time after being made uneasy by the spectre. A storm would get up and the wind, howling well, would lash the window sometimes carrying the salt spray from a very high tide which it flung against the great panes of glass. That was a satisfaction to Mr. Willy and within him something stirred and rose and met the storm and effaced the spectre and other phantoms which were really vague regrets. But the worst that happened against the window was that from time to time a little bird, sometimes but not often a seabird, flung itself like a stone against the strong glass of the window and fell, killed by the passion of its flight. This grieved Mr. Willy, and he could not sit unmoved when the bird flew at the clear glass and was met by death. When this happened, he arose from his chair, opened the glass door at the far end of the window, descended three or four steps and sought in the grasses for the body of the bird. But the bird was dead, or it was dying, its small bones were smashed, its head was broken, its beak split, it was killed by the rapture of its flight. Only once Mr. Willy found the bird a little stunned and picked it up. He cupped the bird's body in his hands and carried it into the house.

Looking up through the grasses at the edge of the rough terrace that descended to the beach, a man watched him return into the house, carrying the bird. Still looking obliquely through the grasses the man watched Mr. Willy enter the room and vanish from view. Then Mr. Willy came again to the door, pushed it open, and released the bird which flew away, who knows where. He closed the door, locked it, and sat down on the chair facing east beside the window and began to read his newspaper. Looking over his paper he saw, to the east, the city of Vancouver deployed over rising ground with low roofs and high buildings and at the apex the tall Electric Building which at night shone like a broad shaft of golden light.

This time, as evening drew on, the man outside went away because he had other business.

Mr. Willy's investment broker was named Gerald Wardho. After a time he said to Mr. Willy in a friendly but respectful way, "Will you have lunch with me at the Club tomorrow?" and Mr. Willy said he would. Some time later Gerald Wardho said, "Would you like me to put you up at the Club?"

Mr. Willy considered a little the life which he had left and did not want to re-enter and also the fact that he had only last year resigned his membership in three clubs, so he said, "That's very good of you, Wardho, but I think not. I'm enjoying things as they are. It's a novelty, living in a vacuum . . . I like it, for a time anyway."

"Yes, but," said Gerald Wardho, "you'd be some time on the waiting list. It wouldn't hurt — "

"No," said Mr. Willy, "no."

Mr. Willy had, Wardho thought, a distinguished appearance or perhaps it was an affable accustomed air, and so he had. When Mrs. Wardho said to her husband, "Gerry, there's not an extra man in this town and I need a man for Saturday," Gerald Wardho said, "I know a man. There's Willy."

Mrs. Wardho said doubtfully, "Willy? Willy who? Who's Willy?"

Her husband said, "He's fine, he's okay, I'll ask Willy."

"How old is he?"

"About a hundred . . . but he's okay."

"Oh-h-h," said Mrs. Wardho, "isn't there anyone anywhere unattached young any more? Does he play bridge?"

"I'll invite him, I'll find out," said her husband, and Mr. Willy said he'd like to come to dinner.

"Do you care for a game of bridge, Mr. Willy?" asked Gerald Wardho.

"I'm afraid not," said Mr. Willy kindly but firmly. He played a good game of bridge but had no intention of entering servitude again just yet, losing his freedom, and being enrolled as what is called a fourth. Perhaps later; not yet. "If you're having bridge I'll come another time. Very kind of you, Wardho."

"No no no," said Gerald Wardho, "there'll only be maybe a table of bridge for anyone who wants to play. My wife would be disappointed."

"Well thank you very much. Black tie?"

"Yes. Black tie," said Gerald Wardho.

And so, whether he would or no, Mr. Willy found himself invited to the kind of evening parties to which he had been accustomed and which he had left behind, given by people younger and more animated than himself, and he realized that he was on his way to becoming old odd man out. There was a good deal of wood ash at these parties — that is, behind him the spectre arose, falling to pieces when he looked at it, and said "So this is what you came to find out on this coast, so far from home, is it, or is there something else. What else is there?" The spectre was not always present at these parties but sometimes awaited him at home and said these things.

One night Mr. Willy came home from an evening spent at Gerald Wardho's brother-in-law's house, a very fine house indeed. He had left lights burning and began to turn out the lights before he went upstairs. He went into the living-room and before turning out the last light gave a glance at the window which had in the course of the evening behaved in its accustomed manner. During the day the view through the window was clear or cloudy, according to the weather or the light or absence of light in the sky; but there it was — the view — never quite the same though, and that is owing to

17

the character of oceans or of any water, great or small, and of light. Both water and light have so great an effect on land observed on any scene, rural urban or wilderness, that one begins to think that life, that a scene, is an illusion produced by influences such as water and light. At all events, by day the window held this fine view as in a frame, and the view was enhanced by ships at sea of all kinds, but never was the sea crowded, and by birds, clouds, and even aeroplanes in the sky — no people to spoil this fine view. But as evening approached, and moonless night, all the view (illusion again) vanished slowly. The window, which was not illusion, only the purveyor of illusion, did not vanish, but became a mirror which reflected against the blackness every detail of the shallow living-room. Through this clear reflection of the whole room, distant lights from across the water intruded, and so chains of light were thrown across the reflected mantelpiece, or a picture, or a human face, enhancing it. When Mr. Willy had left his house to dine at Gerald Wardho's brother-in-law's house the view through the window was placidly clear, but when he returned at 11.30 the window was dark and the room was reflected from floor to ceiling against the blackness. Mr. Willy saw himself entering the room like a stranger, looking at first debonair with such a gleaming shirt front and then — as he approached himself — a little shabby, his hair perhaps. He advanced to the window and stood looking at himself with the room in all its detail behind him.

Mr. Willy was too often alone, and spent far too much time in that space which lies between the last page of the paper or the turning-off of the radio in surfeit, and sleep. Now as he stood at the end of the evening and the beginning of the night, looking at himself and the room behind him, he admitted that the arid feeling which he had so often experienced lately was probably what is called loneliness. And yet he did not want another woman in his life. It was a long time since he had seen a woman whom he wanted to take home or even to see again. Too much smiling. Men were all right, you talked to them about the market, the emergence of the Liberal Party, the impossibility of arriving anywhere with those people while that fellow was in office, nuclear war (instant hells opened deep in everyone's mind and closed again), South Africa where Mr. Willy was born, the Argentine where Mr. Wardho's brother-in-law had spent many years — and then everyone went home.

Mr. Willy, as the months passed by, was dismayed to find that he had entered an area of depression unknown before, like a tundra, and he was a little frightened of this tundra. Returning from the dinner party he did not at once turn out the single last light and go upstairs. He sat down on a chair beside the window and at last bowed his head upon his hands. As he sat there, bowed, his thoughts went very stiffly (for they had not had much exercise in that direction throughout his life), to some area that was not tundra but that area where there might be some meaning in creation which Mr. Willy supposed must be the place where some people seemed to find a God, and perhaps a personal God at that. Such theories, or ideas, or passions had never been of interest to him, and if he had thought of such theories, or ideas, or passions he would have dismissed them as invalid and having no bearing on life as it is lived, especially when one is too busy. He had formed the general opinion that people who hold such beliefs were either slaves to an inherited convention, hypocrites, or nit-wits. He regarded such people without interest, or at least he thought them negligible as he

18

returned to the exacting life in hand. On the whole, though, he did not like them. It is not easy to say why Mr. Willy thought these people were hypocrites or nit-wits because some of them, not all, had a strong religious faith, and why he was not a hypocrite or nit-wit because he had not a strong religious faith; but there it was.

As he sat on and on looking down at the carpet with his head in his hands he did not think of these people, but he underwent a strong shock of recognition. He found himself looking this way and that way out of his aridity for some explanation or belief beyond the non-explanation and non-belief that had always been sufficient and had always been his, but in doing this he came up against a high and solid almost visible wall of concrete or granite, set up between him and a religious belief. This wall had, he thought, been built by him through the period of his long life, or perhaps he was congenitally unable to have a belief; in that case it was no fault of his and there was no religious belief possible to him. As he sat there he came to have the conviction that the absence of a belief which extended beyond the visible world had something to do with his malaise; yet the malaise might possibly be cirrhosis of the liver or a sort of delayed male menopause. He recognized calmly that death was as inevitable as tomorrow morning or even tonight and he had a rational absence of fear of death. Nevertheless his death (he knew) had begun, and had begun — what with his awareness of age and this malaise of his — to assume a certainty that it had not had before. His death did not trouble him as much as the increasing tastelessness of living in this tundra of mind into which a belief did not enter.

The man outside the window had crept up through the grasses and was now watching Mr. Willy from a point rather behind him. He was a morose man and strong. He had served two terms for robbery with violence. When he worked, he worked up the coast. Then he came to town and if he did not get into trouble it was through no fault of his own. Last summer he had lain there and, rolling over, had looked up through the grasses and into — only just into — the room where this guy was who seemed to live alone. He seemed to be a rich guy because he wore good clothes and hadn't he got this great big window and — later, he discovered — a high-price car. He had lain in the grasses and because his thoughts always turned that way, he tried to figger out how he could get in there. Money was the only thing that was any good to him and maybe the old guy didn't keep money or even carry it but he likely did. The man thought quite a bit about Mr. Willy and then went up the coast and when he came down again he remembered the great big window and one or two nights he went around and about the place and figgered how he'd work it. The doors was all locked, even that glass door. That was easy enough to break but he guessed he'd go in without warning when the old guy was there so's he'd have a better chance of getting something off of him as well. Anyways he wouldn't break in, not that night, but if nothing else offered he'd do it some time soon.

Suddenly Mr. Willy got up, turned the light out, and went upstairs to bed. That was Wednesday.

On Sunday he had his first small party. It seemed inevitable if only for politeness. Later he would have a dinner party if he still felt sociable and inclined. He invited the Wardhos and their in-laws and some other couples. A Mrs. Lessways asked if she might bring her aunt and he said yes. Mrs. Wardho said might she bring her niece who was arriving on Saturday to meet her fiancé who was due next week from Hong Kong, and the Wardhos were going to give the two young people a quiet wedding, and Mr. Willy said "Please do." Another couple asked if they could bring another couple.

Mr. Willy, surveying his table, thought that Mrs. Ogden had done well. "Oh I'm so glad you think so," said Mrs. Ogden, pleased. People began to arrive. "Oh!" they exclaimed without fail, as they arrived, "what a beautiful view!" Mrs. Lessways' aunt who had blue hair fell delightedly into the room, turning this way and that way, acknowledging smiles and tripping to the window. "Oh," she cried turning to Mr. Willy in a fascinating manner, "isn't that just lovely! Edna says you're quite a recluse! I'm sure I don't blame you! Don't you think that's the loveliest view Edna . . . oh how d'you do how d'you do, isn't that the loveliest view? . . . " Having paid her tribute to the view she turned away from the window and did not see it again. The Aunt twirled a little bag covered with iridescent beads on her wrist. "Oh!" and "Oh!" she exclaimed, turning, "My dear how *lovely* to see you! I didn't even know you were back! Did you have a good time?" She reminded Mr. Willy uneasily of his wife. Mr. and Mrs. Wardho arrived accompanied by their niece Sylvia.

A golden girl, thought Mr. Willy taking her hand, but her young face surrounded by sunny curls was stern. She stood, looking from one to another, not speaking, for people spoke busily to each other and the young girl stood apart, smiling only when need be and wishing that she had not had to come to the party. She drifted to the window and seemed (and was) forgotten. She looked at the view as at something seen for the first and last time. She inscribed those notable hills on her mind because had she not arrived only yesterday? And in two days Ian would be here and she would not see them again.

A freighter very low laden emerged from behind a forest and moved slowly into the scene. So low it was that it lay like an elegant black line upon the water with great bulkheads below. Like an iceberg, thought Sylvia, and her mind moved along with the freighter bound for foreign parts. Someone spoke to her and she turned. "Oh thank you!" she said for her cup of tea.

Mr. Willy opened the glass door and took with him some of the men who had expressed a desire to see how far his property ran. "You see, just a few feet, no distance," he said.

After a while day receded and night came imperceptibly on. There was not any violence of reflected sunset tonight and mist settled down on the view with only distant dim lights aligning the north shore. Sylvia, stopping to respond to ones and twos, went to the back of the shallow room and sat down behind the out-jut of the fireplace where a wood fire was burning. Her mind was on two levels. One was all Ian and the week coming, and one — no thicker than a crust on the surface — was this party and all these people talking, the Aunt talking so busily that one might think there was a race on, or news to tell. Sylvia, sitting in the shadow of the corner and thinking about her approaching lover, lost herself in this reverie, and her lips, which had been so stern, opened slightly in a tender smile. Mr. Willy who was serving drinks from the dining-room where Mrs. Ogden had left things ready, came upon her and, struck by her beauty, saw a different sunny girl. She looked up at him. She took her drink from him with a soft and tender smile that was grateful and happy and was only partly for him. He left her, with a feeling of beauty seen.

20

Sylvia held her glass and looked towards the window. She saw, to her surprise, so quickly had black night come, that the end of the room which had been a view was now a large black mirror which reflected the glowing fire, the few lights, and the people unaware of the view, its departure, and its replacement by their own reflections behaving to each other like people at a party. Sylvia watched Mr. Willy who moved amongst them, taking a glass and bringing a glass. He was removed from the necessities, now, of conversation, and looked very sad. Why does he look sad, she wondered and was young enough to think, he shouldn't look sad, he is well off. She took time off to like Mr. Willy and to feel sorry that he seemed melancholy.

People began to look at their watches and say good-bye. The Aunt redoubled her vivacity. The women all thanked Mr. Willy for his tea party and for the beautiful beautiful view. They gave glances at the window but there was no view.

When all his guests had gone, Mr. Willy, who was an orderly man, began to collect glasses and take them into the kitchen. In an armchair lay the bag covered with iridescent beads belonging to the Aunt. Mr. Willy picked it up and put it on a table, seeing the blue hair of the Aunt. He would sit down and smoke for a while. But he found that when, lately, he sat down in the evening beside the window and fixed his eyes upon the golden shaft of the Electric Building, in spite of his intention of reading or smoking, his thoughts turned towards this subject of belief which now teased him, eluded, yet compelled him. He was brought up, every time, against the great stone wall, how high, how wide he knew, but not how thick. If he could, in some way, break through the wall which bounded the area of his aridity and his comprehension, he knew without question that there was a light (not darkness) beyond, and that this light could in some way come through to him and alleviate the sterility and lead him, lead him. If there were some way, even some conventional way — although he did not care for convention — he would take it in order to break the wall down and reach the light so that it would enter his life; but he did not know the way. So fixed did Mr. Willy become in contemplation that he looked as though he were graven in stone.

Throughout the darkened latter part of the tea party, the man outside had lain or crouched near the window. From the sands, earlier, he had seen Mr. Willy open the glass door and go outside, followed by two or three men. They looked down talking, and soon went inside again together. The door was closed. From anything the watcher knew, it was not likely that the old guy would turn and lock the door when he took the other guys in. He'd just close it, see.

As night came on the man watched the increased animation of the guests preparing for departure. Like departing birds they moved here and there in the room before taking flight. The man was impatient but patient because when five were left, then three, then no one but the old guy who lived in the house, he knew his time was near. (How gay and how meaningless the scene had been, of these well-dressed persons talking and talking, like some kind of a show where nothing happened — or so it might seem, on the stage of the lighted room from the pit of the dark shore.)

The watcher saw the old guy pick up glasses and take them away. Then he came back into the room and looked around. He took something out of a chair and put it on a table. He stood still for a bit, and then he found some kind of a paper and sat down in the chair facing eastward. But the paper drooped in his hand and then it dropped to

21

the floor as the old guy bent his head and then he put his elbows on his knees and rested his head in his hands as if he was thinking, or had some kind of a headache.

The watcher, with a sort of joy and a feeling of confidence that the moment had come, moved strongly and quietly to the glass door. He turned the handle expertly, slid inside, and slowly closed the door so that no draught should warn his victim. He moved cat-like to the back of Mr. Willy's chair and quickly raised his arm. At the selfsame moment that he raised his arm with a short blunt weapon in his hand, he was aware of the swift movement of another person in the room. The man stopped still, his arm remained high, every fear was aroused. He turned instantly and saw a scene clearly enacted beside him in the dark mirror of the window. At the moment and shock of turning, he drew a sharp intake of breath and it was this that Mr. Willy heard and that caused him to look up and around and see in the dark mirror the intruder, the danger, and the victim who was himself. At that still moment, the telephone rang shrilly, twice as loud in that still moment, on a small table near him.

It was not the movement of that figure in the dark mirror, it was not the bell ringing close at hand and insistently. It was an irrational and stupid fear lest his action, reproduced visibly beside him in the mirror, was being faithfully registered in some impossible way that filled the intruder with fright. The telephone ringing shrilly, Mr. Willy now facing him, the play enacted beside him, and this irrational momentary fear caused him to turn and bound towards the door, to escape into the dark, banging the glass door with a clash behind him. When he got well away from the place he was angry — everything was always against him, he never had no luck, and if he hadn't a lost his head it was a cinch he coulda done it easy.

"Damn you!" shouted Mr. Willy in a rage, with his hand on the telephone, "you might have broken it! Yes?" he said into the telephone, moderating the anger that possessed him and continuing within himself a conversation that said It was eighteen inches away, I was within a minute of it and I didn't know, it's no use telephoning the police but I'd better do that, it was just above me and I'd have died not knowing. "Yes? Yes?" he said impatiently, trembling a little.

"Oh," said a surprised voice, "it is Mr. Willy, isn't it? Just for a minute it didn't sound like you Mr. Willy that was the *loveliest* party and what a lovely view and I'm sorry to be such a nuisance I kept on ringing and ringing because I thought you couldn't have gone out so soon" (tinkle tinkle) "and you couldn't have gone to bed so soon but I do believe I must have left my little bead bag it's not the *value* but . . . " Mr. Willy found himself shaking more violently now, not only with death averted and the rage of the slammed glass door but with the powerful thoughts that had usurped him and were interrupted by the dangerous moment which was now receding, and the tinkling voice on the telephone.

"I have it here. I'll bring it tomorrow," he said shortly. He hung up the telephone and at the other end the Aunt turned and exclaimed "Well if he isn't the rudest man I never was treated like that in my whole life d'you know what he . . . "

Mr. Willy was in a state of abstraction.

He went to the glass door and examined it. It was intact. He turned the key and drew the shutter down. Then he went back to the telephone in this state of abstraction. Death or near-death was still very close, though receding. It seemed to

22

him at that moment that a crack had been coming in the great wall that shut him off from the light but perhaps he was wrong. He dialled the police, perfunctorily not urgently. He knew that before him lay the hardest work of his life — in his life but out of his country. He must in some way and very soon break the great wall that shut him off from whatever light there might be. Not for fear of death oh God not for fear of death but for fear of something else.

Earle Birney

Born in Calgary in 1904, Earle Birney attended high school in Banff and in Creston,
B.C. He graduated in 1926 from the University of British Columbia with an honours
degree in English; subsequently he attended the universities of California, London,
and Toronto; he received a doctorate from Toronto in 1936 with a dissertation on
Chaucer's irony. From 1936 to 1942 he taught English at University College, Toronto,
and was literary editor of the Canadian Forum. *He served with the Canadian Army*
during the Second World War in England and Holland; his experience of war is
reflected in "The Road to Nijmegen" and in his picaresque novel Turvey *(1949). In*
1946 he returned to the University of British Columbia, where he taught English and
provided much of the initiative for the establishment of a department of Creative
Writing, the first of its kind in Canada. In 1965-1966 he was Writer-in-Residence at the
University of Toronto; the following year he held the same position at the University
of Waterloo. His extensive travels in Europe, Latin America, and the Far East have
provided subjects for several of his recent poems. In addition to eight volumes of
poetry, two of which have won Governor-General's Awards, and two novels, he has
published scholarly articles on medieval English literature, written reviews, and given
radio talks. The Creative Writer, *from which the essay "Experimentation Today" is*
taken, contains a series of talks delivered over CBC radio in 1965.

Birney's career as a poet has been long and eclectic. His subject matter is varied,
and, of all the poets in this period, he has been one of the most consistently interested
in formal experiments. His early poem "David" (1941) is fairly traditional; it shows
affinities with the later narratives of E. J. Pratt both in its manner and in its concern
with the theme of man confronting the forces of nature. But his experimental
interests, especially in the possibilities of Old English alliterative verse, were also
evident early in his career in "Anglosaxon Street." In the nineteen-sixties the theories
of the Black Mountain poets about the importance of the ear and of "breath" rather
than of metrics in determining the form of a poem influenced him; one result of this
was his decision to eliminate punctuation in the revised versions of his poems in
Selected Poems *(1966). He has also experimented with concrete poetry; b p Nichol*
has called him "the real forerunner of concrete in Canada." [1]

Another aspect of Birney's experimentation has been his practice of continually
revising his poems. The texts of all the poems, except the last included here, are from
Selected Poems; *the date which Birney includes after each poem indicates the time of*

its composition. This version, however, often differs considerably from the original one.

Footnotes

[1.] *b p Nichol, ed.,* The Cosmic Chef *(Ottawa: 1970), p. 79.*

David

I

David and I that summer cut trails on the survey,
All week in the valley for wages, in air that was steeped
In the wail of mosquitoes, but over the sunalive week-ends
We climbed, to get from the ruck of the camp, the surly

Poker, the wrangling, the snoring under the fetid
Tents, and because we had joy in our lengthening coltish
Muscles, and mountains for David were made to see over,
Stairs from the valleys and steps to the sun's retreats.

II

Our first was Mount Gleam. We hiked in the long afternoon
To a curling lake and lost the lure of the faceted
Cone in the swell of its sprawling shoulders. Past
The inlet we grilled our bacon, the strips festooned

On a poplar prong, in the hurrying slant of the sunset.
Then the two of us rolled in the blanket while round us the cold
Pines thrust at the stars. The dawn was a floating
Of mists till we reached to the slopes above timber, and won

To snow like fire in the sunlight. The peak was upthrust
Like a fist in a frozen ocean of rock that swirled
Into valleys the moon could be rolled in. Remotely unfurling
Eastward the alien prairie glittered. Down through the dusty

Skree on the west we descended, and David showed me
How to use the give of shale for giant incredible
Strides. I remember, before the larches' edge,
That I jumped a long green surf of juniper flowing

Away from the wind, and landed in gentian and saxifrage
Spilled on the moss. Then the darkening firs
And the sudden whirring of water that knifed down a fern-hidden
Cliff and splashed unseen into mist in the shadows.

III

One Sunday on Rampart's arête a rainsquall caught us,
And passed, and we clung by our blueing fingers and bootnails
An endless hour in the sun, not daring to move
Till the ice had steamed from the slate. And David taught me

How time on a knife-edge can pass with the guessing of fragments
Remembered from poets, the naming of strata beside one,
And matching of stories from schooldays. . . . We crawled astride
The peak to feast on the marching ranges flagged

By the fading shreds of the shattered stormcloud. Lingering
There it was David who spied to the south, remote,
And unmapped, a sunlit spire on Sawback, an overhang
Crooked like a talon. David named it the Finger.

That day we chanced on the skull and the splayed white ribs
Of a mountain goat underneath a cliff-face, caught
On a rock. Around were the silken feathers of hawks.
And that was the first I knew that a goat could slip.

IV

And then Inglismaldie. Now I remember only
The long ascent of the lonely valley, the live
Pine spirally scarred by lightning, the slicing pipe
Of invisible pika, and great prints, by the lowest

26

Snow, of a grizzly. There it was too that David
Taught me to read the scroll of coral in limestone
And the beetle-seal in the shale of ghostly trilobites,
Letters delivered to man from the Cambrian waves.

V

On Sundance we tried from the col and the going was hard.
The air howled from our feet to the smudged rocks
And the papery lake below. At an outthrust we balked
Till David clung with his left to a dint in the scarp,

Lobbed the iceaxe over the rocky lip,
Slipped from his holds and hung by the quivering pick,
Twisted his long legs up into space and kicked
To the crest. Then grinning, he reached with his freckled wrist

And drew me up after. We set a new time for that climb.
That day returning we found a robin gyrating
In grass, wing-broken. I caught it to tame but David
Took and killed it, and said, "Could you teach it to fly?"

VI

In August, the second attempt, we ascended The Fortress,
By the forks of the Spray we caught five trout and fried them
Over a balsam fire. The woods were alive
With the vaulting of mule-deer and drenched with clouds all the morning,

Till we burst at noon to the flashing and floating round
Of the peaks. Coming down we picked in our hats the bright
And sunhot raspberries, eating them under a mighty
Spruce, while a marten moving like quicksilver scouted us.

VII

But always we talked of the Finger on Sawback, unknown
And hooked, till the first afternoon in September we slogged
Through the musky woods, past a swamp that quivered with frog-song,
And camped by a bottle-green lake. But under the cold

27

Breath of the glacier sleep would not come, the moon-light
Etching the Finger. We rose and trod past the feathery
Larch, while the stars went out, and the quiet heather
Flushed, and the skyline pulsed with the surging bloom

Of incredible dawn in the Rockies. David spotted
Bighorns across the moraine and sent them leaping
With yodels the ramparts redoubled and rolled to the peaks,
And the peaks to the sun. The ice in the morning thaw

Was a gurgling world of crystal and cold blue chasms,
And seracs that shone like frozen saltgreen waves.
At the base of the Finger we tried once and failed. Then David
Edged to the west and discovered the chimney; the last

Hundred feet we fought the rock and shouldered and kneed
Our way for an hour and made it. Unroping we formed
A cairn on the rotting tip. Then I turned to look north
At the glistening wedge of giant Assiniboine, heedless

Of handhold. And one foot gave. I swayed and shouted.
David turned sharp and reached out his arm and steadied me,
Turning again with a grin and his lips ready
To jest. But the strain crumbled his foothold. Without

A gasp he was gone. I froze to the sound of grating
Edge-nails and fingers, the slither of stones, the lone
Second of silence, the nightmare thud. Then only
The wind and the muted beat of unknowing cascades.

VIII

Somehow I worked down the fifty impossible feet
To the ledge, calling and getting no answer but echoes
Released in the cirque, and trying not to reflect
What an answer would mean. He lay still, with his lean

Young face upturned and strangely unmarred, but his legs
Splayed beneath him, beside the final drop,
Six hundred feet sheer to the ice. My throat stopped
When I reached him, for he was alive. He opened his grey

28

Straight eyes and brokenly murmured, "Over . . . over."
And I, feeling beneath him a cruel fang
Of the ledge thrust in his back, but not understanding,
Mumbled stupidly, "Best not to move," and spoke

Of his pain. But he said, "I can't move . . . If only I felt
Some pain." Then my shame stung the tears to my eyes
As I crouched, and I cursed myself, but he cried,
Louder, "No, Bobbie! Don't ever blame yourself.

I didn't test my foothold." He shut the lids
Of his eyes to the stare of the sky, while I moistened his lips
From our water flask and tearing my shirt into strips
I swabbed the shredded hands. But the blood slid

From his side and stained the stone and the thirsting lichens,
And yet I dared not lift him up from the gore
Of the rock. Then he whispered, "Bob, I want to go over!"
This time I knew what he meant and I grasped for a lie

And said, "I'll be back here by midnight with ropes
And men from the camp and we'll cradle you out." But I knew
That the day and the night must pass and the cold dews
Of another morning before such men unknowing

The ways of mountains could win to the chimney's top.
And then, how long? And he knew . . . and the hell of hours
After that, if he lived till we came, roping him out.
But I curled beside him and whispered, "The bleeding will stop.

You can last." He said only, "Perhaps. . . . For what? A wheelchair,
Bob?" His eyes brightening with fever upbraided me.
I could not look at him more and said, "Then I'll stay
With you." But he did not speak, for the clouding fever.

I lay dazed and stared at the long valley,
The glistening hair of a creek on the rug stretched
By the firs, while the sun leaned round and flooded the ledge,
The moss, and David still as a broken doll.

I hunched to my knees to leave, but he called and his voice
Now was sharpened with fear. "For Christ's sake push me over!

If I could move . . . or die. . . . " The sweat ran from his forehead,
But only his eyes moved. A hawk was buoying

Blackly its wings over the wrinkled ice.
The purr of a waterfall rose and sank with the wind.
Above us climbed the last joint of the Finger
Beckoning bleakly the wide indifferent sky.

Even then in the sun it grew cold lying there. . . . And I knew
He had tested his holds. It was I who had not. . . . I looked
At the blood on the ledge, and the far valley. I looked
At last in his eyes. He breathed, "I'd do it for you, Bob."

IX

I will not remember how nor why I could twist
Up the wind-devilled peak, and down through the chimney's empty
Horror, and over the traverse alone. I remember
Only the pounding fear I would stumble on It

When I came to the grave-cold maw of the bergschrund . . . reeling
Over the sun-cankered snowbridge, shying the caves
In the nêvé . . . the fear, and the need to make sure It was there
On the ice, the running and falling and running, leaping

Of gaping greenthroated crevasses, alone and pursued
By the Finger's lengthening shadow. At last through the fanged
And blinding seracs I slid to the milky wrangling
Falls at the glacier's snout, through the rocks piled huge

On the humped moraine, and into the spectral larches,
Alone. By the glooming lake I sank and chilled
My mouth but I could not rest and stumbled still
To the valley, losing my way in the ragged marsh.

I was glad of the mire that covered the stains, on my ripped
Boots, of his blood, but panic was on me, the reek
Of the bog, the purple glimmer of toadstools obscene
In the twilight. I staggered clear to a firewaste, tripped

And fell with a shriek on my shoulder. It somehow eased
My heart to know I was hurt, but I did not faint
And I could not stop while over me hung the range
Of the Sawback. In blackness I searched for the trail by the creek

And found it. . . . My feet squelched a slug and horror
Rose again in my nostrils. I hurled myself
Down the path. In the woods behind some animal yelped.
Then I saw the glimmer of tents and babbled my story.

I said that he fell straight to the ice where they found him.
And none but the sun and incurious clouds have lingered
Around the marks of that day on the ledge of the Finger,
That day, the last of my youth, on the last of our mountains.

Toronto, 1940

Anglosaxon Street

Dawndrizzle ended   dampness steams from
blotching brick and   blank plasterwaste
Faded housepatterns   hoary and finicky
unfold stuttering   stick like a phonograph

Here is a ghetto   gotten for goyim
O with care denuded   of nigger and kike
No coonsmell rankles   reeks only cellarrot
attar of carexhaust   catcorpse and cookinggrease
Imperial hearts   heave in this haven
Cracks across windows   are welded with slogans
There'll Always Be An England   enhances geraniums
and V's for Victory   vanquish the housefly

31

Ho! with climbing sun   march the bleached beldames
festooned with shopping bags   farded flatarched
bigthewed Saxonwives   stepping over buttrivers
waddling back wienerladen   to suckle smallfry

Hoy! with sunslope   shrieking over hydrants
flood from learninghall   the lean fingerlings
Nordic nobblecheeked   not all clean of nose
leaping Commandowise   into leprous lanes

What! after whistleblow!   spewed from wheelboat
after daylong doughtiness   dire handplay
in sewertrench or sandpit   come Saxonthegns
Junebrown Jutekings   jawslack for meat

Sit after supper   on smeared doorsteps
not humbly swearing   hatedeeds on Huns
profiteers politicians   pacifists Jews

Then by twobit magic   to muse in movie
unlock picturehoard   or lope to alehall
soaking bleakly   in beer skittleless
Home again to hotbox   and humid husbandhood
in slumbertrough adding   sleepily to Anglekin
Alongside in lanenooks   carling and leman
caterwaul and clip   careless of Saxonry
with moonglow and haste   and a higher heartbeat

Slumbers now slumtrack   unstinks cooling
waiting brief for milkmaid   mornstar and worldrise

Toronto, 1942

32

The Road to Nijmégen

December my dear on the road to Nijmégen
between the stones and the bitten sky was your face

Not yours at first but only the countenance of lank canals
and gathered stares   too rapt to note my passing
of graves with frosted billy-tins for hats
of bones of tanks beside the stoven bridges
of old men in the mist who hacked at roots
knifing the final chips from a boulevard of stumps.

These for miles and the fangs of homes but more the women
wheeling into the wind on the tireless rims of their cycles
like tattered sailboats tossing over the cobbles
and the children groping in gravel for knobs of coal
or clustered like wintered flies at the back of messhuts
their legs standing like dead stems out of their clogs

Numbed on the long road to mangled Nijmégen
I thought that only the living of others assures us
the gentle and true we remember as trees walking
Their arms reach down from the light of kindness
into this Lazarus tomb

So peering through sleet as we neared Nijmégen
I glimpsed the rainbow arch of your eyes
Over the clank of the jeep   your quick grave laughter
outrising at last the rockets
brought me what spells I repeat as I travel this road
that arrives at no future

and what creed I bring to our daily crimes
to this guilt
in the griefs of the old and the tombs of the young

Holland, January, 1945

From the Hazel Bough

He met a lady
    on a lazy street
hazel eyes
    and little plush feet

her legs swam by
    like lovely trout
eyes were trees
    where boys leant out

hands in the dark and
    a river side
round breasts rising
    with the finger's tide

she was plump as a finch
    and live as a salmon
gay as silk and
    proud as a Brahmin

they winked when they met
    and laughed when they parted
never took time
    to be brokenhearted

but no man sees
    where the trout lie now
or what leans out
    from the hazel bough

Military Hospital, Toronto, 1945 — Vancouver, 1947

Canada: Case History

This is the case of a highschool land
deadset in adolescence
loud treble laughs and sudden fists
bright cheeks   the gangling presence
This boy is oriented well to sports
and the doctors say he's healthy
he's taken to church on Sunday still
and keeps his prurience stealthy
Doesn't like books (except about bears)
collects new coins   old slogans   jets
and never refuses a dare
His Uncle spoils him with candy of course
but shouts him down when he talks at table
You'll note he has some of his French mother's looks
though he's not so witty and no more stable
He's really much more like his Father and yet
if you say so he'll pull a great face
He wants to be different from everyone else
and daydreams of winning the global race
Parents unmarried and living apart
relatives keen to bag the estate
schizophrenia not excluded—
will he learn to grow up before it's too late?

Ottawa, 1945

Bushed

He invented a rainbow but lightning struck it
shattered it into the lake-lap of a mountain
so big his mind slowed when he looked at it

Yet he built a shack on the shore
learned to roast porcupine belly and
wore the quills on his hatband

At first he was out with the dawn
whether it yellowed bright as wood-columbine
or was only a fuzzed moth in a flannel of storm
But he found the mountain was clearly alive
sent messages whizzing down every hot morning
boomed proclamations at noon and spread out
a white guard of goat
before falling asleep on its feet at sundown

When he tried his eyes on the lake   ospreys
would fall like valkyries
choosing the cut-throat
He took then to waiting
till the night smoke rose from the boil of the sunset

But the moon carved unknown totems
out of the lakeshore
owls in the beardusky woods derided him
moosehorned cedars circled his swamps and tossed
their antlers up to the stars
Then he knew   though the mountain slept   the winds
were shaping its peak to an arrowhead
poised

And now he could only
bar himself in and wait
for the great flint to come singing into his heart

1951

The Bear on the Delhi Road

Unreal   tall as a myth
by the road the Himalayan bear
is beating the brilliant air
with his crooked arms
About him two men   bare
spindly as locusts   leap

One pulls on a ring
in the great soft nose   His mate
flicks   flicks with a stick
up at the rolling eyes

They have not led him here
down from the fabulous hills
to this bald alien plain
and the clamorous world   to kill
but simply to teach him to dance

They are peaceful both   these spare
men of Kashmir   and the bear
alive is their living   too
If   far on the Delhi way
around him galvanic they dance
it is merely to wear   wear
from his shaggy body the tranced
wish forever to stay
only an ambling bear
four-footed in berries

It is no more joyous for them
in this hot dust to prance
out of reach of the praying claws
sharpened to paw for ants
in the shadows of deodars
It is not easy to free
myth from reality
or rear this fellow up
to lurch   lurch with them
in the tranced dancing of men

Srinagar, 1958 — Île des Porquerolles, 1959

El Greco: *Espolio*

The carpenter is intent on the pressure of his hand

on the awl   and the trick of pinpointing his strength
through the awl to the wood   which is tough
He has no effort to spare for despoilings
or to worry if he'll be cut in on the dice
His skill is vital to the scene   and the safety of the state
Anyone can perform the indignities   It's his hard arms
and craft that hold the eyes of the convict's women
There is the problem of getting the holes exact
(in the middle of this elbowing crowd)
and deep enough to hold the spikes
after they've sunk through those bared feet
and inadequate wrists he knows are waiting behind him

He doesn't sense perhaps that one of the hands
is held in a curious gesture over him—
giving   or asking   forgiveness?—
but he'd scarcely take time to be puzzled by poses
Criminals come in all sorts   as anyone knows who makes crosses
are as mad or sane as those who decide on their killings
Our one at least has been quiet so far
though they say he talked himself into this trouble
a carpenter's son who got notions of preaching

Well heres a carpenter's son who'll have carpenter sons
God willing   and build what's wanted   temples or tables
mangers or crosses   and shape them decently
working alone in that firm and profound abstraction
which blots out the bawling of rag-snatchers
To construct with hands   knee-weight   braced thigh
keeps the back turned from death

But it's too late now for the other carpenter's boy
to return to this peace before the nails are hammered

Bowen Island, 1960

38

39

Experimentation Today

Marshall McLuhan, our acknowledged philosopher of communications, is also one of our unacknowledged poets. He writes in rhythms and he thinks in images. In his latest book, *Understanding Media*, McLuhan remarks that art, when it's most significant, "is a DEW line, a Distant Early Warning system that can always be relied on to tell the old culture what is beginning to happen to it". I think this is a truth not often faced, especially by Canadian literary critics, and one that must be accepted if we are to understand the creative process.

Living art, like anything else, stays alive only by changing. The young artist must constantly examine the forms and the aesthetic theories he has inherited; he must reject most of them, and he must search for new ones. Literature is all the more alive today because it is changing so rapidly. In fact it's adjusting to the possibility that the printed page is no longer the chief disseminator of ideas, and that authors must find ways to bend the new technological media to artistic purposes. The rebels and experimenters who are forcing these changes are, of course, having to fight the same battles against the same kind of academic critics who attacked the literary revolutionaries of the last generation. In their beginnings, Joyce, Kafka, Rimbaud, Rilke, Pound, Brecht, even Eliot, were pooh-poohed or ignored as cheap and sensational, as mad or frivolous destroyers of sacred tradition. Now these men are the ancient great—and the young writers who find them inadequate are getting the same treatment. Of course, many literary movements in every generation turn out to be blind alleys, but no critic should think himself so perceptive he can always tell the passing fashion from the significant breakthrough. I don't know exactly where the literary Dew Line is this moment, but I'm sure it lies somewhere in the complicated world of today's little-little magazines and small-press chapbooks.

In that world you'll find that many of the poetic and prose techniques which were regarded a few years ago as merely far-out and probably inconsequential are now customary and established ones. To begin with a small example, punctuation in poetry is now used functionally only—or not at all. Syntactical ambiguities are either permitted, or obviated by artful breakings between lines, and blanks or breathing spaces between phrases. Or, if punctuation is used, it may be in company with spelling distortions and enormous variations of type faces and sizes, to signal voice tones simultaneously with visual effects, to reinforce the feeling and meaning of the poem. One Latin-american poet, José Garcia Villa, is particularly known for a series of short verses he called *Comma Poems*, in which all words are separated by commas, to force the reader to accept each word as of equal importance. Here is the conclusion of one of these pieces (in which the poet has been visioning God dancing on a bed of strawberries): "Yet, He, hurt, not, the littlest, one,/But, gave, them, ripeness, all."[1]

Behind such apparently trivial oddities often lie serious and influential theories. Today there's been going on a great affirmation of poetry as something inescapably auditory as well as visual, a creation successful only when it conveys its maker's unique inner voice, a thing to be spoken or chanted or sung, as in the beginnings, with craft and with care, and yet still a poem in space, working on the eye. Why not give the eye as much as it can use to extend the experience of the poem? Modern photo-offset processes, for example, make it possible, without extra expense, for a poet to order almost anything visually he wants on the page, to paint his work in the Oriental tradition, or, following and extending on e. e. cummings, to make the poem itself a sort of etching in print, so adding both to the range and the intensity of the aesthetic communication.

Some of these attitudes lie behind the Projective Verse theories of Charles Olson and the Black Mountain movement—so-called because its chief figures were associated briefly with an experimental college of that name in the United States. Following leads from Ezra Pound and William Carlos Williams, these poets decided to make the single line of a poem its basic unit for sound as well as sight. Like nearly all young American poets, by the end of the Fifties, they had inherited a belief that rhyming and traditional metrical counting are artificial impediments to honest expression; the poet must write to his own inner melody, his unique "voice". But if the line were no longer to set off rhyme or attest to a regular beat, what use was it at all? The Black Mountain poets rejected the anarchism of the old Free Verse writers, whose lines were never good guides to how they read their poems anyway, and they could not accept the indifference to form of any kind shown by the newer Beat poets, who were content to have their longer efforts set as prose, and their shorter pieces in Whitmanesque lines whose length was decreed by the width of the printer's page. Instead, Olson, Robert Creeley and others sought to develop an exact line whose length and accentuation would be determined organically, by the rhythm of the heart beat and by the natural separate exhalations of human breath. This has led them to rather short-line poems, containing only one strong stress, and it has created an agreeable effect of space, simple intensity, and delicate patterning on the page. At least the superficialities of Black Mountain poetry have caught on, and the "look" of it now dominates the little magazines. The Black Mountain in fact has moved from cult to fashion to establishment, in a decade. It's easy, however, to over-simplify its technique and its influence, as I'm having to do, from my own shortness of breath on this program. For some, the theories behind it involve certain principles of Yoga, anti-rational mysticism, and what Ginsberg calls "mind jerks". Some of the best young poets in Canada have emerged out of the Black Mountain movement: George Bowering, Lionel Kearns and John Newlove among others.[2]

As for old-fashioned rhyming and stanza forms, such as the sonnet, no *avant garde* magazines would be caught dead publishing them, or worry a moment about their loss. Robert Duncan, the San Francisco poet and theorist, teaches his followers that "rime" is simply a way of "showing measurable distances between corresponding elements in a poem" and that this can be more subtly and instinctively achieved by a balancing of images and themes in the poem than by the contriving of sound-echoes.[3]

The insistence on the importance of the image is still probably basic to poetic theorizing, though W. C. Williams and some of the Black Mountain writers have tended to begin with the "thing", the precise object from immediate experience which presumably sets the poem going, and to describe that thing as simply and yet minutely and predicatively as possible; if that is well done, the poem itself may be complete, without need of fortification by metaphor or comment or warping into a conscious form. Others, however, following in the mythopoeic movement associated with Robert Graves and going back to Jung, strive to come upon a primordial emblem or a symbol, some call it a "deep image", which can permeate a whole poem and stir that racial memory going back to the cavemen, that Collective Unconscious we are all supposed to have inherited. An exploration of this sort may perhaps be heard going on in these lines from a recent poem of a Canadian writer, James Reaney:

> Existence gives to me . . .
> What does it give to thee?
> He gives to me: a pebble
> He gives to me   a dewdrop
> He gives to me   a piece of string
> He gives to me   a straw
>
> The pebble is a huge dark hill I must climb
> The dewdrop's a great stormy lake you must cross
> The string was a road he could not find
> The straw will be a sign whose meaning they forgot
>
> Hill   lake   road   sign
>
> What was it that quite changed the scene?
>
> The answer is that they met a Tiger
> The answer is that he met a Balloon
>
> Who was the Tiger?   Christ
> Who was the Balloon?   Buddha[4]

As for Beat poetry, despite its great impact a few years ago, it seems now to be a dying vogue. The tone was too often crude,—"nothing counts", said Pound, "but the quality of the emotion",—and with Ginsberg there is mainly quantity. More serious was the lack of anything authentically experimental about the movement. What it did, rather, was to revive some good old traditions, which go back at least as far as *Piers Plowman*, of using a rush of strong words and rhythms to denounce the sinner and warn the innocent. I like the grapes of wrath Ferlinghetti and Corso and Rexroth poured on our murderous society, but I grow quickly weary of the repetitive rhythms and vocabulary, the monotonous shape of the bottles they poured the vintage from. The chief value of the Beats lies, I think, in what, predictably, aroused most of the hullabaloo against them: their insistence on using the four-letter words, or words of whatever size, most loaded with shock value. I think not only that their message demanded the use of such a technique, but that they have helped twentieth-century written English to retrieve at least some of the round tough words of Shakespeare and Chaucer which our square soft Canadian Puritans shudder at, and are still capable of sicking the police on writers for using.

Another continuing trend, not exactly new, is surrealism, a sort of Daliesque effect, juxtaposing incongruous, highly visual details in a dream-like sequence. Technically this mode is at least fifty years old, going back to Tristan Tzara and beyond. But the technique inclines to be used today not as an end in itself, or for dadistic shock, but as an adjunct to satire, as by Roger McGough and Anselm Hollo in London and Joe Rosenblatt in Toronto. In the USSR, in fact, it becomes a protective smokescreen behind which poets like Visnesensky are firing ideological bullets at the Kremlin. Like the Projective Verse writers, the surrealists write "organic" poems, without formal beginnings or ends, but with *centres*, hearts, like living organisms, and bodies as changeable as Metamorpho's.

Another deepening phenomenon of mid-twentieth-century literature is one I've touched on before, the breaking down of the boundaries between genres, even between poetry and prose itself when used for artistic ends. Such margins were always blurred, it's true, but we've now moved into a period when some of our most gifted writers seek deliberately to annihilate all our formal conceptions. The most spectacular example is William Burroughs, the American so-called anti-novelist. The current issue of a London experimental journal, called *My Own Magazine*, contains a new work of Burroughs, "The Dead Star". This is set up in newspaper columns of mimeographed material superimposed on numbered grid paper. The columns are solid except for blurred photos reproduced from New York tabloids of the Thirties illustrating some of the more sensational gangster shootings. At first glance, the text is a jumble of disconnected and fragmentary quotations from the news-stories of those times, with special emphasis on the killing of Dutch Schultz. Here is a random extract, somewhat shortened:

> Captain Clark's screeching
> tape recordings and the
> charred, remanents (*sic*) of
> 35 M gun. Look for picture
> Death of Stonewall Jackson
> The song is ended . . . smear
> red with the blood of
> old movies I am dying
> here . . . but the melody
> lingers on . . . dim street
> lights . . . a black cadillac
> in 1920 roads . . . fading
> street a distant sky . . . but
> the melody lingers on . . .
> this way to the river . . .
> the slayers ran to their own
> car . . . extra dry Martini made
> with *Tribunal* Vermouth
> . . . Que tal, Henrique? . . .
> —a name not clear—was light
> ing a fire . . . Winds of
> Vietnam . . . (fight tuberculosis folks . . . [5]

But the perceptive listener may have noted, even from such a short extract, that there are curious poetic aromas rising from this stew, and that in fact it's not a stew at all but a powerfully blended collage or mosaic. Further reading of "The Dead Star" will reveal that Burroughs is taking a deep look into an aspect of the sociology of America, into that U.S.A. which, in the last half-century, has produced a new epos of gangster heroes, a bloody mythology of their very real deaths, a utopian triumph of the ad-man and the sick song writer, and a transformation of the old

American dream into a nightmare and a war in Vietnam. His technique is deliberately non-rational, but so is his subject. To label this a work of prose fiction or a satiric poem or an historical documentary or even an anti-novel is to use terms no longer relevant to the kind of verbal-visual philosophical-objectivist experimentation Burroughs is engaged in. And Burroughs is simply an outstanding writer in a movement now affecting hundreds of artists who are trying to transform the modes and exploit the technologies which mass media have made familiar, in order to approach the mass mind and make art meaningful in today's world. They are, as Robert Creeley says, "sighting themselves in history".

The machine, of course, affects us all. Most poets I know, including myself, compose on a typewriter if one is handy, and we don't feel sure the poem will look right till we see it in type. We may also like to voice it and play it back on a tape recorder, and hope to broadcast it over radio. I even think that the great wave of poetry readings, climaxed last summer in that impromptu performance by some of the farthest-out poets of America and Britain in London's huge Albert Hall (filled to overflowing), was a true dividend from radio and television, which have re-accustomed new poets and new audiences to the fact that poetry can be as public an experience as can any other art. I've no doubt too, that the radio, the tape-recorder and the playback have been influences hastening the very evident change-over in poetic styles from the obscure, gnarled and over-concentrated poetry of Hart Crane and the earlier Dylan Thomas to the direct and plain modes of today, the age of the so-called "modern folksong".

Moreover, new alliances between poetry and the machines are being formed yearly. For me one of the most interesting experimentations displayed by some Londoners at the Festival of the Younger Poets of the Commonwealth last September was the exploitation of electronic music as poetic background. Such music is far more controllable, from the poet's point of view, than a jazz combo. The writer can literally tear off a strip of electronic music and keep it subdued to his own purposes, without conflicting with the integrity of the musical performer or composer. There is even something called a poem machine, now, photographs of which appeared in last summer's number of the London art magazine, *Signals*. It's a slowly revolving drum, something like a fat pianola roll, which plays taped music and voice, synchronized with headline-type poems unfolding as the drum turns.

There's also of course the so-called "computer poetry". Recipe: feed the basic rules of syntax and some recurrent rhythmic patterns into a computer, add vocabulary loaded with image words, run the machine long enough, and out come enormous lengths of word-tape arranged in lines. By the operation of statistical chance, such tapes will occasionally produce passages with sufficient unity of theme and image and enough provocative overtones to warrant their being clipped out and presented as poems. English professors who are outraged or terror-struck by such affairs, or reject them scornfully as machine-made, betray their misunderstanding of the nature of poetry. The computer, used this way, is simply an enormously complicated typewriter. The poem is still being made by poetically-sensitized human beings — by the linguistic expert who chooses the data words and, above all, by the editor of the tape, the critic-perceiver who extracts the poem from the surrounding gibberish. Even

44

when you "make" your own poem longhand, you don't make its form, you find it. Some of these poems are, in fact, much better than many I've been reading recently in such fashionable American poetry journals as Chicago *Poetry*, under the signatures of so-called leading American poets.

In any case, I see nothing sacrilegious or unpoetic in any search by a creatively-minded person into the total resources of his society as aids towards the expression of what he wants to say to that society, or even to himself. When it comes to taking LSD or other drugs, new or old, the poet, of course, must be careful that he really is understanding and controlling the power he's invoking for the stimulation of his imagination and the releasing of the doors of his perception. Smoking marihuana, for example, will certainly not turn him into a drug-addict, despite what Canadian law-makers appear to think, and it may induce highly poetic experiences in the smokers; but it may also put him in a state where he becomes temporarily indifferent to pursuing the hard work of converting the experience to poems. As to the actually addictive drugs, the artist who uses them, legally or illegally, seems to be caught in a self-deteriorating process in which creativity is ultimately one of the casualties.

There's still another world of poetic experimentation today, based on a growing awareness of the primitive unity of all the arts. For example, an increasing number of poets and solo dancers are entering into collaborations for dance-reading productions, in which the recited poem forms the script for the choreography of the dancer. There is also, of course, the more complex and more ancient thing-of-art produced when a dance or opera company performs in close relationship with song-and-word creators, as in Edith Sitwell's *Façade* or in *West Side Story*, or in the sort of composition which Stravinsky would have created with Dylan Thomas, if the latter had lived another year. Verbal art today is constantly going out to the other arts for aid in reaching the primitive sensuousness of man.

Again, though the matching of words and music is as old as the clanging of shields to the war-song, and the blowing of reeds to the sorcerer's chant, we mid-century westerners have displayed far more than traditional delight in poetry-music, in the neo-realistic operas of composers like Menotti, in the invention of a whole new mode of "folk-song" and the rise to fame of Bob Dylan, the most widely heard poet alive in the English-speaking world.

Poets have also been working with the film-makers, when they get a chance, from as early at least as the Auden-Grierson combination which produced that fine English documentary, the *Night Mail*. On the whole, however, neither television nor cinema seems as yet to have inspired the sort of collaboration with writers which leads to literature of permanence. On the other hand through tapes and recordings and radio broadcasts the poet has acquired an enormous amplifier for his voice, and mass-circulation opportunities.

Sculptors are even inviting poets to write on their statuary these days, and poems are also turning up on furniture. Why not in weaving and on dress designs? The October, 1965, issue of the *Bulletin* for the London Institute of Contemporary Arts has a full page illustration of a poem in bold face newstype printed on poster-size sheets pasted in such a way as to cover entirely a large sewing machine. Personally I'm still trying to get time to construct a poem from clippings out of a single issue of the *Toronto Daily Star* which will be pasted onto a mobile specially constructed by a team

45

of sculptors. Perhaps we can make something that will create a spell to haul the warm spring sun back sooner in Canada, the way Eskimo poets make chants to go with string figures they weave, to exorcize the Arctic night and make sure that daylight returns at all. At any rate, I seriously and happily look forward to the day when rooms will swing with mobile poems, and the lobbies of our public buildings will be hung with verses inworked with murals, and engraved with things more verbally exciting and more "depth involving" than the names of founders, or sinister fingers pointing to toilets.

What about poems and paintings? Oriental cultures married these thousands of years ago and a proper Chinese poem, to this day, is something painted on the paper as a visual design (which includes both title and signature), and is in harmony with the poet's theme. Moreover, the units of the design, the carefully executed, brush-stroked and beautiful ideographs, carry not only the meaning but often the formalized vestiges of the original picture still behind the word itself. I think the great renewal of interest by the west in Chinese and Japanese poetry has in turn been one of the influences at work in the new emphasis on visuality in poetry today. The Gutenberg world forgot the close relation of painter and writer that existed in the great manuscript pages of medieval bookmakers, but the profusion of visual media now at the writer's back, and the exciting pioneering of artists themselves, have brought us into an era that is neither Gutenberg's nor Caxton's. Yet, despite what my friend Marshall McLuhan is saying, I contend it is still a world of literature. So far we haven't found new William Blakes or Rossettis, with the ability to create great books that are both poems and paintings, but we do have hundreds of poets today who are "swinging" with the visual arts, writing poems *about* paintings, particularly non-objective paintings, or poems *to* painters, or, as I've said, making designs of all sorts out of the poems themselves, even shimmering moire designs (following the lead of OP Art), or designs so visual only the titles require us to think of them as poems. The cool movements of the moment in this connection are what are known as Concrete Poetry and Found Poetry.

Although some dismiss concrete poems as nothing more than acrostics and crossword puzzles, this vogue contains some serious aesthetic theorizings. To quote its chief British practitioner, the Scot, Ian Hamilton Finlay, concrete poetry is "concerned with a structure of small nuances".[6] A single word may be taken, broken into syllables or letters but so arranged as to suggest many other words which extend the force of the original one, and the whole made into a design of a provocative nature in itself. One of the French concrete poets, Pierre Garnier, cheerfully admits that his work cannot be read out loud. You take it in with the eye, as you do with a billboard; the total effect is the accumulation of words as seen. The word itself is the magic, as Charles Olson once said. An American proponent of concrete poetry explains that "letters and junctures retain their physical identities . . . ; poetry here aspires not to the condition of music but to that of spatial art".[7] It doesn't seek to demolish language but to make language yield those enjoyments offered the viewer of non-objective painting.

Found poetry, on the other hand, seems at first glance an anarchist rather than collectivist fashion. Certainly it assaults the very idea of creation as a slow controlled shaping, and asserts art to be a subjective, even momentary, illusion in the eye of the individual beholder. Aesthetic form is, in a sense, always there; the artist merely

46

isolates it. Just as a stone, or a rusted pair of braces off a garbage dump, once an artist frees them from their typical environment, can be offered as *objet d'arts*, (if the artist sees them as such), so poems may be "created" merely by extracting paragraphs from newspapers, phrases from advertisements, fragments of novels, letters, scientific articles, anything. Even as a can of Campbell Soup became, when Andy Warhol meticulously duplicated it on canvas, a famous modern painting, so the text of the label of the same can might emerge as a Found Peom. The Toronto poet, John Colombo, has recently published a book of excerpts from the political speeches of William Lyon Mackenzie, which he has arranged in lines of verse, following the basic rhetorical rhythms of Toronto's first revolutionary. There is a Greenwich Village poet, Lowell Conway, who has been printing a series of "found Haikus"; he claims that this Japanese form (five syllables followed by seven followed by five) is endemic in contemporary American advertising copy and movie dialogue. One of his discoveries is:

> Caution: no refund
> or adjustment will be made
> without this receipt. [8]

Conway admits, however, that he has grown tired of merely finding poems and has taken to tampering, to interweaving two or three found poems to produce a sort of super-satire. This activity has taken him out of the Found Poem class into another, but still very Camp one at the moment, that of Pop Poetry. This is a movement seeking, like Pop Art, to bridge the gap between High and Low culture, by offering subject matter immediately relevant and true to ordinary people's lives. However, Conway, like many in this movement, is not content with mere neo-realism. He wants to make his Pop poetry both exciting and socially important. An example of his new style, called "Eros 1965", appears in the September *Cavalier*:

> Does she . . .
>   (persons under 16 not admitted)
>
> Does she or . . .
>   (caution: contents under pressure)
>
> Does she or doesn't
>   (please pay when served)
>
> Does she or doesn't she?
>   (this offer void in states where prohibited)
>
> Only her hairdresser knows . . .
>   (a sticky roll-on, a messy spray)
>
> Only her hairdresser knows for . . .
>   (no one will be served without proper identification)
>
> Only her hairdresser knows for sure.
>
> And he'd really rather have a Buick this year.

47

My space is ended, and there is time merely to mention the experimentation of Michael McLure, who invents his own "beast" language in an effort to get at the magic of the poetic voice itself, by way of the syllables or the phonemes behind the word; and to make a bow to the new dramatic forms of Pinter and Paul Ableman in England, in which several characters stand on a stage and speak lines, alternately or in unison, which have no consecutive meaning.

If all this leaves you convinced at the end that writers are mad, dissatisfied, rebellious, restless, word-obsessed, emotional non-conformists, this is partly what I've been trying to say all these times. I hope, however, that you have also come to agree with me that the artist-writer is on life's side nevertheless, and essential to its victory.

Footnotes

[1.] *Comma Poem No. 145; Signals*, June/July, 1965.
[2.] The poems and critical essays of Olson, Creeley and their movement (including Olson's 1950 essay on "Projective Verse") may be approached through Donald M. Allen's anthology, *The New American Poetry*, New York, Grove, 1960.
[3.] See Frank Davey's "Rime", summarizing Duncan's theories, in *Evidence* (Toronto), No. 9, 1965.
[4.] *Gifts (Literary Review*, Summer, 1965) by permission of James Reaney and *The Literary Review*. For the theory of the "deep image" see the essays of George Dowden and Jerome Rothenberg in *The Eleventh Finger* (London), Autumn, 1965.
[5.] Quoted from *My Own Magazine*, No. 13, August, 1965, by kind permission of Jeff Nuttall, editor.
[6.] Ian Hamilton Finlay, letter in *Glasgow Review*, Summer, 1965. See also the special Concrete number of *Extra Verse* (London), Summer, 1965.
[7.] Barbara Smith (Bennington College) in the same issue of the *Glasgow Review.*
[8.] This and the succeeding quotations from the work of Lowell Conway appeared in *Cavalier*, September, 1965, and are reprinted here by kind permission of that magazine and the author.

Hugh MacLennan

Hugh MacLennan was born in 1907 on Cape Breton Island, where his father was a doctor in the mining community of Glace Bay. In 1914 the family moved to Halifax; MacLennan received his schooling there and took a B.A. in Classics at Dalhousie University. On his graduation in 1929, he won a Rhodes scholarship to Oxford in order to continue his classical studies; in 1935 he received a doctorate from Princeton University. Unable to obtain a university teaching post, he taught Latin and History at Lower Canada College in Montreal from 1935 to 1945. He then gave up teaching for several years and supported himself and his wife entirely by his writing. In 1951 he became a part-time lecturer in English at McGill University, where he now teaches full-time.

MacLennan has won considerable public recognition in Canada. He has been awarded five Governor-General's Awards for his novels and collections of essays; he has also won the Lorne Pierce Medal for Literature and an Order of Canada Medal and has been elected a Fellow of the Royal Society of Canada. His novels, though sometimes structurally flawed, represent the most sustained effort which any contemporary writer has made to study in fiction important aspects of Canadian society. His first book, Barometer Rising *(1941), deals with Canada's emergence from British domination;* Two Solitudes *(1945) focuses on Anglo-French relations in Canada;* The Precipice *(1948) compares small-town Ontario life with American urban life;* Each Man's Son *(1951) examines the Scottish-Calvinist conscience;* Return of the Sphinx *(1967) discusses Quebec separatism.* The Watch that Ends the Night *(1959) stands somewhat apart from this group of "thesis-novels"; although it analyses the political radicalism of the nineteen-thirties, its primary themes are personal and spiritual.*

As an essayist, MacLennan has written both familiar and formal essays on a wide variety of subjects—education, cultural history, literature, for example; he frequently returns, however, to questions related to an identity for the Canadian nation. The selection included here was the keynote address at a symposium on the "de-Canadian-ization" of university faculties held at Sir George Williams University in Montreal in May, 1969. The issue which MacLennan discusses here was first raised by Professors Robin Mathews and James Steele of Carleton University in December, 1968, when they compiled the figures to which MacLennan refers in his address and called for a quota on foreign professors.[1] They received both strong opposition and strong support in Canadian universities and among the public at large. MacLennan takes a definite point of view in this controversy, but is, at the same time, clearly aware of the difficulties which his nationalist position entails.

Footnotes

[1] *Robin Mathews and James Steele, eds.,* The Struggle for Canadian Universities: A Dossier *(Toronto: 1969), pp. 1-20.*

Address to the Montreal Symposium on De-Canadianization

If I have ever accepted an assignment less congenial than my present one, I am unable to recall it. The title of this symposium speaks for itself and its implications are enormous and conflicting. They involve the individual futures of thousands of academics. They actually involve the viability of the Canadian nation, a commodity of which she has always been improvident, but now may have carried her pitcher one time too often to the well. Our conscience, our sensibilities, our notion of courtesy are deeply strained by this issue. I hate the idea that I may appear to be hostile to American friends of whom I am fond, or to American colleagues whom I esteem and know to be dedicated men. I am sure you all feel exactly the same about this aspect of today's symposium as I do myself.

Perhaps I should define my present assignment as I understand it. Though I am a member of the academic community, I would prefer you to think that I am speaking as an ordinary Canadian citizen. I have no expert knowledge to offer you. For basic information I have relied mainly on the facts and figures compiled by Professors Mathews and Steele. I am speaking now as I have often done in the past on the issue of the identity of our country, and identity is no abstraction. The instinct to assert and maintain it ranks second only to the instinct to eat when you are hungry. The struggle to assert and maintain it has caused most of the wars and all of the triumphs of human civilization, and a man would have to be blind to the lessons of history and biology to pretend otherwise. Identity — we can add this, too — is almost as basic and essential to the human group as it is to the individual.

It seems to be grievous — something I never dreamed could ever happen in this way — that the unending struggle for the Canadian identity should once again find its arena in our universities. However, this is what has happened. Therefore it seems desperately important that this crisis, which has come upon us so suddenly that it was here before we even knew it, should be faced with the maximum of understanding and the minimum of prejudice. Above all it is vital that any measures taken to deal with it should be undertaken with the scrupulous care of a person who is handling a delicate, intricate and wonderful organism. For that is what a university is, and that is also what it is in danger of ceasing to be.

But having admitted this, let us not turn our eyes away from certain shameful, bitter facts. Suddenly, and everywhere, the university has become a battleground in which mysterious forces have exploded and which unscrupulous power-seekers have exploited. The atmosphere of many a campus today is poisoned with slogans which far too often are uttered as proven truths. Character assassination has become the routine weapon of too many student and faculty politicians. Reason and logic have been swamped by animal passions. Our natural unwillingness to believe that people would contaminate science and philosophy, to say nothing of the teaching of youth, with political propaganda has paralyzed the energies of many of us, and this paralysis may be partially a cause of the particular crisis we are met here to discuss. For a long time we failed to realize — and who can blame us? — what it means that the modern multi-university should have become the focus of some of the worst hatreds and passions which divide the post-war world. Yet this has happened, and if it has happened — with one notable exception — with less virulence than in Germany, Italy, Japan, France and the United States, there is no guarantee that Good Old Canada, trailing as usual behind the prevailing fashions, may not find herself a victim like the others. The atmosphere, we may as well admit, is polluted here, too. And it is in that atmosphere that we are met here today.

You know, and I know, what will be said about us for even daring to raise the subject of today's symposium. Professors Mathews and Steele have already had a nasty foretaste of this. And therefore I would like to say that never in the history of the Canadian academy has there been a finer example of just and dedicated courage than that displayed by these two men. I am sure they hated having to do what they had to do just as much as I hate having to face the implications of what they have told to us and to the nation.

If Kant was right when he said that duty can be recognized as something you do not do gladly, then we will seldom have a better chance of doing our duty than we have now. It is painful to be misunderstood and be quoted out of context, but we are certain to be misunderstood and quoted out of context. In some quarters we will be called parochial, illiberal and paranoiac. We will be accused of preferring nationalism to quality — but of that I intend to say more later. It will be said that we betray the ideal of the international university, although the international university as it existed in the Middle Ages disappeared in the nineteenth century. We will outrage more than one embattled idealist who refuses to face reality. Just as liberals a generation ago leaped to Wendell Willkie's One World slogan — and he meant this in the social sense — so do the idealistic successors of that earlier generation accept in a spirit of brotherhood McLuhan's assertion that we live in an electronic village. Therefore, so the emotional reasoning goes, there are no boundaries any more and anyone who acts as though they still exist runs contrary to progress.

However, there are boundaries a-plenty today, more than ever in human history. While Willkie toured the world hypnotizing himself with his own good will, Stalin, who had fixed him with his obsidian eye and told him how much he liked him, lost no time in establishing the Iron Curtain between Russia and the West, and included behind it some sixty million peoples of whom only a tiny minority wished to be there. And now, in the era of McLuhan, it is difficult to recognize the unifying effects of electronics in Nigeria, South Africa, South America, Cuba, Indonesia, the Russo-Chinese borderlands, or even the campus of a North American university.

Since this is so, what is the point in pretending it is not so, or of denying that the conception of a boundary lies so deep within the genetic inheritance that it is probably ineradicable? Let me put the situation in a single sentence written by a brother novelist, Mordecai Richler, the current writer in residence in this university. Why does Richler's *The Apprenticeship of Duddy Kravitz* go straight to the core of the human experience? In many respects Duddy is one of the most disagreeable characters in Canadian literature, but he is nonetheless a character absolutely universal. The quest of this status-less, mannerless youth seeking a place of his own strikes a universal chord in all humanity. Duddy's inspiration came from a remark his grandfather kept repeating to him from his earliest childhood: "A man without land, Duddel, is nobody." And neither is a nation anything but a geographical expression unless it is able to control its own communications and above all to control its education and the service to which it enlists its universities in the moulding of its people.

For at least a century and a half this idea has been accepted in practice by every nation in the world. Paradoxically, the only way a modern university can truly serve the international community is by first serving its own community. This is true because it is out of its own community that it grows; because it is its own community that supports it; because no community on earth can be loved and understood by foreigners in precisely the same way as by those people who have been born and bred in it, or have elected to become permanent citizens of it because they love and understand it, too. Just as Shakespeare, the supreme world poet, was a profound Englishman, so are certain world universities the repositories and expressions of their nation's profoundest conscience and genius — Bologna in Italy, the Sorbonne in France, Oxford and Cambridge in England, Uppsala in Sweden, Heidelberg in Germany, Harvard and several others in the United States, the Hebrew University in Israel. The only way a university can become a harmonizer and a civilizer within the human chaos is by becoming harmonious within itself.

Surely what I have so far said is practically self-evident. Yet in the atmosphere now prevailing, I feel, and I am sure that you also feel, a very powerful inhibition. So many people everywhere are sniping at the United States that the word "anti-American" has an ugly sound, and deservedly so. Americans have been so well-meaning, so generous and efficient that they are naturally sensitive to any nuance of an attack on their good intentions, and we, their closest neighbours, are more sensitive than they guess about incurring the suspicion that we can be numbered among those who bite them. I think it a statement of simple fact that there is no anti-Americanism in Canada as this idea is understood elsewhere. Rather, there is a nervous unwillingness to protect and develop ourselves in all areas where we may even appear to be acting contrary to American interests. As I am a veteran in this dubious no man's land, and once again am making myself a target, perhaps I may be forgiven if I speak personally for a few minutes.

52

I am not now, and never have been, anti-American, but this does not commit me to the assumption that it is my duty to place American problems, upon which I can have no influence whatever, before Canadian problems which I may perhaps be able to influence a little. During our times of trouble at McGill, for instance, I know I have been called a reactionary by some ardent young American colleagues, recently arrived, for refusing to join with them and some of our internationally-minded student activists in a continuous assault on our Principal because, so they believed, he was serving an Establishment which in turn served the military-industrial Establishment of the United States. If Lester Pearson as Prime Minister was unable to influence ex-President Johnson's Viet Nam policy, I failed to see what chance poor Principal Robertson had of doing any better. Meanwhile in Canada we have had acute internal problems of our own which only we can solve, and in this spill-over of American griefs within our universities, however international those griefs may be in their implications, I must say with regret that our universities have had their native energies badly distracted. Why, I used to ask myself a few years ago, were Canadian students and teachers demonstrating for the civil rights movement and an end to the Viet Nam war — areas in which their activities could only arouse resentment in the bulk of the American people if for no other reason than that they were not Americans — while at the same time they did hardly anything to meet the racial and cultural divisions which threatened the existence of Canada, and which to some extent still threaten it? Emphatically, I am not anti-American when I think like this. As a novelist I have always had a warmer reception from American reviewers than from those in my own country, and for this I have been profoundly grateful. But I have always believed, probably by instinct, in the validity of the border, in the old New England maxim that good fences make good neighbours. Thirty-four years ago when I graduated with a Ph.D. from Princeton, it never occurred to me to think that the chairman of my department was unjust when he told me that he could make no effort to place me in a university in the United States, because at that time academic jobs were as scarce as snowballs in summer and his first duty was to graduates who were his own fellow-citizens.

But when I returned to Canada I encountered for the first time a Canadian attitude which makes us unique among the nations of the world. There was a vacancy in my field in Dalhousie, my old Canadian university, and I applied for it. I was then told by one of my former professors, who had become chairman of the department, that he was surprised that I had come to him. Did I not know that an Englishman had applied for this position and was sure to get it? I asked what the Englishman's record was, being perfectly prepared to give way if it was better than my own. I discovered that it was practically the same as my own had been at Oxford and that he had no advanced degree beyond that. Needless to say he got the job. Nor could I get a job anywhere in a Canadian university, and finally I settled for teaching school at $25 a week.

It seemed to me then, and it still does, that this was a curious attitude for my old teacher to have taken. But in those days it was a typically Canadian one.

Now I will come to the nub of this symposium. You all have the brochure furnished us over the signatures of Professors Beissel, Dudek and Gnarowski containing the figures researched, I presume, by Professors Steele and Mathews. For the record, let me repeat what seem to me the most important of these figures. In 1961, approximately 75% of faculty in Canadian universities were Canadian. In 1968, by September, this proportion had dropped to 49% and has almost certainly dropped further since then. This current year, Canadian universities made about 2,642 new appointments. Of these appointments 1,013 were Americans, 545 British, 722 others.

The truly devastating statistic is the one which indicates that only 362 were Canadians — *the smallest single group.*

I submit that within any nation in the world, with the possible exception of Nigeria and the Gold Coast before they became independent, figures like these would be regarded as beyond belief.

The question naturally arises, how did such an incredible disproportion come about? Earlier this week Opposition Leader Stanfield, referring to this situation as one of the gravest threats to Canada's future, implied that our universities had been unable to engage more of our own people because their expansion-rate, especially that of the new ones, had been so rapid that our own graduate schools were unable to graduate enough candidates to fill the positions. As I have not been able to obtain the complete text of Mr. Stanfield's speech — if speech it was — I may be misquoting him. But one thing at least is certain: there was no serious lack these past three years of adequately trained Canadians to fill many of our academic vacancies.

Looking once again at the figures given in the brochure, we see that between 1965 and 1967, Canada produced a total of 14,151 individuals with advanced degrees, of whom 1,837 were Ph.D.'s and 12,312 were M.A.'s. And we note further that of this group only 1,320 found jobs in Canadian universities. The final statistic is the most shocking of all: last year Canadian universities engaged only 9.5% of the total Canadians available to fill academic positions.

If these figures are true, and I can only presume they are, I don't think I exaggerate when I say that they suggest a programme of national suicide.

The next question naturally arises: how did such a situation come about? It has been widely suggested that the American draft system has been the chief cause of Canada's sudden attractiveness in the eyes of so many of our young American academic friends, for we must presume that by far the largest percentage of these academic appointments have gone to young scholars and scientists and not to international specialists for whom the whole world competes. But after many conversations with American colleagues, I am inclined to doubt that this explanation is the basic one or even the right one. Quite possibly this sudden influx results from the overflow of a domestic American market already saturated. This is a new phenomenon. When I was a graduate student in the United States in the 1930's, graduate student populations were extremely small. Moreover, there were no more than seven or eight universities whose graduate schools had great prestige all the way across the board. As a matter of fact these same universities still retain that prestige. Harvard, Yale, Princeton, the Hopkins, Chicago, M.I.T., Berkeley — the number of these élite institutions has been certainly increased, but I wonder how substantially it has been increased. And I cannot fail to ask myself the question why, if young Americans beginning an academic career could obtain a position in the United States, where they would be paid more than here, they should be crossing the border in such alarming numbers to work in another country which has never interested Americans before save as a source of investment and raw materials?

Another possibility is that our own graduate candidates are generally inferior to those in average or minor graduate colleges south of the border. In some subjects they may be — though I rather doubt it — but across the board I believe this is a preposterous suggestion, because for decades the great lament in Canada has been the brain-drain that occurred automatically every year when we had far fewer universities than we have now, a much smaller population and were unable to furnish jobs for some of our best people.

The second reason for this overwhelming influx of foreign scholars has been, as usual, our typical Canadian casualness, our deplorable habit of never waking up to situations until they become desperate. And I suggest that our situation is going to become a good deal more desperate than it is now unless something is done about it very quickly.

At the moment the magic word in universities is "democratization". I am not going to discuss the desirability or the undesirability of this development, but I am stating it as a fact we all recognize. Not only are students being admitted to senates, steering committees and departmental meetings; in many universities departments have become virtual parliamentary assemblies in which all colleagues, regardless of their age, experience and reputation, have equal voting rights in deciding academic policies and standards, which in turn influence the policies and standards of the university as a whole.

Since this is the case, it is idle to pretend that the preponderance of senior Canadians in the academic departments can keep our universities Canadian in character much longer. As more and more Americans enter the departments, as the balance swings more and more away from native teachers, this will mean only one thing — that the departments will be split down the middle with the Americans in control of the majority factions. I say this with regret and sadness, not only because it is human nature that this should occur, but because I have already seen it occurring with my own eyes, and have even seen some departments which are so entirely Americanized that they operate within the university as a whole as though they were still in the United States. This means that soon, and in some departments it has already happened, the dwindling number of Canadians in our faculties are being reduced to colonial status. It means more for the future. As like always tends to elect like, it means that in the future more and more Americans will be hired and more and more Canadians will have to leave the country or give up the academic life entirely.

This situation, which has come about as suddenly as the physicists' Big Bang, is bound to have catastrophic results both within the nation and within the delicate, nervous organism of our university system. It will not only make Canadian faculty members increasingly discontented and bitter; when its implications are known, it will outrage the Canadian taxpayer. He will ask, make no mistake about it, why he should finance the erosion of his own society, why he should pay out enormous sums for the training of his own people who are denied jobs in his own universities.

What can be done about this specifically is a complex problem, and I presume some solutions will be suggested this afternoon. I take it for granted that in the near future

55

this crisis will become the subject of one of the most important national debates in our history, for the violence within universities, the changes within them, are now front-page news all over the world. The only possible solution here is the one suggested already by Professors Mathews and Steele — that a quota system be established and adhered to. What percentage that will be is of course subject to debate. And whatever quota may be decided upon, of this we may be certain, it will be far, far more generous to foreigners than any existing quota in any other nation. But a quota will have to be established if our universities are to remain Canadian, and my own suggestion is that it should be enacted by law passed by our provincial governments. They, after all, are the chief paymasters of the university today. I speak ruefully when I predict that the Canadian universities, if left to their own devices, would never under any circumstances, least of all existing ones, take a measure of this sort on their own initiative and make it stick.

Now, two more things must be said before I finish. Neither Professors Mathews and Steele, nor anyone of us here, in any way whatever wishes to refuse a warm welcome to American and foreign scholars within our midst. A university, to be a good one, must always have foreign scholars and scientists on its faculties. And when it admits them, it should treat them exactly as it would treat its own native teachers. But for this very reason it should be strong enough in its native majority to be able truly to welcome them, and that majority is what this nation must protect and if necessary create — a strong enough native majority on our faculties to guarantee both our control of policy and our grateful goodwill to those others we invite to work with us. If we fail to secure such a majority, and secure it soon, it takes no clairvoyance to foretell a disastrously unhappy situation for all concerned, for our visitors no less than for ourselves. For the territorial imperative will be sure to assert itself if it is excessively violated, and if it should come to that, then Canadians will behave as it has always made people behave when their own destinies have been taken out of their hands. The volume of ill-will that would then ensue would be something so unpleasant that I cannot bring myself to contemplate it.

Irving Layton

Born in Rumania in 1912, Irving Layton (Lazarovitch) came to Montreal with his family when he was a year old. He was educated at Baron Byng High School and Macdonald College. During World War II he served in the Canadian army. After the war he took an M.A. in political science from McGill University, taught high school in Montreal, and lectured part-time at Sir George Williams University. During these years he was associated with John Sutherland and Louis Dudek in editing First Statement *and with Dudek and Raymond Souster in founding the influential Contact Press. In 1967 he was Writer-in-Residence at the University of Guelph. He now teaches in Toronto at York University.*

Throughout his career Layton has willingly engaged in public controversy. He has attacked the values of the middle class in Canada and the academic tradition in Canadian poetry. In his recent volumes, The Shattered Plinths *(1968) and* The Whole Bloody Bird *(1969), there are a number of pro-Israeli poems inspired by the "six-day war" between Egypt and Israel in June, 1967. In "Above All, Avoid Halitosis," Layton points out, despite the influence that American poetry has had on him, that the liberating ideas of the Black Mountain poets are themselves in danger of becoming foundations of a new academic tradition.*

Layton sees nothing inconsistent in his dual role as poet and controversialist, for he, like Shelley and Blake, conceives of the poet as a prophet, one of the "unacknowledged legislators of the world."[1] His numerous prefaces, such as that to A Red Carpet for the Sun *(1959) reprinted here, make this clear. In the polemical foreword to* Balls for a One-Armed Juggler *(1963) he also says:*

> *Because he is a prophet, the poet must take into himself all the moral diseases, all the anguish and terror of his age, so that from them he can forge the wisdom his tortured fellowmen need to resist the forces dragging them down to the inhuman and the bestial. No doubt it is more pleasant for the contemporary poet to put that cup aside or hand it on to others; more pleasant to regard himself as a surrogate for the displaced clergyman or priest, breathing spasmodically before the True, the Good, and the Beautiful. Or even to think of himself as a picturesque rebel or a colorful bohemian who livens up the parties of jaded suburbanites, or as a scholar and wit. More pleasant; also more applaudable by university presidents, literary scribes, and culture-philistines. But the penalty for this fiddle-faddling is the seepage of life out of his poetry. The age has left him behind, and the best he can give us today are consolatory beautiful mouthings and clever semantic riddles to provide profitable employment for hordes of English profs.[2]*

Layton's output is both voluminous and uneven. Since his first volume, Here and Now, appeared in 1946, he has produced twenty-two volumes of poetry. His most important collections are A Red Carpet for the Sun (1959) and Collected Poems (1965). Eli Mandel argues that Layton's unevenness is an essential aspect of his contempt for the traditional values of literary criticism. "Layton's genius," he suggests, "is as much for the occasional, the off-hand, the anti-literary, the ephemeral, the journalistic, as for the profoundly aesthetic structure."[3]

But if Layton's poems are not always profound, their variety is unfailingly interesting. He writes tender lyrics, witty satires, and carefully crafted, mythopoeic poems like the sonnet sequence "A Tall Man Executes a Jig." Layton's most profound poems are those, like "A Tall Man Executes a Jig," that both shock the reader into an awareness of his evil and shake him into a celebration of his physical and imaginative energy. "Whatever Else Poetry is Freedom," shouts Layton. And Layton's eclectic freedom makes his voice one of the most important in Canadian poetry today.

Footnotes

[1] *Percy Bysshe Shelley,* Complete Works, *eds., R. Ingpen and W. E. Peck (London: 1965), VII, p. 140.*
[2] *Irving Layton,* Balls for a One-Armed Juggler *(Toronto: 1963), p. 20.*
[3] *Eli Mandel,* Irving Layton *(Toronto: 1969), p. 15.*

The Birth of Tragedy

And me happiest when I compose poems.
      Love, power, the huzza of battle
      are something, are much;
yet a poem includes them like a pool
      water and reflection.
In me, nature's divided things—
      tree, mould on tree—
      have their fruition;
I am their core. Let them swap,
bandy, like a flame swerve
I am their mouth; as a mouth I serve.

And I observe how the sensual moths
        big with odour and sunshine
        dart into the perilous shrubbery;
or drop their visiting shadows
        upon the garden I one year made
of flowering stone to be a footstool
        for the perfect gods:
        who, friends to the ascending orders,
sustain all passionate meditations
and call down pardons
for the insurgent blood.

A quiet madman, never far from tears,
        I lie like a slain thing
        under the green air the trees
inhabit, or rest upon a chair
        towards which the inflammable air
tumbles on many robins' wings;
        noting how seasonably
        leaf and blossom uncurl
and living things arrange their death,
while someone from afar off
blows birthday candles for the world.

Song for Naomi

Who is that in the tall grasses singing
By herself, near the water?
I can not see her
But can it be her
Than whom the grasses so tall
Are taller,
My daughter,
My lovely daughter?

Who is that in the tall grasses running
Beside her, near the water?
She can not see there
Time that pursued her

In the deep grasses so fast
And faster
And caught her,
My foolish daughter.

What is the wind in the fair grass saying
Like a verse, near the water?
Saviours that over
All things have power
Make Time himself grow kind
And kinder
That sought her,
My little daughter.

Who is that at the close of the summer
Near the deep lake? Who wrought her
Comely and slender?
Time but attends and befriends her
Than whom the grasses though tall
Are not taller,
My daughter,
My gentle daughter.

The Bull Calf

The thing could barely stand. Yet taken
from his mother and the barn smells
he still impressed with his pride,
with the promise of sovereignty in the way
his head moved to take us in.
The fierce sunlight tugging the maize from the ground
licked at his shapely flanks.
He was too young for all that pride.
I thought of the deposed Richard II.

"No money in bull calves," Freeman had said.
The visiting clergyman rubbed the nostrils
now snuffing pathetically at the windless day.

"A pity," he sighed.
My gaze slipped off his hat toward the empty sky
that circled over the black knot of men,
over us and the calf waiting for the first blow.

Struck,
the bull calf drew in his thin forelegs
as if gathering strength for a mad rush . . .
tottered . . . raised his darkening eyes to us,
and I saw we were at the far end
of his frightened look, growing smaller and smaller
till we were only the ponderous mallet
that flicked his bleeding ear
and pushed him over on his side, stiffly,
like a block of wood.

Below the hill's crest
the river snuffled on the improvised beach.
We dug a deep pit and threw the dead calf into it.
It made a wet sound, a sepulchral gurgle,
as the warm sides bulged and flattened.
Settled, the bull calf lay as if asleep,
one foreleg over the other,
bereft of pride and so beautiful now,
without movement, perfectly still in the cool pit,
I turned away and wept.

On Seeing the Statuettes of Ezekiel and Jeremiah in the Church of Notre Dame

They have given you French names
    and made you captive, my rugged
troublesome compatriots;
    your splendid beards, here, are epicene,
plaster white
        and your angers
unclothed with Palestinian hills quite lost
in this immense and ugly edifice.

You are bored — I see it — sultry prophets
    with priests and nuns
(What coarse jokes must pass between you!)
    and with those morbidly religious
i.e. my prize brother-in-law
          ex-Lawrencian
pawing his rosary, and his wife
sick with many guilts.

Believe me I would gladly take you
    from this spidery church
its bad melodrama, its musty smell of candle
    and set you both free again
in no make-believe world
        of sin and penitence
but the sunlit square opposite
alive at noon with arrogant men.

Yet cheer up Ezekiel and you Jeremiah
    who were once cast into a pit;
I shall not leave you here incensed, uneasy
    among alien Catholic saints
but shall bring you from time to time
        my hot Hebrew heart
as passionate as your own, and stand
with you here awhile in aching confraternity.

Whatever Else Poetry is Freedom

Whatever else poetry is freedom.
Forget the rhetoric, the trick of lying
All poets pick up sooner or later. From the river,
Rising like the thin voice of grey castratos — the mist;
Poplars and pines grow straight but oaks are gnarled;
Old codgers must speak of death, boys break windows;
Women lie honestly by their men at last.

And I who gave my Kate a blackened eye
Did to its vivid changing colours
Make up an incredible musical scale;
And now I balance on wooden stilts and dance

And thereby sing to the loftiest casements.
See how with polish I bow from the waist.
Space for these stilts! More space or I fail!

And a crown I say for my buffoon's head.
Yet no more fool am I than King Canute,
Lord of our tribe, who scanned and scorned;
Who half-deceived, believed; and, poet, missed
The first white waves come nuzzling at his feet;
Then damned the courtiers and the foolish trial
With a most bewildering and unkingly jest.

It was the mist. It lies inside one like a destiny.
A real Jonah it lies rotting like a lung.
And I know myself undone who am a clown
And wear a wreath of mist for a crown;
Mist with the scent of dead apples,
Mist swirling from black oily waters at evening,
Mist from the fraternal graves of cemeteries.

It shall drive me to beg my food and at last
Hurl me broken I know and prostrate on the road;
Like a huge toad I saw, entire but dead,
That Time mordantly had blacked; O pressed
To the moist earth it pled for entry.
I shall be I say that stiff toad for sick with mist
And crazed I smell the odour of mortality.

And Time flames like a paraffin stove
And what it burns are the minutes I live.
At certain middays I have watched the cars
Bring me from afar their windshield suns;
What lay to my hand were blue fenders,
The suns extinguished, the drivers wearing sunglasses.
And it made me think I had touched a hearse.

So whatever else poetry is freedom. Let
Far off the impatient cadences reveal
A padding for my breathless stilts. Swivel,
O hero, in the fleshy groves, skin and glycerine,
And sing of lust, the sun's accompanying shadow
Like a vampire's wing, the stillness in dead feet—
Your stave brings resurrection, O aggrievèd king.

Keine Lazarovitch 1870 — 1959

When I saw my mother's head on the cold pillow,
Her white waterfalling hair in the cheeks' hollows,
I thought, quietly circling my grief, of how
She had loved God but cursed extravagantly his creatures.

For her final mouth was not water but a curse,
A small black hole, a black rent in the universe,
Which damned the green earth, stars and trees in its stillness
And the inescapable lousiness of growing old.

And I record she was comfortless, vituperative,
Ignorant, glad, and much else besides; I believe
She endlessly praised her black eyebrows, their thick weave,
Till plagiarizing Death leaned down and took them for his
    mould.

And spoiled a dignity I shall not again find,
And the fury of her stubborn limited mind;
Now none will shake her amber beads and call God blind,
Or wear them upon a breast so radiantly.

O fierce she was, mean and unaccommodating;
But I think now of the toss of her gold earrings,
Their proud carnal assertion, and her youngest sings
While all the rivers of her red veins move into the sea.

A Tall Man Executes a Jig

I

So the man spread his blanket on the field
And watched the shafts of light between the tufts
And felt the sun push the grass towards him;
The noise he heard was that of whizzing flies,

64

The whistlings of some small imprudent birds,
And the ambiguous rumbles of cars
That made him look up at the sky, aware
Of the gnats that tilted against the wind
And in the sunlight turned to jigging motes.
Fruitflies he'd call them except there was no fruit
About, spoiling to hatch these glitterings,
These nervous dots for which the mind supplied
The closing sentences from Thucydides,
Or from Euclid having a savage nightmare.

II

Jig jig, jig jig. Like minuscule black links
Of a chain played with by some playful
Unapparent hand or the palpitant
Summer haze bored with the hour's stillness.
He felt the sting and tingle afterwards
Of those leaving their unorthodox unrest,
Leaving their undulant excitation
To drop upon his sleeveless arm. The grass,
Even the wildflowers became black hairs
And himself a maddened speck among them.
Still the assaults of the small flies made him
Glad at last, until he saw purest joy
In their frantic jiggings under a hair,
So changed from those in the unrestraining air.

III

He stood up and felt himself enormous.
Felt as might Donatello over stone,
Or Plato, or as a man who has held
A loved and lovely woman in his arms
And feels his forehead touch the emptied sky
Where all antinomies flood into light.
Yet jig jig jig, the haloing black jots
Meshed with the wheeling fire of the sun:
Motion without meaning, disquietude
Without sense or purpose, ephemerides
That mottled the resting summer air till
Gusts swept them from his sight like wisps of smoke.
Yet they returned, bringing a bee who, seeing
But a tall man, left him for a marigold.

IV

He doffed his aureole of gnats and moved
Out of the field as the sun sank down,
A dying god upon the blood-red hills.
Ambition, pride, the ecstasy of sex,
And all circumstance of delight and grief,
That blood upon the mountain's side, that flood
Washed into a clear incredible pool
Below the ruddied peaks that pierced the sun.
He stood still and waited. If ever
The hour of revelation was come
It was now, here on the transfigured steep.
The sky darkened. Some birds chirped. Nothing else.
He thought the dying god had gone to sleep:
An Indian fakir on his mat of nails.

V

And on the summit of the asphalt road
Which stretched towards the fiery town, the man
Saw one hill raised like a hairy arm, dark
With pines and cedars against the stricken sun
— The arm of Moses or of Joshua.
He dropped his head and let fall the halo
Of mountains, purpling and silent as time,
To see temptation coiled before his feet:
A violated grass snake that lugged
Its intestine like a small red valise.
A cold-eyed skinflint it now was, and not
The manifest of that joyful wisdom,
The mirth and arrogant green flame of life;
Or earth's vivid tongue that flicked in praise of earth.

VI

And the man wept because pity was useless.
"Your jig's up; the flies come like kites," he said
And watched the grass snake crawl towards the hedge,
Convulsing and dragging into the dark
The satchel filled with curses for the earth,
For the odours of warm sedge, and the sun,
A blood-red organ in the dying sky.
Backwards it fell into a grassy ditch

Exposing its underside, white as milk,
And mocked by wisps of hay between its jaws;
And then it stiffened to its final length.
But though it opened its thin mouth to scream
A last silent scream that shook the black sky,
Adamant and fierce, the tall man did not curse.

VII

Beside the rigid snake the man stretched out
In fellowship of death; he lay silent
And stiff in the heavy grass with eyes shut,
Inhaling the moist odours of the night
Through which his mind tunnelled with flicking tongue
Backwards to caves, mounds, and sunken ledges
And desolate cliffs where come only kites,
And where of perished badgers and racoons
The claws alone remain, gripping the earth.
Meanwhile the green snake crept upon the sky,
Huge, his mailed coat glittering with stars that made
The night bright, and blowing thin wreaths of cloud
Athwart the moon; and as the weary man
Stood up, coiled above his head, transforming all.

Confederation Ode

Like an old, nervous and eager cow
my country
is being led up to the bull
of history

The bull has something else
on his mind
and ignores her;
still, dazed by her wagging tail, in good time
he must unsheathe
his venerable tool
for the long-awaited consummation

Certainly it will be the biggest
bang-up affair
within the memory of centenarians,
and seismologists have been alerted
everywhere
to record the shocks and tremors

Emissaries
are fanning out to advise
younger and older statesmen around the globe:
take note, finally our brindled Elsie
is mating history

For everyone coming to watch
this extraordinary event
there can be standing room only
for himself
and a single bag of overcharged peanuts

Poor dear
what will she do
the day after
when she looks in a pool
and sees
the same bland face,
the same dull wrinkles between the horns
and the relieved bull
even more indifferent than before?

Above All, Avoid Halitosis

Since Americans believe
        there's a gimmick for everything
even for writing poetry
        you   must watch   your breath;
Don't look now
                but I think
certain English profs
        are looking in   your direction;

they'll want to know
                        what you did with
it;
where   your breath   went.
Also gargle on occasion
A sweet breath never hurt anyone

Foreword to *A Red Carpet for the Sun*

This volume contains all the poems I wrote between 1942 and 1958 that I wish to preserve. They are taken from twelve collections I have published during this period; except for retouching lightly two or three poems I have left them stand as they were. To these I have added the following poems: "The Warm Afterdark," which I wrote in the summer of 1957, and "Divinity," "A Bonnet for Bessie," "Love Is an Irrefutable Fire," "Young Girls Dancing at Camp Lajoie," "For Mao Tse-Tung: A Meditation on Flies and Kings," and "My Flesh Comfortless," which I wrote the summer following, after the publication of my last volume, *A Laughter in the Mind*. Looking back upon this period — how to say this tongue-in-cheek yet mean it; how to make love with a hot potato in one's mouth — I see my work as an effort to achieve a definition of independence. Not, though, of disaffiliation. Aristotle was surely wrong: it isn't reason but cruelty distinguishes our species. Man is not a rational animal, he's a dull-witted animal who loves to torture. However, I have my share in the common disgrace; project along with others the fearful rigidities, crippling and comforting, of family, state, and religion. The free individual — independent and gay — is farther from realization than he ever was. Still, in a world where corruption is the norm and enslavement universal, all art celebrates him, prepares the way for his coming. Poetry, by giving dignity and utterance to our distress, enables us to hope, makes compassion reasonable.

Why are people destructive and joy-hating? Is it perception of the unimportance of their lives finally penetrating the bark of their complacency and egotism? The slow martyrdom of sexual frustration? The feeling they're objects of use and not of love? The knowledge they're marked out for death, their resentment hardening with their arteries? Whichever is the reason, they can't for long endure the sight of a happy man. You might as wisely light a match in a room filled with cyclopropane as go among them with a pleased expression. Tear it off your face they must, let their fingers be crushed in the attempt. Because many poets have averted their eyes from this radical evil, they strike me as insufferable blabbermouths. They did not retch enough; were too patient, courteous, civilized. A little brutality would have made them almost men.

My extraction has made me suspicious of both literature and reality. Let me explain. My father was an ineffectual visionary; he saw God's footprint in a cloud and lived only for his books and meditations. A small bedroom in a slum tenement, which in the torrid days steamed and blistered and sweated, he converted into a tabernacle for the Lord of Israel; and here, like the patriarch Abraham, he received his messengers. Since there was nothing angelic about me or his other children, he no more noticed us than if we had been flies on a wall. Had my mother been as otherworldly as he was, we should have starved. Luckily for us, she was not; she was tougher than nails, shrewd and indomitable. Moreover, she had a gift for cadenced vituperation; to which, doubtless, I owe my impeccable ear for rhythm. With parents so poorly matched and dissimilar, small wonder my entelechy was given a terrible squint from the outset. I am not at ease in the world (what poet ever is?); but neither am I fully at ease in the world of the imagination. I require some third realm, as yet undiscovered, in which to live. My dis-ease has spurred me on to bridge the two with the stilts of poetry, or to create inside me an ironic balance of tensions. Unlike Keats, I have not wished to escape into the unreal domain of the nightingale nor to flee, as the more cowardly do, from imagination to fact. Mercifully all poetry, in the final analysis, is about poetry itself; creating through its myriad forms a world in which the elements of reality are sundered; are, as it were, preserved for a time in suspension.

Yet this rift reflects something actual and objective, is as tensing and generative as that of the Hebrew and pagan in Occidental civilization. A real division exists in the human world where at certain points art and life, like thought and instinct, are hostile to each other. It's a truism to say normal people do not write poetry. Philistinism is the permanent basis of human existence: a world in which everyone was an artist or a philosopher would perish in a week. The Canadian philistine, of course, enjoys advantages — his Anglo-Saxon connection, numbers, natural resources, prosperity — philistines of other countries may perhaps envy. But human life anywhere on this planet very wisely preserves itself by spawning more stenographers, trade-union bosses, military leaders, hashslingers, and second-rate presidents than it does poets. The aesthete, nursing incurable ego-wounds, has the relationship down pat — life is the raw material for art! I can't persuade myself this is so. In my very bones I feel it isn't. Art also finally crumbles and falls back into life as the water-lily's brightness crumbles into the pondscum that surrounds it. Though art transcends pain and tragedy, it does not negate them, does not make them disappear. Whatever its more perfervid devotees may think and write, poetry does not exorcise historical dynamism, macabre cruelty, guilt, perversity, and the pain of consciousness.

Each poem that thumbs its nose at death is a fusion of accident and destiny. As such it is a structure in which the bronzed, athletic philistine is not interested. In any event, he can live without it. For accidents he has insurance policies; for destiny, his image of Napoleon, should he be a profound intellectual suburbanite; the assurances of dialectical materialism, if he is a Marxist proletarian. Before these, the poet unwilling to act as choirboy or morale-builder must appear ailing, furtive, hysterical; one who bumps his forehead against a wall, then exclaims: "Look at the lovely bump I have! Isn't the shape of it glorious? Aren't the colours extraordinarily beautiful?" (That's the sort of poetry the genteel and "cultured" especially like. The poet, of course, *should* strike his head against the wall of men's ferocity and senselessness, but let him yell and curse; not whimper, not bleat.) At this point Byron's contempt and Nietzsche's for the poet becomes understandable; my mother's commonsensical expletives begin ringing in my ears. And so rapturously, too, does he sing of his griefs, this poet, while the dull muttonheads pick their teeth or mount their females. Miserable clown! Can one think of anything more ludicrous? ironic? zany? Squeaking and throbbing, chittering and twittering; demon-driven or driven by their peacock vanity — so the poets, or so I sometimes see them, even the best of them. "What have these jigging fools to do with wars?" Shakespeare understood. Patricians or mob, what have they to do with the joy and wonder that is poetry: they are far happier killing or intriguing to kill. Too long have poets sung with blocked noses, their suffocating complaints and sudden euphoric sneezes filling the indifferent air. They deceive themselves — would they might deceive the hard-faced and heartless. Nevertheless the world remembers them, needs them. They alone are authentic. Bypassing the philistine suburbs of purgatory, they alone have the imagination to commute between heaven and hell.

So what I've written — besides my joy in being alive to write about them — has been about this singular business of human evil; the tension between Hebrew and pagan, between the ideal and real. The disorder and glory of passion. The modern tragedy of the depersonalization of men and women. About a hideously commercial civilization spawning hideously deformed monstrosities. Modern women I see cast in the role of furies striving to castrate the male; their efforts aided by all the malignant forces of a technological civilization that has rendered the male's creative role of revelation superfluous — if not an industrial hazard and a nuisance. We're being feminized and proletarianized at one and the same time. This is the inglorious age of the mass-woman. Her tastes are dominant everywhere — in theatres, stores, art, fiction, houses, furniture — and these tastes are dainty and trivial. Dionysus is dead: his corpse seethes white-maggotty with social workers and analysts. Not who is winning the Cold War is the big issue confronting mankind, but this: Will the Poet, as a type, join the Priest, the Warrior, the Hero, and the Saint as melancholy museum pieces for the titillation of a universal babbitry? It could happen.

The poems in this collection are all leaves from the same tree. A certain man living between 1942 and 1958 wrote them. That man is now dead, and even if he could be resurrected wouldn't be able to write them in the way they were written. Nor would he want to. They belong to a period of my life that is now behind me: a period of testing, confusion, ecstasy. Now there is only the ecstasy of an angry middle-aged man growing into courage and truth. Unlike the scholar or literary historian who writes about life, the poet enjoys it, *lives* it. Lives it with such intensity that he is often unable to say coherently or in plain words what the experience was like. I have in these paragraphs tried to set down those things that have most violently engaged my feelings and entered into the composition of my poems. For me, a poet is one who explores new areas of sensibility. If he has the true vocation he will take risks; for him there can be no "dogmatic slumbers." It will not do to repeat oneself, life is fluid and complex, and become with Housman or Jeffers a one-note Johnny. Or having grown respectable, to trot out a sterile moralism or religiosity, that favourite straw of poets with declining powers. I too have seen the footprint in the cloud, though somewhat gorier than my father saw it. When all is said, I have no choice but to walk after it.

Lac Provost, Que.
August 30, 1958

Hugh Garner

Hugh Garner was born in Yorkshire in 1913 and came to Toronto in 1919, where he attended Danforth Technical School. During the Depression of the nineteen-thirties he worked at a series of manual jobs until 1937 when he went to Spain to fight on the side of the Loyalists in the Spanish Civil War. He was a machine-gunner in the Abraham Lincoln Battalion of the International Brigade. From 1940 to 1945 he served in the Canadian navy. His earliest stories appeared in the Canadian Forum *in 1936, but he did not publish again until after the war. Since then he has written several novels, short stories, and essays. Two of his novels,* Cabbagetown *(1950) and* Silence on the Shore *(1962), are set in working-class districts of Toronto.* Hugh Garner's Best Stories *(1963), a selection of his short stories which includes "One-Two-Three Little Indians," won a Governor-General's Award.*

Garner's experiences during the Depression gave him a good deal of sympathy with the lower classes in contemporary society, a sympathy which is manifest in much of his fiction. In many cases his settings are urban, and his characters are very much products of the east end of Toronto, a district with which Garner is thoroughly familiar. But he is also capable of writing about the rural poor. "One-Two-Three Little Indians," one of his most powerful stories, explores the debilitating effects on the Indian of the adoption of white values and the indifference of well-intentioned whites to the sufferings of the Indians. Garner does not write to promote a particular social ideology, however; here, as in his best work, his method is simply to present an action and let the humanity of his characters speak for itself.

One-Two-Three Little Indians

After they had eaten, Big Tom pushed the cracked and dirty supper things to the back of the table and took the baby from its high chair carefully, so as not to spill the flotsam of bread crumbs and boiled potatoes from the chair to the floor.

He undressed the youngster, talking to it in the old dialect, trying to awaken its interest. All evening it had been listless and fretful by turns, but now it seemed to be soothed by the story of Po-chee-ah, and the Lynx, although it was too young to understand him as his voice slid awkwardly through the ageless folk-tale of his people.

For long minutes after the baby was asleep he talked on, letting the victorious words fill the small cabin so that they shut out the sounds of the Northern Ontario night: the buzz of mosquitoes, the far-off bark of a dog, the noise of the cars and transport trucks passing on the gravelled road.

The melodious hum of his voice was like a strong soporific, lulling him with the return of half-forgotten memories, strengthening him with the knowledge that once his people had been strong and brave, men with a nation of their own, encompassing a million miles of teeming forest, lake and tamarack swamp.

When he halted his monologue to place the baby in the big brass bed in the corner the sudden silence was loud in his ears, and he cringed a bit as the present suddenly caught up with the past.

He covered the baby with a corner of the church-donated patchwork quilt, and lit the kerosene lamp that stood on the mirrorless dressing table beside the stove. Taking a broom from a corner he swept the mealtime debris across the doorsill.

This done, he stood and watched the headlights of the cars run along the trees bordering the road, like a small boy's stick along a picket fence. From the direction of the trailer camp a hundred yards away came the sound of a car engine being gunned, and the halting note-tumbles of a clarinet from a tourist's radio. The soft summer smell of spruce needles and wood smoke blended with the evening dampness of the earth, and felt good in his nostrils, so that he filled his worn lungs until he began to cough. He spat the resinous phlegm into the weed-filled yard.

It had been this summer smell, and the feeling of freedom it gave, which had brought him back to the woods after three years in the mines during the war. But only part of him had come back, for the mining towns and the big money had done more than etch his lungs with silica: they had also brought him pain and distrust, and a wife who had learned to live in gaudy imitation of the boomtown life.

When his coughing attack subsided he peered along the path, hoping to catch a glimpse of his wife Mary returning from her work at the trailer camp. He was becoming worried about the baby, and her presence, while it might not make the baby well, would mean that there was someone else to share his fears. He could see nothing but the still blackness of the trees, their shadows interwoven in a sombre pattern across the mottled ground.

He re-entered the cabin and began washing the dishes, stopping once or twice to cover the moving form of the sleeping baby. He wondered if he could have transmitted his own wasting sickness to the lungs of his son. He stood for long minutes at the side of the bed, staring, trying to diagnose the child's restlessness into something other than what he feared.

His wife came in and placed some things on the table. He picked up a can of pork-and-beans she had bought and weighed it in the palm of his hand. "The baby seems pretty sick," he said.

She crossed the room, and looked at the sleeping child. "I guess it's his teeth."

He placed the pork-and-beans on the table again and walked over to his chair beside the empty stove. As he sat down he noticed for the first time that his wife was beginning to show her pregnancy. Her squat form had sunk lower, and almost filled the shapeless dress she wore. Her brown ankles were puffed above the broken-down heels of the dirty silver dancing pumps she was wearing.

"Is the trailer camp full?" he asked.

"Nearly. Two more Americans came about half an hour ago."

"Was Billy Woodhen around?"

"I didn't see him, only Elsie," she answered. "A woman promised me a dress tomorrow if I scrub out her trailer."

"Yeh." He saw the happiness rise over her like a colour as she mentioned this. She was much younger than he was — twenty-two years against his thirty-nine — and her dark face had a fullness that is common to many Indian women. She was no longer pretty, and as he watched her he thought that wherever they went the squalor of their existence seemed to follow them.

"It's a silk dress," Mary said, as though the repeated mention of it brought it nearer.

"A silk dress is no damn good around here. You should get some overalls," he said, angered by her lack of shame in accepting the cast-off garments of the trailer women.

She seemed not to notice his anger. "It'll do for the dances next winter."

"A lot of dancing you'll do," he said pointing to her swollen body. "You'd better learn to stay around here and take care of the kid."

She busied herself over the stove, lighting it with newspapers and kindling. "I'm going to have some fun. You should have married a grandmother."

He filled the kettle with water from an open pail near the door. The baby began to cough, and the mother turned it on its side in the bed. "As soon as I draw my money from Cooper I'm going to get him some cough syrup from the store," she said.

"It won't do any good. We should take him to the doctor in town tomorrow."

"I can't. I've got to stay here and work."

He knew the folly of trying to reason with her. She had her heart set on earning the silk dress the woman had promised.

After they had drunk their tea he blew out the light, and they took off some of their clothes and climbed over the baby into the bed. Long after his wife had fallen asleep he lay in the darkness listening to a ground moth beating its futile wings against the glass of the window.

They were awakened in the morning by the twittering of a small colony of tree sparrows who were feasting on the kitchen sweepings of the night before. Mary got up and went outside, returning a few minutes later carrying a handful of birch and poplar stovewood.

He waited until the beans were in the pan before rising and pulling on his pants. He stood in the doorway scratching his head and absorbing the sunlight through his bare feet upon the step.

The baby awoke while they were eating their breakfast.

"He don't look good," Big Tom said as he dipped some brown sauce from his plate with a hunk of bread.

"He'll be all right later," his wife insisted. She poured some crusted tinned milk from a tin into a cup and mixed it with water from the kettle.

Big Tom splashed his hands and face with cold water, and dried himself on a soiled shirt that lay over the back of a chair. "When you going to the camp, this morning?"

"This afternoon," Mary answered.

"I'll be back by then."

He took up a small pile of woven baskets from a corner and hung the handles over his arm. From the warming shelf of the stove he pulled a bedraggled band of cloth, into which a large goose feather had been sewn. Carrying this in his hand he went outside and strode down the path toward the highway.

He ignored the chattering sauciness of a squirrel that hurtled up the green ladder of a tree beside him. Above the small noises of the woods could be heard the roar of a transport truck braking its way down the hill from the burnt-out sapling covered ridge to the north. The truck passed him as he reached the road, and he waved a desultory greeting to the driver, who answered with a short blare of the horn.

Placing the baskets in a pile on the shoulder of the road he adjusted the corduroy band on his head so that the feather stuck up at the rear. He knew that by so doing he became a part of the local colour, "a real Indian with a feather'n everything," and also that he sold more baskets while wearing it. In the time he had been living along the highway he had learned to give them what they expected.

The trailer residents were not yet awake, so he sat down on the wooden walk leading to the shower room, his baskets resting on the ground in a half circle behind him.

After a few minutes a small boy descended from the door of a trailer and stood staring at him. Then he leaned back inside the doorway and pointed in Big Tom's direction. In a moment a man's hand parted the heavy curtains on the window and a bed-mussed unshaven face stared out. The small boy climbed back inside.

A little later two women approached on the duckboard walk, one attired in a pair of buttock-pinching brown slacks, and the other wearing a blue chenille dressing gown. They circled him warily and entered the shower room. From inside came the buzz of whispered conversation and the louder noises of running water.

During the rest of the morning several people approached and stared at Big Tom and the baskets. He sold two small ones to an elderly woman. She seemed surprised when she asked him what tribe he belonged to, and instead of answering in a monosyllable he said, "I belong to the Algonquins, Ma'am." He also got rid of one of his forty-five cent baskets to the mother of the small boy who had been the first one up earlier in the day.

A man took a series of photographs of him with an expensive-looking camera, pacing off the distance and being very careful in setting his lens openings and shutter speeds.

"I wish he'd look into the camera," the man said loudly to a couple standing nearby, as if he were talking about an animal in a cage.

"You can't get any good picshus around here. Harold tried to get one of the five Dionney kids, but they wouldn't let him. The way they keep them quints hid you'd think they was made of china or somep'n," a woman standing by said.

She glanced at her companion for confirmation.

"They want you to *buy* their picshus," the man said. "We was disappointed in 'em. They used to look cute before, when they was small, but now they're just five plain-looking kids."

"Yeah. My Gawd, you'd never believe how homely they got, would you, Harold? An' everything's pure robbery in Callander. You know, Old Man Dionney's minting money up there. Runs his own souvenir stand."

"That's durin' the day, when he's got time," her husband said.

The man with the camera, and the woman, laughed.

After lunch Big Tom watched Cooper prepare for his trip to North Bay. "Is there anybody going fishing, Mr. Cooper?" he asked.

The man took the radiator cap off the old truck he was inspecting, and peered inside.

"Mr. Cooper!"

"Hey?" Cooper turned and looked at the Indian standing behind him, hands in pockets, his manner shy and deferential. He showed a vague irritation as though he sensed the overtone of servility in the Indian's attitude.

"Anybody going fishing?" Big Tom asked again.

"Seems to me Mr. Staynor said he'd like to go," Cooper answered. His voice was kind, with the amused kindness of a man talking to a child.

The big Indian remained standing where he was, saying nothing. His old second-hand army trousers drooped around his lean loins, and his plaid shirt was open at the throat, showing a grey high-water mark of dirt where his face washing began and ended.

"What's the matter?" Cooper asked. "You seem pretty anxious to go today."

"My kid's sick. I want to make enough to take him to the doctor."

Cooper walked around the truck and opened one of the doors, rattling the handle in his hand as if it was stuck. "You should stay home with it. Make it some pine-sap syrup. No need to worry, it's as healthy as a bear cub."

Mrs. Cooper came out of the house and eased her bulk into the truck cab. "Where's Mary?" she asked.

"Up at the shack," answered Big Tom.

"Tell her to scrub the washrooms before she does anything else. Mrs. Anderson, in that trailer over there, wants her to do her floors." She pointed across the lot to a large blue and white trailer parked behind a Buick.

"I'll tell her," he answered.

The Coopers drove between the whitewashed stones marking the entrance to the

76

camp, and swung up the highway, leaving behind them a small cloud of dust from the pulverized gravel of the road.

Big Tom fetched Mary and the baby from the shack. He gave his wife Mrs. Cooper's instructions, and she transferred the baby from her arms to his. The child was feverish, its breath noisy and fast.

"Keep him warm," she said. "He's been worse since we got up. I think he's got a touch of the 'flu."

Big Tom placed his hand inside the old blanket and felt the baby's cheek. It was dry and burning to his palm. He adjusted the baby's small weight in his arm and walked across the camp and down the narrow path to the shore of the lake where the boats were moored.

A man sitting in the sternsheets of a new-painted skiff looked up and smiled at his approach. "You coming out with me, Tom?" he asked.

The Indian nodded.

"Are you bringing the papoose along?"

Big Tom winced at the word "papoose", but he answered, "He won't bother us. The wife is working this afternoon."

"O.K. I thought maybe we'd go over to the other side of the lake today and try to get some of them big fellows at the creek mouth. Like to try?"

"Sure," the Indian answered, placing the baby along the wide seat in the stern, and unshipping the oars.

He rowed silently for the best part of an hour, the sun beating through his shirt causing the sweat to trickle coldly down his back. At times his efforts at the oars caused a constriction in his chest, and he coughed and spat into the water.

When they reached the mouth of the creek across the lake, he let the oars drag and leaned over to look at the baby. It was sleeping restlessly, its lips slightly blue and its breath laboured and harsh. Mr. Staynor was busy with his lines and tackle in the bow of the boat.

Tom picked the child up and felt its little body for sweat.

The baby's skin was bone dry. He picked up the bailing can from the boat bottom and dipped it over the side. With the tips of his fingers he brushed some of the cold water across the baby's forehead. The child woke up, looked at the strange surroundings, and smiled up at him. He gave it a drink of water from the can. Feeling reassured now he placed the baby on the seat and went forward to help the man with his gear.

Mr. Staynor fished for a half hour or so, catching some small fish and a large black bass, which writhed in the bottom of the boat. Big Tom watched its gills gasping its death throes, and noted the similarity between the struggles of the fish and those of the baby lying on the seat in the blanket.

He became frightened again after a time, and he turned to the man in the bow and said, "We'll have to go pretty soon. I'm afraid my kid's pretty sick."

"Eh! We've hardly started," the man answered. "Don't worry, there's not much wrong with the papoose."

77

Big Tom lifted the child from the seat and cradled it in his arms. He opened the blanket, and shading the baby's face, allowed the warm sun to shine on its chest. He thought, if I could only get him to sweat; everything would be all right then.

He waited again as long as he dared, noting the blueness creeping over the baby's lips, before he placed the child again on the seat and addressed the man in the bow. "I'm going back now. You'd better pull in your line."

The man turned and felt his way along the boat. He stood over the Indian and parted the folds of the blanket, looking at the baby. "My God, he is sick, Tom! You'd better get him to a doctor right away!" He stepped across the writhing fish to the bow and began pulling in the line. Then he busied himself with his tackle, stealing glances now and again at the Indian and the baby.

Big Tom turned the boat around, and with long straight pulls on the oars headed back across the lake. The man took the child in his arms and blew cooling drafts of air against its fevered face.

As soon as they reached the jetty below the tourist camp, Tom tied the boat's painter to a stump and took the child from the other man's arms.

Mr. Staynor handed him the fee for a full afternoon's work. "I'm sorry the youngster is sick, Tom," he said. "Don't play around. Get him up to the doctor in town right away. We'll try her again tomorrow afternoon."

Big Tom thanked him. Then, carrying the baby and unmindful of grasping hands of the undergrowth, he climbed the path through the trees. On reaching the parked cars and trailers he headed in the direction of the large blue and white one where his wife would be working.

When he knocked, the door opened and a woman said, "Yes?" He recognized her as the one who had been standing nearby in the morning while his picture was being taken.

"Is my wife here?" he asked.

"Your wife; Oh, I know now who you mean. No, she's gone. She went down the road in a car a few minutes ago."

The camp was almost empty, most of the tourists having gone to the small bathing beach farther down the lake. A car full of bathers was pulling away to go down to the beach. Big Tom hurried over and held up his hand until it stopped. "Could you drive me to the doctor in town?" he asked. "My baby seems pretty sick."

There was a turning of heads within the car. A woman in the back seat began talking about the weather. The driver said, "I'll see what I can do, Chief, after I take the girls to the beach."

Big Tom sat down at the side of the driveway to wait. After a precious half hour had gone by and they did not return, he got to his feet and started up the highway in the direction of town.

His long legs pounded on the loose gravel of the road, his anger and terror giving strength to his stride. He noticed that the passengers in the few cars he met were pointing at him and laughing, and suddenly he realized that he was still wearing the feather in the band around his head. He reached up, pulled it off, and threw it in the ditch.

When a car or truck came up from behind him he would step off the road and raise his hand to beg a ride. After several passed without pausing he stopped this useless time-wasting gesture and strode ahead, impervious to the noise of their horns as they approached him.

Now and again he placed his hand on the baby's face as he plodded along, reassuring himself that it was still alive. It had been hours since it had cried or shown any other signs of consciousness.

Once, he stepped off the road at a small bridge over a stream, and making a crude cup with his hands, tried to get the baby to drink. He succeeded only in making it cough, harshly, so that its tiny face became livid with its efforts to breathe.

It was impossible that the baby should die. Babies did not die like this, in their father's arms, on a highway that ran fifteen miles north through a small town, where there was a doctor and all the life-saving devices to prevent their deaths.

The sun fell low behind the trees and the swarms of black flies and mosquitoes began their nightly forage. He waved his hand above the fevered face of the baby, keeping them off, while at the same time trying to waft a little air into the child's tortured lungs.

But suddenly, with feelings as black as hell itself, he knew that the baby was dying. He had seen too much of it not to know now, that the child was in an advanced stage of pneumonia. He stumbled along as fast as he could, his eyes devouring the darkening face of his son, while the hot tears ran from the corners of his eyes.

With nightfall he knew that it was too late. He looked up at the sky where the first stars were being drawn in silver on a burnished copper plate, and he cursed them, and cursed what made them possible.

To the north-west the clouds were piling up in preparation for a summer storm. Reluctantly he turned and headed back down the road in the direction he had come.

It was almost midnight before he felt his way along the path through the trees to his shack. It was hard to see anything in the teeming rain, and he let the water run from his shoulders in an unheeded stream, soaking the sodden bundle he still carried in his arms.

When he reached the shanty he opened the door and fell inside. He placed the body of his son on the bed in the corner. Then, groping around the newspaper-lined walls, he found some matches in a pocket of his mackinaw and lit the lamp. With a glance around the room he knew that his wife had not yet returned, so he placed the lamp on the table under the window and headed out again into the rain.

At the trailer camp he sat down on the rail fence near the entrance to wait. Some lights shone from the small windows of the trailers and from Cooper's house across the road. The illuminated sign said: COOPER'S TRAILER CAMP — Hot And Cold Running Water, Rest Rooms. FISHING AND BOATING — INDIAN GUIDES.

One by one, as he waited, the lights went out, until only the sign lit up a small area at the gate. He saw the car's headlights first, about a hundred yards down the road. When it pulled to a stop he heard some giggling, and Mary and another Indian girl, Elsie Woodhen, staggered out into the rain.

A man's voice shouted through the door, "See you again, sweetheart. Don't forget next Saturday night." The voice belonged to one of the French-Canadians who worked at a creosote camp across the lake.

Another male voice shouted, "Wahoo!"

The girls clung to each other, laughing drunkenly, as the car pulled away.

They were not aware of Big Tom's approach until he grasped his wife by the hair and pulled her backwards to the ground. Elsie Woodhen screamed, and ran away in the direction of the Cooper house. Big Tom bent down as if he was going to strike at Mary's face with his fist. Then he changed his mind and let her go.

She stared into his eyes and saw what was there. Crawling to her feet and sobbing hysterically she left one of her silver shoes in the mud and limped along towards the shack.

Big Tom followed behind, all the anguish and frustration drained from him, so that there was nothing left to carry him into another day. Heedless now of the coughing that tore his chest apart, he pushed along in the rain, hurrying to join his wife in the vigil over their dead.

W.O. Mitchell

William Ormond Mitchell was-born in Weyburn, Saskatchewan in 1914, and educated at the universities of Manitoba and Alberta. He taught school in Alberta for a number of years and then settled in High River to devote his time to writing. He is now Writer-in-Residence at the University of Calgary.

Mitchell's first novel, Who Has Seen the Wind (1947), is a story of a boy growing up in a Prairie town and confronting the facts of God, death, and human society. Mitchell is, however, perhaps best known as the creator of the series Jake and the Kid which ran on CBC radio and television for a number of years. The volume of stories, Jake and the Kid (1962), from which the following selection is taken, is based on this series. It won the Leacock Medal for Humour.

Mitchell is a strongly regional writer; his best writing evokes the physical and social environment of the Canadian Prairies. He is also profoundly interested in the impact of a child's environment on his imagination, and his rich gift for comic characterization depends, in part, on the incongruities of the adult world as seen through the eyes of a child. In "Two Kinds of Sinner," Jake, the hired man, is necessary for the comic resolution of the conflict between the Kid and Doc Toovey; only Jake perfectly understands the Kid's desires and at the same time possesses the adult wiliness necessary to realize them.

Two Kinds of Sinner

Ever since Ma quit cutting my hair for me, I go in to Repeat Golightly's. He lets me sit right on the chair; he doesn't put that board across any more. Most of the time Jake, our hired man, takes me to town in the democrat, and he was in the barbershop the afternoon Doc Toovey got to talking how his paint horse, Spider, could run the gizzard out of Auction Fever.

The afternoon the argument with Doc Toovey started, Jake had got his shave and was sitting next to Old Man Gatenby whilst Repeat cut my hair. I had my head tilted, with my chin on my chest, and was looking up from under, the way you do, when Repeat swung me around. Then I could see myself over the tonic bottles and the clock with its numbers all backward and Doc Toovey just in the doorway.

Doc runs the Crocus Hay and Feed and Livery. He is a horse and cattle vet, and he has very white hair and a very red face that is all the time smiling. His eyes will put you in mind of oat seeds, sort of.

"Anybody ahead of me?" he asked. His voice is kind of smily too.

"There's four shaves waitin'," Repeat said; "there's four fellas waitin' to git their shave."

"That's fine," Doc said, and he sat down in the chair between Old Man Gatenby and Jake. Jake slid over a little; he isn't so fussy about Doc Toovey; Doc would steal the well out of a person's yard when they weren't looking, Jake says. Jake has old-timer eyes that are squinty from looking into the sun an awful lot. He is pretty near always right.

Repeat went back to work on my hair. "She was smart," he said. "She was a smart little mare." He was talking about Dish Face, the black hackney he used to have in the early days.

"I knew a real smart horse once," Jake said. "Wasn't no hot blood neither — just an ordinary work horse. He run for Parliament on the Lib'ral ticket."

Doc stopped with a plug of tobacco halfway to his mouth. "That's plum foolish." He bit a corner off.

"The heck it is," said Jake. "He was a real bright horse, an' when he seen all the combines an' tractors comin' West he — what else was there fer him to do but go into politics?"

"Well — " Doc leaned sideways in his chair and spit into the spittoon. "I ain't interested in smart horses. But you take running horses, like my paint. He can run."

" 'Bout as fast as a one-arm fella on a handcar," said Jake.

Doc Toovey smiled at Jake. "Ain't nothing around here can beat him."

"That right?" said Jake.

"The kid here has got a nice-looking horse," said Repeat. "I say this here kid's horse is a nice look — "

"I've seen him," said Doc. "He ain't no match for Spider." He smiled at me.

"He can nail Spider's hide to a fence post," I said. "Recess time out at Rabbit Hill he — "

"You wasn't int'rested in findin' out, was you?" Jake asked Doc real polite.

"Might be." Doc spit again. "Might even put a little bet on it."

"How much?" Jake asked him.

"Whatever you want."

"Fifty dollars," said Jake, "and Repeat holds the money."

"I'll hold her," said Repeat, letting me down out of the chair. "You fellas can give her to me and I'll hold her fer you."

"Fine," said Doc. Both him and Jake reached into their pockets.

They worked it out we were going to hold the race next Saturday along the C.P.R. tracks behind Hig Wheeler's lumberyards. When they were done Doc climbed into the barber chair.

"You ain't next," said Repeat. "I say you ain't the — "

"That's all right," said Doc. "Those others ain't in a hurry."

"I'm in a hell of a hurry," said Old Man Gatenby.

"I don't really need a four-bit haircut, Repeat." Doc smiled up at him. "Just give her a sort of a neck trim. Fifteen cents."

Going out home I sat with Jake in the democrat, watching Baldy's hindquarters tipping first one side then the other, real regular but sort of jerky, like Miss Henchbaw when she leads the singing at Rabbit Hill with her stick. Jake didn't say anything for a long way. By the road a meadow lark spilled some notes off of a strawstack. A jack rabbit next to the bar pit undid himself for a few hops then sat startled, with his black-tipped ears straight up.

Jake spit curvey into the breeze. "I wouldn't say nothin' to yer maw."

"About Fever racin' Doc's paint, Spider?"

"Yep."

The rabbit went bouncing to beat anything over the bald-headed prairie. Over to the right of the road a goshawk came sliding down real quiet, slipping his black shadow over the stubble.

"Way yer maw looks at it, bettin' ain't right. I guess next to eatin' tobacco, yer maw hates gamblin'. I wouldn't say nothin' to her — ain't like you was doing the bettin'. All you're doin' is racing." Jake turned to me. "Like she's always sayin', 'Gents don't bet, an' gents don't chaw.'" He spit, and slapped the reins. "Git yer nose out of it, Baldy."

Jake turned to me again. "Fever's gonna run that there long-geared Spider right into the ground!"

All that week I raced Fever — at recess — after four; and like he always does, he beat everything at Rabbit Hill. At home Jake worked on him till he started dandy nine times out of ten. When he finished the distance he wasn't blowing hardly at all, and stepped away all dancy, like he was walking on eggs.

"He'll do," Jake said.

Then Ma found out. She came out to the shed whilst I was washing up for supper.

"I was talking with Mrs. Fotheringham today, son." She waited like she wanted me to say something. I pretended I was getting soap out of my ears. "On the phone," Ma said.

I poured out the basin into the slop pail.

"Mrs. Fotheringham was talking to Doctor Fotheringham. He was talking with Mr. Golightly. She told me there was to be a race Saturday."

"Did she?" I said.

"Yes." Ma's dark eyes were looking right at me. "Between Fever and Dr. Toovey's horse."

I could feel my face getting burny.

"There is some money involved. Fifty dollars. Is that right?"

I jerked my head.

"Why did you do it, son?"

I didn't get any answer out.

"You knew I wouldn't approve. You know what I think of that sort of thing. You know it's wrong, don't you?"

I said, yes, I guessed I did.

"I blame you just as much as I do Jake. I'm beginning to think Auction Fever's not good for you."

"Oh yes he is, Ma!"

"Not if he's going to get you mixed up in — in —gambling."

I looked down at my boots.

"I honestly think I'd just as soon see you chewing tobacco, son!" Ma turned away. At the kitchen door she swung around again. "There's not to be a race Saturday or any day. Not with Doctor Toovey's horse or any horse!"

She gave it to Jake too. She told him to call the race off because it was immoral. That means bad. Jake kicked, but it didn't do him any good.

We found Doc Toovey leaning against his livery stable. His tobacco cud had bulged out the side of his face, so his smile was sort of lopsided. "All set to get beat in that race?" he called.

"Ain't gonna be no race," Jake said.

"Huh!"

"Kid's maw won't let him."

"Well — " Doc smiled down to me — "that's just too bad."

"It is," Jake said.

" 'Course, you'd have lost your 50 dollars anyway."

"Huh!"

"This way you don't prolong the agony."

"What you mean?"

"You called off the race," said Doc. "I didn't. Don't expect to get your money back, do you?"

"I shore as hell do!"

Doc spit, and a little puff of dust came up. "Well, you ain't getting it."

Jake looked at Doc all smily; he looked at the manure fork leaning against the stable wall; he looked back at Doc Toovey again. Real quiet, he said, "You'd look awful funny with that there stickin' outa yer wishbone, Doc."

"Would I?" Doc kept right on smiling.

Later when Jake told Repeat Golightly, Repeat said:

"Ain't much you can do, Jake. I say if he don't want to leave you have the money there ain't much you can — "

Jake slammed out of the barbershop, me right behind.

84

Ma didn't give an inch. She's sure set against betting — and chewing tobacco.

The next time we were in to Crocus we met Doc Toovey in front of the Royal Bank.

"Got a new critter today, Jake," he said. "Bent Golly sold him to me. Figgered you might like to race the kid's buckskin against him."

Jake pushed on past.

"I'd have to get odds," Doc called after us. "He's a mule!"

The next time was in Snelgrove's bakery, when Doc saw me and Jake through the window, eating ice cream. He came in and he said he had a jack rabbit he wanted to put up against Fever. A week later he asked Jake if he thought Fever might give a prairie chicken a good run. Jake mumbled something under his breath.

" 'Course you might be scared, same as you were the time before, and want to back out of it," Doc said. "If you haven't got the guts — "

"Guts!" Jake yelled. "We got 'em all right! We'll show you! That there race is on again! Same place, same distance, and double the bet, you scroungin', stubble-jumpin', smily-faced son of a hardtail!"

Afterward I said to Jake:

"What'll Ma — "

"We're racin'," Jake said.

"But, Ma won't — "

"Yer maw figgers 'tain't right, but what that there — what that — what he's doin' to us is plum immortal too, an' if I got to take my pick between two kinds of a sinner, I know which kind I'm takin'!"

And that was how come we ended up behind Hig Wheeler's the next Saturday, all set to race Fever and the paint. Jake and me brought Fever in behind the democrat. At the last moment Ma decided to come with us. Jake told her we were getting Fever's hind shoes fixed.

We left Ma at Mrs. Fotheringham's, then we headed for the race.

Half the folks from Crocus were there, and nearly everyone from Rabbit Hill district. Jake and Doc Toovey weren't the only ones betting.

Mr. MacTaggart, that is mayor of Crocus, he was the starter and he sent Johnny Totcoal down to the Western Grain Elevator, where we had to make the turn. That turn had bothered Jake a lot when we were working out Fever. Spider was a cow horse and could turn on a dime. "He's got you there," Jake had said to me, "but I got a little trick to even that up." Then he'd showed me how to grab the horn with both hands and up into the saddle without touching a foot to the stirrup. Doc hadn't kicked when Jake told him the race ought to be from a standing start beside the horses. I guess he figured a small kid couldn't get up as fast as he could with his longer legs.

"Now, fellas," Mr. MacTaggart was saying, "you start from here, each one beside his horse. When I say 'go,' into the saddle and down to the stake by the Western Grain Elevator, then around an' back."

Doc nodded and smiled; he had a chew of tobacco the size of a turkey hen's egg. Looking at the paint horse I felt sort of grasshoppery to my stomach; my knees weren't so good either. Doc's Spider was long in the leg, and he looked like he could line out if he wanted to.

"Real pretty." Doc had his hand on Fever's neck, stroking his gold hide and running his fingers through his silver mane. "But that don't make 'em run any faster."

If being ugly made a horse fast, I was thinking that jug head of Doc's must be a whirlwind!

"How old is he?" Doc was up at Fever's head now.

"Two and a half."

Doc lifted Fever's lip and looked inside.

"Let that there horse alone!" Jake had left Mr. MacTaggart and come up.

"Just looking at his teeth," said Doc.

"Only ones he's got," said Jake. "Keep yer han's off that horse!"

"Ready, fellas?" Mr. MacTaggart called.

Doc jumped back beside Spider. I put both hands on top of the saddle horn.

"GO!"

I jumped into that saddle like a toad off a hot stove, and I dug my heels into Fever and gave him the leather both sides. He jumped straight into a gallop. Looking back I saw Doc's leg just coming down over the saddle.

Fever had his head up and was fighting like anything. "Come on, Fever!" I yelled at him. His head came down again and he threw his shoulders into it. Then Spider and Doc were beside us, and Fever had his head up again. Doc passed us, and Fever wasn't running at all! He was trying, but I'd seen old Baldy do better.

"Please, Fever — *please!*" I leaned down over his neck. "Come on, boy!" He threw back his head, and I felt something wet on my check — foam blowing back.

Spider reached the stake five lengths ahead of us. He made the turn like you snap your fingers. We were halfway down the second lap when the paint went across the finish line. Doc was over by Repeat Golightly when I climbed down from Fever.

Poor Fever's sides were heaving, and he was still tossing his head, and me, I wished I wasn't a human being at all.

"He didn't run, Jake! He didn't run a bit."

"Some horses are like that," said Doc. He watched Jake feeling Fever's front legs. "When they get up against something good they quit."

"This horse ain't no quitter!" Jake had straightened up. "There's somethin' fishy about this — "

"Jake!" That was Ma, with her face all red and her eyes brighter than anything. Jake saw Ma and he swallowed and kind of ducked. She grabbed me by the arm, hard. "You've deliberately disobeyed me, son! You've — Jake!"

Jake had hold of Fever's nose and was sticking his finger in it. "I'm lookin' fer somethin'," Jake said. "Somebody went an' — "

"I forbade you to race that horse and you went ahead, against my wishes! I — it — " Ma had got so tangled up in her britching she couldn't talk.

"Mebbe a sponge," Jake said. "Cuts off their wind."

"Ma, Auction Fever he didn't run at — "

"That's enough!" Ma yanked on my arm. "I know now that I can't —" She stared at me, and it was like her face froze over all of a sudden.

"What have you got in your mouth?"

I didn't have anything in my mouth.

She jerked around to Jake. "The most despicable thing I've ever seen!"

"They claim water in their ear — "

"Teaching my son to chew tobacco!"

"Chew tobacco!" Jake's mouth dropped open and his eyes bugged.

Ma stepped forward and she stuck out her finger. It came away from the corner of my mouth, all brown. "There!"

"Now jist a minnit," said Jake. "Take it easy."

"Betting is bad enough — but — chewing — "

"Don't give him that money!" Jake's face was all lit up like he'd eaten a sunset. Repeat looked over at him, with the money he'd been going to give Doc still in his hand.

Jake walked across to Fever. He pulled out Fever's underlip. He looked, then he lifted the lip, grunted, and stuck his crooked finger in. It came out with the biggest jag of chewing tobacco I ever saw.

"Well, now," Jake said as he walked toward Doc, "ain't that interestin'? Horse that's fussy about chewin' tobacco. Wouldn't be Black Stag like you had in your mouth before the race — before you took a look at Fever's teeth?"

"I don't know what you're talking about." Doc was smiling, but it was a pretty sick-looking smile.

"The hell you don't!"

"Doctor Toovey!" That was Ma, and the way she was looking at Doc you could easy tell she used to be a schoolteacher. "Did you or did you not put a — a — cud of chewing tobacco in my — in that horse's mouth?"

I knew how Doc felt — like when the whole room gets quiet and Miss Henchbaw is looking right at you and you know you're in for it.

"Makes 'em slobber," said Jake. "Then they swallow it down an' it cuts their wind."

"Will the horse be all right, Jake?" Ma asked.

"Shore," said Jake. "Won't hurt him none. 'Fact he's all right now."

Ma's face sort of tightened. She whirled back to Doc. "You are going to race! You will climb up on that horse and run an honest race against my son! Don't interrupt, Doctor Toovey."

"I ain't — that kid don't weigh more'n a grasshopper — "

"He hasn't put on any weight since you first arranged the race," Ma snapped.

Doc looked at Jake and the other folks around him; folks from our section aren't so fussy about seeing a kid and his horse get diddled.

You should of felt Fever under me that second race! He ran smooth, with his silver mane flying and his neck laid out. He ran like the wind over the edge of the prairie coming to tell everybody they can't live forever — slick as the wind through a field of wheat — slicker than peeled saskatoons. He's the only horse living, Jake says, with three gears in high. He's the only horse can make my throat plug up that way and my chest nearly bust.

Doc Toovey ought to have known better. My Fever is a Gent. And Gents don't chaw!

Margaret Avison

Margaret Avison was born in Galt, Ontario in 1918. She spent part of her youth in Alberta and graduated in English Language and Literature from Victoria College, University of Toronto, in 1940. She has worked as a research assistant and librarian. In 1963 she returned to the University of Toronto for graduate work. She subsequently lectured in English at Scarborough College until 1968, when she began working full-time for a Presbyterian Church Mission in Toronto.

Her first poems were published in 1939; since then her work has appeared in Canadian Forum, Contemporary Verse, *and in American periodicals like* Origin *and* Poetry. *Her total output, though excellent, is small; her first volume of poems,* Winter Sun, *did not appear until 1960. It won a Governor-General's Award. Her second volume,* The Dumbfounding, *appeared in 1966. The issue of* Origin *for January, 1962 contains thirteen of her poems.*

Though some of her poems present a surface of apparently wilful obscurity, she rewards careful attention. She is interested in the paradoxical nature of time and space, but she is anything but abstract; her poems often begin and end with the perceiving eye.[1] "Nobody stuffs the world in at your eyes," she says in "Snow"; "the optic heart must venture." Perception, therefore, is active, not passive, and the adventures of the "optic heart," in which the relationship between the external world and the consciousness of the perceiver is explored, are major themes in her poetry. Many of the poems in The Dumbfounding *are explicitly Christian and have been compared to poems by Hopkins, Donne, and Herbert.[2] Her perception in them is directed toward an apprehension of the Incarnation, the continuing point of intersection of a closely observed physical world and the "far country" of the spirit.*

Footnotes

[1]. *Milton Wilson, "The Poetry of Margaret Avison,"* Canadian Literature, *2 (Autumn, 1959), 47.*
[2]. *Ernest Redekop,* Margaret Avison *(Toronto: 1970), p. 109.*

Neverness
or
The One Ship Beached on
One Far Distant Shore

Old Adam, with his fist-full of plump earth,
His sunbright gaze on his eternal hill
Is not historical:
His tale is never done
For us who know a world no longer bathed
In the harsh splendour of economy.
We millions hold old Adam in our thoughts
A pivot for the future-past, a core
Of the one dream that never goads to action
But stains our entrails with nostalgia
And wrings the sweat of death in ancient eyes.

The one-celled plant is not historical.
Leeuwenhoek peered through his magic window
And in a puddle glimpsed the tiny grain
Of firmament that was before the Adam.

I'd like to pull that squinting Dutchman's sleeve
And ask what were his thoughts, lying at night,
And smelling the sad spring, and thinking out
Across the fulness of night air, smelling
The dark canal, and dusty oat-bag, cheese,
And wet straw-splintered wood, and rust-seamed leather
And pearly grass and silent deeps of sky
Honey-combed with its million years' of light
And prune-sweet earth
Honey-combed with the silent worms of dark.
Old Leeuwenhoek must have had ribby thoughts
To hoop the hollow pounding of his heart
Those nights of spring in 1600-odd.
It would be done if he could tell it us.

The tissue of our metaphysic cells
No magic window yet has dared reveal.
Our bleared world welters on

Far past the one-cell Instant. Points are spread
And privacy is unadmitted prison.

Why, now I know the lust of omnipresence!
You thousands merging lost,
   I call to you
Down the stone corridors that wall me in.

I am inside these days, snug in a job
In one of many varnished offices
Bleak with the wash of daylight
And us, the human pencils wearing blunt.
Soon I'll be out with you,
Another in the lonely unshut world
Where sun blinks hard on yellow brick and glazed,
On ads in sticky posterpaint
   And fuzzy
      At midday intersections.
The milk is washed down corded throats at noon
Along a thousand counters, and the hands
That count the nickel from a greasy palm
Have never felt an udder.
   The windy dark
That thrums high among towers and nightspun branches
Whirs through our temples with a dry confusion.
We sprawl abandoned into disbelief
And feel the pivot-picture of old Adam
On the first hill that ever was, alone,
And see the hard earth seeded with sharp snow
And dream that history is done.

*   *   *

And if that be the dream that whortles out
Into unending night
Then must the pivot Adam be denied
And the whole cycle ravelled and flung loose.
Is this the Epoch when the age-old Serpent
Must writhe and loosen, slacking out
To a new pool of Time's eternal sun?
O Adam, will your single outline blur
At this long last when slow mist wells
Fuming from all the valleys of the earth?
Or will our unfixed vision rather blind
Through agony to the last gelid stare
And none be left to witness the blank mist?

The Butterfly

An uproar,
a spruce-green sky, bound in iron,
the murky sea running a sulphur scum,
I saw a butterfly, suddenly.
It clung between the ribs of the storm, wavering,
and flung against the battering bone-wind.
I remember it, glued to the grit of that rain-strewn beach
that glowered around it, swallowed its startled design
in the larger iridescence of unstrung dark.

That wild, sour air, those miles of crouching forest, that moth
when all enveloping space
is a thin glass globe, swirling with storm
tempt us to stare, and seize analogies.
The Voice that stilled the sea of Galilee
overtoned by the new peace, the fierce subhuman peace
of such an east sky, blanched like Eternity.

The meaning of the moth, even the smashed moth, the
meaning of the moth—
can't we stab that one angle into the curve of space
that sweeps so unrelenting, far above,
towards the subhuman swamp of under-dark?

New Year's Poem

The Christmas twigs crispen and needles rattle
Along the windowledge.
      A solitary pearl
Shed from the necklace spilled at last week's party
Lies in the suety, snow-luminous plainness
Of morning, on the windowledge beside them.
And all the furniture that circled stately
And hospitable when these rooms were brimmed
With perfumes, furs, and black-and-silver
Crisscross of seasonal conversation, lapses
Into its previous largeness.
      I remember
Anne's rose-sweet gravity, and the stiff grave
Where cold so little can contain;
I mark the queer delightful skull and crossbones
Starlings and sparrows left, taking the crust,
And the long loop of winter wind
Smoothing its arc from dark Arcturus down
To the bricked corner of the drifted courtyard,
And the still windowledge.
      Gentle and just pleasure
It is, being human, to have won from space
This unchill, habitable interior
Which mirrors quietly the light
Of the snow, and the new year.

Butterfly Bones;
or Sonnet Against Sonnets

The cyanide jar seals life, as sonnets move
towards final stiffness. Cased in a white glare
these specimens stare for peering boys, to prove
strange certainties. Plane dogsled and safari
assure continuing range. The sweep-net skill,
the patience, learning, leave all living stranger.
Insect — or poem — waits for the fix, the frill
precision can effect, brilliant with danger.
What law and wonder the museum spectres
bespeak is cryptic for the shivery wings,
the world cut-diamond-eyed, those eyes' reflectors,
or herbal grass, sunned motes, fierce listening.
Might sheened and rigid trophies strike men blind
like Adam's lexicon locked in the mind?

Snow

Nobody stuffs the world in at your eyes.
The optic heart must venture: a jail-break
And re-creation. Sedges and wild rice
Chase rivery pewter. The astonished cinders quake
With rhizomes. All ways through the electric air
Trundle candy-bright disks; they are desolate
Toys if the soul's gates seal, and cannot bear,
Must shudder under, creation's unseen freight.
But soft, there is snow's legend: colour of mourning
Along the yellow Yangtze where the wheel
Spins an indifferent stasis that's death's warning.
Asters of tumbled quietness reveal
Their petals. Suffering this starry blur
The rest may ring your change, sad listener.

Apocalyptic?

"We must accept the baptism of the gutter"
(Yeats). "We must love one another or die"
(some other poet). "We must eat and marry
And give our children college educations,
Write fair insurance for our wives and die
If possible before retirement," say
The despised who despise in innocence.
Accept, yes. Choose what we accept. *And* die.
Create yes, even if genes
Are marbled through with radioactive rays
And promise a millenium of cripples
And fools of God (will they do better?). Praise
The light, that we can breathe it, and defy
All mustiness around the living I.
This treadmill turns by us, and of itself.
For just this sparrow time, we tramp in day,
Our one arc under the magnificent sky.
If love first turn the doggedness to dance
Then staggers on the why, still monuments
Hover oblique to a descending wheel.
Figures of fun before us and behind
Glimpse wry stone silhouettes, and find an eye
Emptily searching theirs. Old scores for hautboy
Sing from forgotten winters. The faint cry
Where the wheel verges upwards peals
A splendour in our hearts. An amnesty
No prince declared yet shines. The old man reels.
Love in absurdity rocks even just men down
And doom is luminous today.

Grammarian on a Lakefront Parkbench

Skewer my heart and I am less transfixed
than with this gill that sloughs and slumps
in a spent sea. Flyspecked and dim
my lighthouse signals when no ships could grind.
Sargassos of inheritance thrid through
choked day, swollen to almost total swamp.
Could I be pierced and spun,
pronged for a Midway,
that would be leaping.
             But not life.
White-teethed after their plates of kale, these smilers
stroll across triangles of blue, rectangles
of purple-blue, collages of green-blue
and shellack orange. All their newspaper sky
squints through the milky midday Sunday
to read them, carelessly,
Confusing saddle-pears and sundecks.
The vintage elms wither by moral accident.

The Swimmer's Moment

For everyone
The swimmer's moment at the whirlpool comes,
But many at that moment will not say
"This is the whirlpool, then."
By their refusal they are saved
From the black pit, and also from contesting
The deadly rapids, and emerging in
The mysterious, and more ample, further waters.
And so their bland-blank faces turn and turn
Pale and forever on the rim of suction
They will not recognize.
Of those who dare the knowledge
Many are whirled into the ominous centre
That, gaping vertical, seals up
For them an eternal boon of privacy,
So that we turn away from their defeat
With a despair, not for their deaths, but for
Ourselves, who cannot penetrate their secret
Nor even guess at the anonymous breadth
Where one or two have won:
(The silver reaches of the estuary).

95

Waking Up

Monkey colour, morning smokes from
the pond. Looped and festooned
with fawn heraldic rags
trees wait. Seawall of day
deafens the turmoil the true seafarer,
the Wanderer, fronts. High grass
rides crest; a spill
of grains casts stone-age shadows on the bluffs.
Selvedge of water mirrors
the always first light.
Like soil no inchworm's excremental course
has rendered friable,
today, mute quantum
of all past pitted against sun,
weighs, a heft of awareness, on
tallow, brawn, auricle,
iris. Till monkey-
grinder habit turning his organ
grinds out curbs, scurrying,
dust,
day.

First

Excessive gladness can drag
the 3-dimensional uncircumferenced circle
out of its sublime true
unless contrition also past all bound
extend it.

In the mathematics of God
there are percentages beyond one hundred.

His new creation is
One, whole, and a
beginning.

The Dumbfounding

When you walked here,
took skin, muscle, hair,
eyes, larynx, we
withheld all honor: "His house is clay,
how can he tell us of his far country?"

Your not familiar pace
in flesh, across the waves,
woke only our distrust.
Twice-torn we cried "A ghost"
and only on our planks counted you fast.

Dust wet with your spittle
cleared mortal trouble.
We called you a blasphemer,
a devil-tamer.

The evening you spoke of going away
we could not stay.
All legions massed. You had to wash, and rise,
alone, and face
out of the light, for us.

You died.
We said,
"The worst is true, our bliss
has come to this."

When you were seen by men
in holy flesh again
we hoped so despairingly for such report
we closed their windpipes for it.

Now you have sought
and seek, in all our ways, all thoughts,
streets, musics — and we make of these a din
trying to lock you out, or in,
to be intent. And dying.

Yet you are
constant and sure,
the all-lovely, all-men's-way
to that far country.

Winning one, you again
all ways would begin
life: to make new
flesh, to empower
the weak in nature
to restore
or stay the sufferer;

lead through the garden to
trash, rubble, hill,
where, the outcast's outcast, you
sound dark's uttermost, strangely light-brimming, until
time be full.

George Grant

George Parkin Grant was born in Toronto in 1918. He studied at Queen's University and Oxford and taught in the department of Philosophy at Dalhousie University from 1947 to 1960. In 1961 he moved to McMaster University, where he now teaches in the departments of Religion and Political Science. In 1959 he published Philosophy in the Mass Age, *a series of essays on moral philosophy originally delivered as radio talks.*

Grant has a reputation as one of the most articulate spokesmen, along with Donald Creighton, of a conservative view of Canadian history. "To be a Canadian," he says in Lament for a Nation *(1965), "was to build, along with the French, a more ordered and stable society than the liberal experiment in the United States."[1] Elsewhere he defines liberalism as "a set of beliefs which proceed from the central assumption that man's essence is his freedom and therefore that what chiefly concerns man in this life is to shape the world as we want it."[2] He argues that the inevitable result of the growth of liberal, profit-oriented values was to destroy the attitudes that had created the country in the first place and thus to make Canadian independence impossible. Ironically, his views have received as much attention from people on the left wing of Canadian politics as from people who call themselves conservatives.*

"Canadian Fate and Imperialism," originally published in Canadian Dimension, *was reprinted in Grant's volume of essays,* Technology and Empire *(1969). In this essay he focuses on the homogenizing effects which modern technology has on historical traditions, and the problems which technology and the ideal of material progress pose for Canada's survival. He begins with a discussion of a contemporary issue — the war in Vietnam — but, characteristically, he brings to bear on his examination of Canada's relationship to this issue an extensive knowledge of the whole intellectual tradition of Western Europe.*

Footnotes

[1]. *George Grant,* Lament for a Nation *(Toronto: 1965), p. 4.*
[2]. *George Grant,* Technology and Empire *(Toronto: 1969), p. 114.*

Canadian Fate and Imperialism

To use the language of fate is to assert that all human beings come into a world they did not choose and live their lives within a universe they did not make. If one speaks in this way, one is often accused either of being pessimistic or of holding a tragic view of life. Neither of these accusations is correct. To say that one holds a tragic view of life would be to follow Nietzsche in thinking that Dionysian tragedy was a higher stance than that of Socrates; I do not think this. And the words optimistic and pessimistic are surely most accurately used, following Leibniz, to describe what one thinks about the nature of things, whether the world is good or not. It is quite possible to use the word "fate," and to think that "nature" is good, and not contradict oneself. It is in my opinion a sensible way to talk about events, though obviously it is far from the liberal dogmas within which most people are taught to think.

A central aspect of the fate of being a Canadian is that our very existing has at all times been bound up with the interplay of various world empires. One can better understand what it is to be Canadian if one understands that interplay. As no serious person is interested in history simply as antiquarianism but only as it illumines one's search for the good in the here and now, let me set the problem in its most contemporary form — Vietnam. What our fate is today becomes most evident in the light of Vietnam. It is clear that in that country the American empire has been demolishing a people, rather than allowing them to live outside the American orbit.

The Americans are forced to that ferocious demolition because they have chosen to draw the line against the Chinese empire in a country where nationalism and communism have been in large measure identified. How does this affect Canadians? On the one hand, many Canadians, whether their moral traditions come from Judaism, Christianity, the liberal enlightenment or a mixture, are not yet so empty that they can take lightly the destruction of a people — even in the case of Asians. On the other hand, the vast majority of Canadians are a product of western civilization and live entirely within the forms and assumptions of that enterprise. Today the enterprise of western civilization finds its spearhead in the American empire. In that sense our very lives are inevitably bound up in the meeting of that empire with the rest of the world, and the movements of war which draw the limits in that meeting. The depth of that common destiny with the Americans is shown in the fact that many Canadians who are forced to admit the sheer evil of what is being done in Vietnam say at the same time that we have no choice but to stand with the Americans as the pillar of western civilization. Beyond this kind of talk is of course the fact that this society is above all a machine for greed, and our branch plant industry is making a packet out of the demolition of Vietnam.

Our involvement is much deeper than the immediate profits of particular wars. Our very form of life depends on our membership in the western industrial empire which is centred in the U.S.A. and which stretches out in its hegemony into parts of western

Europe and which controls South America and much of Africa and Asia. Somewhere in the minds of nearly all Canadians there is the recognition that our present form of life depends on our place as second class members of that system. By "second class" I do not imply a low status, because there are a large number of classes within it. It is much nicer to be a Canadian than a Brazilian or a Venezuelan, or for that matter an Englishman.

Indeed our involvement in the American empire goes deeper than a simple economic and political basis; it depends on the very faith that gives meaning and purpose to the lives of western men. To most Canadians, as public beings, the central cause of motion in their souls is the belief in progress through technique, and that faith is identified with the power and leadership of the English-speaking empire in the world.

This then is why our present fate can be seen with such clarity in the glaring light of Vietnam. The very substance of our lives is bound up with the western empire and its destiny, just at a time when that empire uses increasingly ferocious means to maintain its hegemony. The earlier catastrophes and mass crimes of the age of progress could be interpreted as originating entirely with other peoples, the Germans, or the Russians. They could be seen as the perverse products of western ideology — national socialism or communism. This can no longer be said. What is being done in Vietnam is being done by the English-speaking empire and in the name of liberal democracy.

Not only in our present but in our origins, Canada was made by western empires. We were a product of two north-western empires as they moved out in that strange expansion of Europe around the world. It is essential to emphasize that they were north-western. Hegel's language is here the clearest. He speaks of the "germanische Geist," and in using those words he does not mean the German spirit. He means geographically those European lands whose rivers flow into the North Atlantic. He means the particular secularising Christianity which characterized those lands. He understands that the dominant spirit of the modern age is no longer in the mediterranean peoples, but has passed northward and westward to the Abendland.

If one is to understand Canada one must understand the history of those empires — and not simply in terms of what they did, but in terms of the spirit which drove them to such enormous motion. If one is to pick the society where modernity first makes its appearance in a more than individual way, one must pick England. To understand English modernity one must look above all at that unique meeting of Calvinist Protestantism and the new secular spirit of the Renaissance. That secular spirit can be seen in the new physical science whose origins we identify with Galileo, and in the new moral science of Machiavelli. It was the liberals' superficial interpretation of what we call the Renaissance to see such thinkers as a return to the Greeks, when they were a profound turning away from the ancients. The role of Calvinism in making possible the capitalism which has shaped the western world has been described by Weber.[1] He sees with great clarity how Calvinism provided the necessary ethic for capitalism; what he does not understand is that deeper movement of the mind in which the Puritans were open to the new physical and moral science in a way the older Christianity was not. You can see this acceptance taking place in the seventeenth century. At the end of the sixteenth century, Shakespeare writes: "to set the murderous Machiavell' to school." But during the seventeenth century, Bacon, Hobbes and Locke have achieved the terrible task of making Machiavelli widely respectable, and the new secular, moral and physical science is particularly welcomed by the Protestants. The union of the new secularism and Protestantism brought forth the first great wave of social modernity in England and its empire.

These days when we are told in North America that capitalism is conservative, we should remember that capitalism was the great dissolvent of the traditional virtues and that its greatest philosophers, Hobbes and Locke, Smith and Hume, were Britishers. In the appeal to capitalism as the tradition it is forgotten that the capitalist philosophers dissolved all ideas of the sacred as standing in the way of the emancipation of greed. For example, the criticism of any knowable teleology by Hume not only helped to liberate men to the new natural science, but also liberated them from knowledge of any purposes which transcended the economically rational. It is not surprising that North America was won by the English empire rather than the French. It is enough to read John Nef's book about the differing uses of iron in England and France in the seventeenth century. Despite the work of Henri IV, Richelieu and Colbert, France was not to the same degree an initiator of capitalism and modernity. The French who were left as an enclave on the shores of the St. Lawrence came from an earlier tradition, before France had initiated the second great wave of modernity with Rousseau and the French Revolution. What is so endearing about the young French Canadians revolting against their tradition is that they sometimes write as if Voltaire's *Candide* had come off the press last week instead of two hundred years ago. One's enchantment is however limited by the knowledge that their awakening to modernity, which seems to them an expression of independence, in fact leaves them wide open to conquest by a modernity which at its very heart is destructive of indigenous traditions. Of course, many stylish French Canadian liberals are quite clear that their espousal of the modern does not consistently include any serious interest in the continuance of their own traditions, including even language.

Although the English who conquered North America were of a more modern tradition than the French left in their enclave, it must be remembered that there was always a strong losing party in all the great public events in which modernity put its stamp on English society. Progressivist historians do not write much about the losers of history, because belief in progress often implies the base assumption that to lose is to have failed to grasp the evolving truth. Nevertheless, the losers existed and they are worth reading now that we see what kind of society the winners have made. We can read what Hooker wrote against the Puritans and the society they would build. Above all, the views of the losing party can be found in the greatest of English prose stylists. Swift was a comic genius because he understood with clarity that the victory of the Whigs was not simply a passing political event, but involved new intellectual assumptions. In the quarrel between the ancients and the moderns, Swift knew why he accepted the ancients against the new moral science of Hobbes and Locke.

Though the empire of the English was the chief of the early driving forces towards modernity, many traditions from before the age of progress remained alive in parts of English society, and some of these existed in an inchoate way in the early

English-speaking peoples of this country. It would be balderdash to imply that the early English-speaking leaders of Canada had a firm tradition like their French compatriots, or that they were in any sense people who resisted modernity with the clarity of Swift. Most of the educated among the Loyalists were that extraordinary concoction, straight Locke with a dash of Anglicanism. They were above all a product of the English empire, and the victory of modernity had long since been decided in favour of the Whigs. What can be fairly said, however, is that they were not so given over to modernity as were the leaders of the U.S., particularly insofar as the Americans had incorporated in their revolution a mixture of Locke with elements of Rousseau. The fact that the Canadians had consciously refused the break with their particular past meant that they had some roots with tradition, even though that tradition was the most modern in Europe up till the eighteenth century. Indeed, when one reads the speeches of those founders whom we celebrated in 1967, one is aware of their continual suspicion of the foundations of the American republic, and of their desire to build a political society with a clearer and firmer doctrine of the common good than that at the heart of the liberal democracy to the south. (One would never know this from what one reads about our founders in our liberal text books.)

Nevertheless, having asserted these differences, what is far more important is to repeat that the English empire was a dominant source of modernity. The early Canadian settlers may have wanted to be different from the Americans in detail but not in any substantial way which questioned that modernity. I emphasize this for a personal reason. A couple of years ago I wrote a book about the dissolution of Canadian sovereignty. These days when psychologising is the chief method for neutralising disagreeable opinions, my psyche was interpreted as harking back in nostalgia to the British empire and old fashioned Canada. This was the explanation of why I did not think that the general tendencies of modern society were liable to produce human excellence. In this era when the homogenising power of technology is almost unlimited, I do regret the disappearance of indigenous traditions, including my own. It is true that no particularism can adequately incarnate the good. But is it not also true that only through some particular roots, however partial, can human beings first grasp what is good and it is the juice of such roots which for most men sustain their partaking in a more universal good? Still, regret, however ironical, is not an adequate stance for living and is an impossible stance for philosophy. Conservatism is a practical stance; it must be transcended to reach philosophy. What I said in that book was that the belief that human excellence is promoted by the homogenising and universalising power of technology is the dominant doctrine of modern liberalism, and that that doctrine must undermine all particularisms and that English-speaking Canada as a particular is wide open to that doctrine.

In the nineteenth century the European empires modernised themselves. Nearly all those aspects of their cultures from before the age of progress disappeared. The fact that England came into that century with a vast empire (despite its loss of the American colonies), and as the pioneer of industrialism, meant that it started with an enormous advantage over the other modernising empires. In some ways it was this sense of advantage and unquestioned power which made it indifferent to immediate political control in Canada. But after 1870 industrial and imperial competition was the order of the day and England threw itself into the wild scramble for more possessions and greater imperial control to counter the growing strength of its European rivals. The imperialism of the last half of the nineteenth century is modern man (man as Hobbes has said he is) realising his potentialities. The culmination of that European process was the war of 1914.

Canada as always was involved in the general western fate. Just read how English-speaking Canadians from all areas and all economic classes went off to that war hopefully and honestly believing that they were thereby guaranteeing freedom and justice in the world. Loyalty to Britain and loyalty to liberal capitalist democracy was identified with loyalty to freedom and justice. For example, I have met people from Cape Breton who were so cut off from the general world in 1914 that they thought that Queen Victoria was still reigning and took for granted it was their duty to fight for her. When one thinks what that war was in fact being fought about, and the slaughter of decent men of decent motive which ensued, the imagination boggles. As that war spelled out the implicit violence of the West, it also spelled out Canadian fate.

First, it killed many of the best English-speaking Canadians and left the survivors cynical and tired. I once asked a man of that generation why it was that between the wars of 1914 and 1939 Canada was allowed to slip into the slough of despond in which its national hope was frittered away to the U.S. by Mackenzie King and the Liberal party. He answered graphically: "We had our guts shot away in France." The energy of that generation was drained away in that conflict so that those who returned did not have the vitality for public care, but retreated into the private world of money making. Canada's survival has always required the victory of political courage over immediate and individual economic advantage.

Secondly, English-speaking Canadians in the name of that brutal struggle between empires forced French-speaking Canadians to take part in a way which they knew not to be theirs. If Canada were to exist, English and French-speaking peoples had to have sufficient trust to choose to be together rather than to be Americans. The forcing of the French by fanatics such as Sam Hughes and the culmination of that process in the election of 1917 meant that the French Canadians saw themselves threatened more by English-speaking Canadians than by the deeper threat to the south. Mackenzie King's stand in the election of 1917 must be taken to his political credit, and God knows he needs credit somewhere. In saying that, however, one must remember that between the two great wars King and the Liberal party kept the flames of that hostility alive in Quebec so that they could take the full political benefit from it.

The third great effect of that war in Canada was due to the policies of the ruling classes in Great Britain. In the face of the competition from other European empires, the British ruling classes acted as if their only hope of continuing power was to put their fate into the hands of the American empire. That process is epitomized in the career of Winston Churchill. High rhetoric about partnership among the English-speaking peoples has been used about this process. It cannot, however, cover the fact that Great Britain's chief status in the world today is to do useful jobs for its masters and to be paid for so doing by the support of the pound and the freedom to provide entertainers and entertainment for the empire as a whole. The American empire may

104

be having its difficulties with France and Germany, but it does not have them with Great Britain. Leaving aside the complex question of whether this status was the best that the English could achieve in the circumstances, it is clear that its effect on the possibility of Canada being a nation has been large. The elimination of Great Britain as an independent source of civilisation in the English-speaking world greatly increased the pull of English-speaking Canadians to an identity with the centre of that world in the United States. It is an ambiguity of present Canada that some serious French Canadians now turn to France for support against the English-speaking technological sea. They so turn just as English-speaking Canadians can no longer turn to Great Britain for alternative forms of life to those which press from the south. This present turning is ambiguous because for so long English-speaking Canadians were told by French Canadians that we were not properly Canadian because of our connection with Great Britain. English-speaking Canadians now lean on similar criticism when the great general is welcomed in Quebec.

The supremacy of the American empire in the western world was important for Canada not only in the geographic and economic senses that our nation had to try to exist in the very presence of the empire, but in the much profounder sense that the dominance of the United States is identified with the unequivocal victory of the progressive spirit in the West. The older empires had some residual traditions from before the age of progress — the French more, the British less. The United States is the only society that has none. The American supremacy is identified with the belief that questions of human good are to be solved by technology; that the most important human activity is the pursuit of those sciences which issue in the conquest of human and non-human nature. Anybody who is in university today, and knows where he is, knows both that these are the ends for which the university exists and that the universities are becoming almost the chief institutions of our system.

The gradual victory of the progressive spirit has taken place in interdependence with an enormous expansion of the western peoples into the rest of the world. The era of modern thought has been the era of western imperialism. Imperialism, like war, is coeval with human existence. But the increasingly externalised view of human life which is the very nature of the progressive spirit has given and will continue to give an enormous impetus to imperialism. As the classical philosophers said, man cannot help but imitate in action his vision of the nature of things. The dominant tendency of the western world has been to divide history from nature and to consider history as dynamic and nature controllable as externality. Therefore, modern men have been extremely violent in their dealings with other men and other beings. Liberal doctrine does not prepare us for this violence because of its identification of technology with evolution, and the identification of evolution with movement of the race to higher and higher morality. Such a doctrine could not understand that an expanding techno-logical society is going to be an imperialist society even when it is run by governments who talk and sometimes act the language of welfare both domestically and internationally. Among advanced liberals, this failure was compounded by the naive account in Marxism of imperialism as simply a product of late capitalism. In the case of the American empire, the vulgarity of the analysis can be seen in the assessments of the presidency of F. D. Roosevelt. The 'right' wing has accused him of being soft about American interests at Yalta; the 'left' wing has seen him as a lover of humanity whose untimely death prevented him from stopping the cold war and building a world based on the principles of the United Nations. In fact under his presidency the U.S. at last moved fully into the imperial role for which its dominant classes had been preparing since John Hay. Our modern way of looking at the world hides from us the reality of many political things; but about nothing is it more obscuring than the inevitable relation between dynamic technology and imperialism.

Of course, what has happened in our immediate era is that the non-western nations have taken on western means, both technical and ideological, as the only way to preserve themselves against the West. They now move from being simply the sufferers of Western dynamism to having an active imperialist role of their own. Indeed Russian and Chinese imperialism present an undoubted challenge to the West. There is equal distortion in the rhetoric of those who see the American empire as the sole source of violence in the world and in the rhetoric of those who see an essentially peaceful western world defending itself against communism. Modern imperialism — with all its ideological and technical resources — may have been invented in the West, but it is not now confined to it.

To live in a world of these violent empires, and in a satellite of the greatest of them, presents complex problems of morality. These problems may be stated thus. In human life there must always be place for love of the good and love of one's own. Love of the good is man's highest end, but it is of the nature of things that we come to know and to love what is good by first meeting it in that which is our own — this particular body, this family, these friends, this woman, this part of the world, this set of traditions, this country, this civilisation. At the simplest level of one's own body, it is clear that one has to love it yet pass beyond concentration on it. To grow up properly is not to be alienated from one's own body; but an adult who does not pay reverence to anything beyond his own body is a narcissist, and not a full human being. In many parts of our lives the two loves need never be in conflict. In loving our friends we are also loving the good. But sometimes the conflict becomes open. An obvious case in our era is those Germans who had to oppose their own country in the name of the good. I have known many noble Jewish and Christian Germans who were torn apart because no country but Germany could really be their own, yet they could no longer love it because of their love of the good.

This is why the present happenings in Vietnam are particularly terrible for Canadians. What is being done there is being done by a society which is in some deep way our own. It is being done by a society which more than any other carries the destiny of the West, and Canadians belong inevitably to that destiny. Canada could only continue to be if we could hold some alternative social vision to that of the great republic. Yet such an alternative would have had to come out of the same stream — western culture. Indeed our failure to find such an alternative is bound up with the very homogenising path of western history. So we are left with the fact. As the U.S. becomes daily more our own, so does the Vietnam war.

The majority of North Americans do not seem to believe that love of their own and love of the good are exposed to stringent conflict in Vietnam. They assume that the

106

structure of our society is essentially good, that it requires to be defended against aggression, and that it is against aggression that the American troops are engaged in Vietnam. They are either not much concerned with the actual history of the conflict, or else have been convinced by propaganda that there is a gallant country, South Vietnam, which is defending itself from aggression with American help. When a more explicit ideology is sought, the position becomes divided at one particular point. Are we to fear the Vietnamese and beyond them the Chinese because they are non-western, or because they are communist? Is it the old Europocentric fear of the Asian hordes under Asian tyranny as a threat to the freedom and right which belong essentially to the West? Or is it because the Asians have taken on communism that they are to be feared? It is not easy to hold these two positions together for the reason that Marxism is an advanced product of the West which appealed to British industry, French revolutionary ideas and German philosophy. Of course many people in North America no longer appeal to any ideology beyond our affluence. They take the line that it's either them or us, and this position is wrapped up in Darwinian packaging which says that any means are permissible that allow us to protect our own.

For a minority, the events in Vietnam must help to push them over that great divide where one can no longer love one's own — where indeed it almost ceases to be one's own. Vietnam is a glaring searchlight exposing the very structure of the imperial society. Even if hopefully the violence there should ease off, the searchlight has still been cast on the structure. We can never be as we were, because what has been done has been done. Some could see the structure of that society before the last years, but Vietnam has been for many the means to a clearer analysis. It has had this result because here are obvious facts which cannot be accounted for within the usual liberal description by which the society is legitimised to its own members and to the world.

Many liberals who do not find the events in Vietnam easy to stomach sometimes talk as if what were happening there were some kind of accident — if only that Texan had not got into the White House, etc., etc. Such a way of thinking is worthy only of journalists. Let us suppose that the American ruling class (through either of its political instruments) comes to see more clearly what a tactical error it has made in Vietnam and allows the war to tail off. It still governs the most powerful empire in the history of the world. It may learn to carry out its policies (e.g. in South America) more effectively and without such open brutalities. But it will have to have its Vietnams if the occasions demand, and we will have to be part of them. A profounder liberal criticism is made by those who say that the health of the western empire is shown by the extent of dissent against war. They maintain that only the traditions of the West make such dissent possible and that that possibility shows us the essential goodness of liberal society. This argument turns on a judgement of fact — an extremely difficult one. Does this dissent in the West present a real alternative of action, or is it simply froth on the surface which is necessary to the system itself as a safety valve? I am not sure. I lean to the position that dissent on major questions of policy is impotent and that the western system has in truth achieved what Michels called "the bureaucratising of dissent."[2]

The word "alienation" has become a cliché to be thrown about in journalistic chitchat. Surely the deepest alienation must be when the civilisation one inhabits no

107

longer claims one's loyalty. It is a rational alienation, and therefore not to be overcome by opting out of the system through such methods as LSD and speed. The ecstasy therein offered is just another package which one buys from the system and which keeps people quiet. Indeed the depth of the alienation is seen in the ambiguity of the words "one's own." To repeat, the events in Vietnam push one towards that divide where one can no longer love one's own — to the point where the civilisation almost ceases to be one's own. Yet it is impossible to give up the word "almost." Think of being the parent or the child of a concentration camp guard. One would want to say: "This person is not my own," and yet one could not. The facts of birth are inescapable. So are the very facts of belonging to the civilisation that has made one. It is this inevitability which leads to the degree of alienation and disgust which some people feel in the present situation.

There is a distinction between those who in their alienation find political hope in loyalty to one of the other empires, and those who cannot find such an alternative. Sartre, for example, takes part in politics, but he takes part in it as seeking the victory of the eastern empires, and is able to do so because of the freedom granted him in the western world. Which of these two positions is more adequate turns on the following question of fact: whether the qualities common to technological empires are more fundamental than their differences. This is not the place to discuss that extremely difficult question. It is clear, however, that the person who says "no" to his own and cannot substitute a hope in some other empire is in a position of much profounder alienation than those who can put their political trust elsewhere.

A similar difference in alienation will be found between those who place expectation in changing our society by reform or revolution and those who do not. Those, such as myself, who think that the drive for radical change in this society tends only to harden the very directions the society is already taking, and who think of the source of revolutionary fervour as arising finally from a further extension of the very modernity which has brought us where we are, inevitably find it more difficult to know how to live in this society than those who have expectations from radical activity.

Some people, particularly some of the young, will say that I have used a lot of words about the obvious. They may say that they have known since they began to think that this society is quite absurd and that sanity requires one to be either indifferent or hostile to it. Why write so long about what is so evident? However, finding that one is hostile or indifferent to a society may be a necessary discovery, but it is always an emasculating one. Man is by nature a political animal and to know that citizenship is an impossibility is to be cut off from one of the highest forms of life. To retreat from loyalty to one's own has the exhilaration of rebellion, but rebellion cannot be the basis for a whole life. Like all civilisations the West is based on a great religion — the religion of progress. This is the belief that the conquest of human and non-human nature will give existence meaning. Western civilisation is now universal so that this religion is nearly everywhere dominant. To question the dominant world religion is indeed to invite an alienation far greater than the simply political.

Nothing here written implies that the increasingly difficult job of preserving what is left of Canadian sovereignty is not worth the efforts of practical men. However disgraceful has been our complicity in the Vietnam War, however disgusting the wealth we have made from munitions for that war, one must still be glad that Canadian forces are not fighting there. This is due to what little sovereignty we still possess. So equally our non-involvement in the imperial adventures elsewhere will continue to depend on the possible maintenance of some waning sovereignty. But what lies behind the small practical question of Canadian nationalism is the larger context of the fate of western civilisation. By that fate I mean not merely the relations of our massive empire to the rest of the world, but even more the kind of existence which is becoming universal in advanced technological societies. What is worth doing in the midst of this barren twilight is the incredibly difficult question.

Footnotes

1. This question is discussed at greater length in the first essay of [Technology and Empire]. Prof. G. E. Wilson has rightly pointed out to me that in emphasizing the importance of the English in this history, I have underestimated the importance of the Dutch.

2. Since this was written some of the evidence is in. Clearly the dissent over the war in the U.S. had some effect on some decisions. It was not only the difficulty of winning the war which convinced the ruling class that the enterprise was a mistake, but also that too many of the influential young were being alienated from the purposes of the society by it. The dissent made this clear. No ruling class could afford to neglect such a circumstance particularly when its society was faced at the same time by a major racial crisis. But it would be wrong to carry the consequences too far. The Democratic party was punished by losing the presidency — but not by the dissenters, rather by the settled and unsettled bourgeois. Dissent was able to expose the folly of defending imperial interests in such a misguided way in Vietnam. But it cannot be effective in turning the U.S. from its course as a great imperial power.

Al Purdy

Born of Loyalist stock in Wooler, a small village in Northumberland County, Ontario, in 1918, Alfred Purdy was educated in Trenton and Belleville. During World War II he served in the R.C.A.F. in Vancouver, where he published his first book of poetry, The Enchanted Echo, in 1944. He married Eurithe Mary Jane Parkhurst in 1941. After the war he worked at manual jobs all across the country; at this time too, he became involved in efforts to unionize workers. Though he continued to write during the fifties, it was not until 1962, when Souster's Contact Press published Purdy's Poems for all the Annettes, that he showed a distinctive poetic voice. Since then he has won a Governor-General's Award for The Cariboo Horses (1965). A trip to Baffin Island resulted in a series of poems about the Canadian Arctic in North of Summer (1967), a book which also contained oil sketches of the Arctic by A. Y. Jackson. Purdy has also edited two anthologies of Canadian poetry and a collection of Canadian views of the United States, The New Romans (1968).

In his introduction to Milton Acorn's I've Tasted My Blood (1969), Purdy says of himself, "If simplistic labels were feasible then . . . I would be a cynical Canadian nationalist, a lyrical Farley Mowat maybe."[1] This is simplistic, of course, but perhaps the "lyrical Farley Mowat" side of Purdy's writing can be seen in his fascination with the land and with the people who live in close contact with it, and in his distrust of the effects of modern technology. His poems often begin with some trivial experience perceived through the eyes of a persona who is awkward and uncertain of himself. But they are also informed by a strong sense of history and myth. Characteristically, in "Lament for the Dorsets," he is conscious of the immemorial history which lies behind the archaeological fragments of Baffin Island and of modern man's difficulty in being able to imagine that history. But the relationship between present and past is left open-ended, as are most things in Purdy's poetry; D. G. Jones says of it that "the meaning is all in the tone of the talk, and the gathering up of details, not in the ending, not in a conclusion."[2] Purdy's use of a persona and his colloquial, conversational style imply that the real subject matter of his poetry is the consciousness of the observer attempting to make sense of an experience.

Footnotes

[1.] Alfred Purdy, "Introduction," I've Tasted My Blood (Toronto: 1969), p. xi.
[2.] D. G. Jones, Butterfly on Rock (Toronto: 1970), p. 171.

Mind Process re a Faucet

The faucet is cool green shadowed spring—
some stocky old water god with
knobby knees sits there making magic—

Or a grim sun-burned Roman engineer
(came with the lease?) kneels in the flooded
kitchen to curse this damned aqueduct—

No such fantasy of metal and water,
not the unreasonable slim princess
crawling continuously from every drop and hiccuping—
But the flash-picture, the idea of faucet.

And I can't make it be
what it isn't by saying,
or take the shape of a word's being.

For multiple identity confuses anyway,
there must be a single total,
all water — torrents of god-stuff.

(Absurd delight in this sort of thing—
as if the sprawled mind was exercising,
asked its sybil self questions — grins derisively
behind the hand at its own shell game.)

Obviously the idea of faucet is its own function,
a lovesome sound (god wot?) dripping thru the night,
concentrating desperately on retaining its faucet shape:
Water, keep thinking WATER, you'll be all right!

Essence? analyse the metal constituents:
nickel-steel, imposed form — but I keep thinking
of mineral molecules before and after they got here,
the lyric rubble, mind that holds and joins—

Mind that gets bloody tired! — you too, reader,
need shock after shock — for myself continuous discovery,
else in the midst of somnolence: defeat after defeat.

Now relax in the cerebral split levels
of mind — and silence on the fourth floor
in an apt. where nothing works very well:

and round the city's misty hemisphere
lights come on like discordant signals,
answered by starry holes in black tissuepaper,
which makes no sense at all—
and the faucet drips.

Montreal, 1961

The Country North of Belleville

Bush land scrub land—
       Cashel Township and Wollaston
Elvezir McClure and Dungannon
green lands of Weslemkoon Lake
where a man might have some
       opinion of what beauty
is and none deny him
       for miles—

Yet this is the country of defeat
where Sisyphus rolls a big stone
year after year up the ancient hills
picnicking glaciers have left strewn
with centuries' rubble
       days in the sun
when realization seeps slow in the mind
without grandeur or self deception in
       noble struggle
of being a fool—

A country of quiescence and still distance
a lean land
            not fat
with inches of black soil on
            earth's round belly—
And where the farms are it's
            as if a man stuck
both thumbs in the stony earth and pulled
                    it apart to make room
enough between the trees
for a wife
            and maybe some cows and
            room for some
of the more easily kept illusions—
And where the farms have gone back
to forest
            are only soft outlines and
            shadowy differences—
Old fences drift vaguely among the trees
            a pile of moss-covered stones
gathered for some ghost purpose
has lost meaning under the meaningless sky
            — they are like cities under water and
the undulating green waves of time are
            laid on them—

This is the country of our defeat and
            yet
during the fall plowing a man
might stop and stand in a brown valley of the furrows
            and shade his eyes to watch for the same
            red patch mixed with gold
            that appears on the same
            spot in the hills
            year after year
            and grow old
plowing and plowing a ten acre field until
the convolutions run parallel with his own brain—

And this is a country where the young
            leave quickly
unwilling to know what their fathers know
or think the words their mothers do not say—

Herschel Monteagle and Faraday
lakeland rockland and hill country
a little adjacent to where the world is
a little north of where the cities are and
sometime
we may go back there
                         to the country of our defeat
Wollaston Elvezir Dungannon
and Weslemkoon lake land
where the high townships of Cashel
                    McClure and Marmora once were—
But it's been a long time since
and we must enquire the way
                    of strangers—

The Cariboo Horses

At 100 Mile House the cowboys ride in rolling
stagey cigarettes with one hand reining
restive equine rebels on a morning grey as stone
— so much like riding dangerous women
          with whiskey coloured eyes—
such women as once fell dead with their lovers
with fire in their heads and slippery froth on thighs
— Beaver and Carrier women maybe or
          Blackfoot squaws far past the edge of this valley
on the other side of those two toy mountain ranges
          from the sunfierce plains beyond—

But only horses
               waiting in stables
hitched at taverns
               standing at dawn
pastured outside the town with
jeeps and fords and chevvys and
busy muttering stake trucks rushing
importantly over roads of man's devising
over the safe known roads of the ranchers
families and merchants of the town—
               On the high prairie

114

are only horse and rider
                wind in dry grass
clopping in silence under the toy mountains
dropping sometimes and
                lost in the dry grass
                golden oranges of dung—

Only horses
          no stopwatch memories or palace ancestors
not Kiangs hauling undressed stone in the Nile Valley
and having stubborn Egyptian tantrums or
Onagers racing thru Hither Asia and
the last Quagga screaming in African highlands
          lost relatives of these
          whose hooves were thunder
the ghosts of horses battering thru the wind
whose names were the wind's common usage
whose life was the sun's
          arriving here at chilly noon
          in the gasoline smell of the
          dust and waiting 15 minutes
          at the grocer's—

Hockey Players

What they worry about most is injuries
                broken arms and legs and
fractured skulls opening so doctors
can see such bloody beautiful things
almost not quite happening in the bone rooms
                as they happen outside—

And the referee?
                He's right there on the ice
not out of sight among the roaring blue gods
of a game played for passionate businessmen
and a nation of television agnostics
who never agree with the referee and applaud
when he falls flat on his face—

On a breakaway
the centre man carrying the puck
his wings trailing a little
                on both sides why
I've seen the aching glory of a resurrection
                in their eyes
                if they score
but crucifixion's agony to lose
—the game?

        We sit up there in the blues
bored and sleepy and suddenly three men
break down the ice in roaring feverish speed and
we stand up in our seats with such a rapid pouring
of delight exploding out of self to join them why
theirs and our orgasm is the rocket stipend
for skating thru the smoky end boards out
of sight and climbing up the appalachian highlands
and racing breast to breast across laurentian barrens
over hudson's diamond bay and down the treeless
                        tundra where
auroras are tubercular and awesome and
stopping isn't feasible or possible or lawful
but we have to and we have to
                    laugh because we must and
stop to look at self and one another but
            our opponent's never geography
                    or distance why
            it's men
            —just men?

And how do the players feel about it
this combination of ballet and murder?
For years a Canadian specific
to salve the anguish of inferiority
by being good at something the Americans aren't—
And what's the essence of a game like this
which takes a ten year fragment of a man's life
replaced with love that lodges in his brain
                and takes the place of reason?
Besides the fear of injuries
is it the difficulty of ever really overtaking
a hard black rubber disc?
Is it the impatient coach who insists on winning?

116

Sportswriters friendly but sometimes treacherous?
—And the worrying wives wanting you to quit and
your aching body stretched on the rubbing table
thinking of money in owner's pocket that might be in yours
the butt-slapping camaraderie and the self indulgence
of allowing yourself to be a hero and knowing
everything ends in a pot-belly—

Out on the ice can all these things be forgotten
in swift and skilled delight of speed?
—roaring out the endboards out the city
streets and high up where laconic winds
whisper litanies for a fevered hockey player—
Or racing breast to breast and never stopping
over rooftops of the world and all together
sing the song of winning all together
sing the song of money all together . . .
                    (and out in the suburbs

there's the six year old kid
whose reflexes were all wrong
who always fell down and hurt himself and cried
and never learned to skate
                    with his friends)—

Innuit

An old man carving soapstone
at the co-op in Frobisher Bay
and in his faded eyes
it is possible to see them
shadowy figures
past the Dorset and pre-Dorset Cultures
5,000 years ago
if you look closely
But the race-soul has drawn back
drawn back
from settlements and landing fields
from white men
into secret vaults

and catacombs of marrow
bone rooms
that reveal nothing
The Innuit which is to say
                    THE PEOPLE
as the Greeks called all foreigners
                    barbaroi
something other than themselves
                    un-GREEK
so the Innuit
                    The People
these unknowable human beings
who have endured 5,000 years
on the edge of the world
a myth from long ago
that reaches into the past
but touches an old man still living
Looking into his eyes
it is possible to see the first hunters
(if you have your own vision)
after the last ice age
moving eastward from Siberia
without dogs or equipment
toward the new country
pausing on the sea-ice
for a moment of rest
then pushing on thru the white smother
— Flying generations
leap and converge on this face
an old man carving soapstone
with the race-soul of The People
THE PEOPLE
moving somewhere
behind his eyes

Pangnirtung

118

Wilderness Gothic

Across Roblin Lake, two shores away,
they are sheathing the church spire
with new metal. Someone hangs in the sky
over there from a piece of rope,
hammering and fitting God's belly-scratcher,
working his way up along the spire
until there's nothing left to nail on—
Perhaps the workman's faith reaches beyond:
touches intangibles, wrestles with Jacob,
replacing rotten timber with pine thews,
pounds hard in the blue cave of the sky,
contends heroically with difficult problems
of gravity, sky navigation and mythopeia,
his volunteer time and labor donated to God,
minus sick benefits of course on a non-union job—

Fields around are yellowing into harvest,
nestling and fingerling are sky and water borne,
death is yodeling quiet in green woodlots,
and bodies of three young birds have disappeared
in the sub-surface of the new county highway—

That picture is incomplete, part left out
that might alter the whole Dürer landscape:
gothic ancestors peer from medieval sky,
dour faces trapped in photograph albums escaping
to clop down iron roads with matched greys:
work-sodden wives groping inside their flesh
for what keeps moving and changing and flashing
beyond and past the long frozen Victorian day.
A sign of fire and brimstone? A two-headed calf
born in the barn last night? A sharp female agony?
An age and a faith moving into transition,
the dinner cold and new-baked bread a failure,
deep woods shiver and water drops hang pendant,
double yolked eggs and the house creaks a little—
Something is about to happen. Leaves are still.
Two shores away, a man hammering in the sky.
Perhaps he will fall.

Lament for the Dorsets

(Eskimos extinct in the 14th century A.D.)

Animal bones and some mossy tent rings
scrapers and spearheads   carved ivory swans
all that remains of the Dorset giants
who drove the Vikings back to their long ships
talked to spirits of earth and water
— a picture of terrifying old men
so large they broke the backs of bears
so small they lurk behind bone rafters
in the brain of modern hunters
among good thoughts and warm things
and come out at night
to spit on the stars

The big men with clever fingers
who had no dogs and hauled their sleds
over the frozen northern oceans
awkward giants
                killers of seal
they couldn't compete with little men
who came from the west with dogs
Or else in a warm climatic cycle
the seals went back to cold waters
and the puzzled Dorsets scratched their heads
with hairy thumbs around 1350 A.D.
— couldn't figure it out
went around saying to each other
plaintively
            "What's wrong? What happened?
            Where are the seals gone?"
And died

Twentieth century people
apartment dwellers
executives of neon death
warmakers with things that explode
— they have never imagined us in their future
how could we imagine them in the past
squatting among the moving glaciers
six hundred years ago
with glowing lamps?

As remote or nearly
as the trilobites and swamps
when coal became
or the last great reptile hissed
at a mammal the size of a mouse
that squeaked and fled

Did they ever realize at all
what was happening to them?
Some old hunter with one lame leg
a bear had chewed
sitting in a caribou skin tent
— the last Dorset?
Let's say his name was Kudluk
carving 2-inch ivory swans
for a dead grand-daughter
taking them out of his mind
the places in his mind
where pictures are
He selects a sharp stone tool
to gouge a parallel pattern of lines
on both sides of the swan
holding it with his left hand
bearing down and transmitting
his body's weight
from brain to arm and right hand
and one of his thoughts
turns to ivory
The carving is laid aside
in beginning darkness
at the end of hunger
after a while wind
blows down the tent and snow
begins to cover him
After 600 years
the ivory thought
is still warm

Raymond Souster

Raymond Souster was born in 1921 in Toronto and educated at the University of Toronto Schools and Humberside Collegiate. He served in the R.C.A.F. during the Second World War. Since then he has lived in Toronto, where he works for a bank. Although he has kept out of the public eye to a much greater extent than some of his contemporaries and colleagues — Irving Layton, for example — he has established a firm place in contemporary Canadian poetry. He has published a number of volumes since 1946; The Colour of the Times: Collected Poems *(1964) won a Governor-General's Award. From 1952 to 1954 he edited* Contact: An International Magazine of Poetry; *its aim was to put Canadian poets in communication with American and European poets. He also collaborated with Irving Layton and Louis Dudek to found Contact Press, which remained in operation until 1967 and was quite important in publishing the early work of such Canadian poets as Al Purdy, Margaret Atwood, John Newlove, and Gwendolyn MacEwen. Souster's continuing interest in bringing new poets and poetry before the public is demonstrated by his editorship of the anthologies* New Wave Canada: The New Explosion in Canadian Poetry *(1966) and* Made in Canada *(1970).*

Souster may be considered a regionalist, since many of his poems are specifically about life in the city of Toronto. This is a subject which he treats in a number of different ways. Souster's city can be a place of comfortable old houses, memories of youth, jazz, and young lovers. But it is also a place of derelicts, prostitutes, personalities warped by the destructive, impersonal forces of modern commercial and industrial society. This does not make him a poet of social protest, for the impersonality of the city is primarily, for Souster, a function of man's capacity to be indifferent to suffering. Against this impersonality, the grim determination to survive represented in "Downtown Corner News Stand" wins his admiration. And in "Maryrose Visits the Stock Exchange" the innocent sensuality of the young girl is seen as being in opposition to the systematized operations of the Stock Exchange.

Like many other modern Canadian poets, Souster has shown himself distrustful of conventional poetic forms and diction. He has long been interested in Black Mountain theories of poetry and like Olson and Creeley he believes that poetic form "is never more than an extension of content."[1] Most of his poems are short; many of them, like "The Six-Quart Basket" which focuses directly on a single clear image, show the influence of Imagism. "Pomegranates in Studio One" suggests some of his ideas about poetry; the poem described in "Pomegranates" is successful because it directs attention to the object rather than to its own clever artifice.

Footnotes

[1] *Charles Olson, "Projective Verse,"* The New American Poetry, *1945-1960, ed., Donald M. Allen (New York: 1960), p. 387.*

The Hunter

I carry the ground-hog along by the tail
all the way back to the farm, with the blood
dripping from his mouth a couple of drops at a time,
leaving a perfect trail for anyone to follow.

The half-wit hired-man is blasting imaginary rabbits
somewhere on our left. We walk through fields steaming after rain,
jumping the mud: and watching the swing of your girl's hips
ahead of me, the proud way your hand holds the gun,
and remembering how you held it
up to the hog in the trap and blew his head in

wonder what fate you have in store for me.

Dominion Square

They wouldn't understand my haste
in getting out of the rain, in leaving this cold
wind-blowing night for the tavern's
warm heart, for its hot, steaming food,
much beer, and the subtle music
of the violin:
                they seem almost part of the rain
like the policeman in the white cape, white rubber boots to the thighs
who stands in the centre of the traffic
and directs with a sure hand:
                    they seem almost part of the night,
these two lovers,
with their slow lingering steps, their total unawareness
of everything in this city but their love, the strength,
      the honest lust in their bodies touching
as they walk across the Square . . . .

Lagoons, Hanlan's Point

Mornings
before the sun's liquid
spilled gradually, flooding
the island's cool cellar,
there was the boat
and the still lagoons,
with the sound of my oars
the only intrusion
over cries of birds
in the marshy shallows,
or the loud thrashing
of the startled crane
rushing the air.

And in one strange
dark, tree-hung entrance,
I followed the sound
of my heart all the way
to the reed-blocked ending,
with the pads of the lily
thick as green-shining film
covering the water.

And in another
where the sun came
to probe the depths
through a shaft of branches,
I saw the skeletons
of brown ships rotting
far below in their burial-ground,
and wondered what strange fish
with what strange colours
swam through these palaces
under the water. . . .

A small boy
with a flat-bottomed punt
and an old pair of oars
moving with wonder
through the antechamber
of a waking world.

Downtown Corner News Stand

It will need all of death to take you from this corner.
It has become your world, and you its unshaved
bleary-eyed, foot-stamping king. In winter
you curse the cold, huddled in your coat from the wind,
you fry in summer like an egg hopping on a griddle;
and always the whining voice, the nervous-flinging arms,
the red face, shifting eyes watching, waiting
under the grimy cap for God knows what
to happen. (But nothing ever does, downtown Toronto
goes to sleep and wakes the next morning
always the same, except a little dirtier.)
And you stand with your armful of Stars and Telys,
the peak of your cap well down against the sun,
and all the city's restless seething river
surges beside you, but not once do you plunge
into its flood, are carried or tossed away:
but reappear always, beard longer than ever, nose running,
to catch the noon editions at King and Bay.

Flight of the Roller-Coaster

Once more around should do it, the man confided . . .

and sure enough, when the roller-coaster reached the peak
of the giant curve above me, screech of its wheels
almost drowned out by the shriller cries of the riders,

instead of the dip and plunge with its landslide of screams,
it rose in the air like a movieland magic carpet,
        some wonderful bird,

and without fuss or fanfare swooped slowly across
        the amusement-park,
over Spook's Castle, ice-cream booths, shooting-gallery.
        And losing no height

made the last yards above the beach, where the cucumber-cool
brakeman in the last seat saluted
a lady about to change from her bathing-suit.

Then, as many witnesses reported, headed leisurely
        out over the water,
disappearing all too soon behind a low-flying flight of clouds.

The Six-Quart Basket

The six-quart basket
one side gone
half the handle torn off

sits in the centre of the lawn
and slowly fills up
with the white fruits of the snow.

This Lizard of Summer

Heat
forked in its tongue

this lizard
of summer

licks
almost lovingly

each inch
of our bodies.

Maryrose Visits the Stock Exchange

If the shouting bothers you
cover your ears, my lady,
if the disorder jars you
reflect that in this disorder
there is strictest order.

Then, when you can't stand
any more of this Interplay
of Commerce, why, move down
to the middle of the floor,
shake your hips a couple
of wonderful times and bring
this whole damn farce
to a paper-strewn halt.

Walking River Ice

Six inches of ice
between me and the gurgle
of unseen water.

Still I walk with care,
a small nagging fear
hard on my heels.
                    No secret,
this river would like me
six inches under
not over its frozen pride.

So Easy to Explain

So easy to explain
why I followed him all the way over
to Bay Street just to be sure
he found the bus terminal . . . .

There for a moment as he stood
helpless at Dundas and Yonge,
blaze of noon slicing at his eyes
still bandaged from the hospital—

I was that man standing there
waiting for a voice to speak,
waiting for a hand held out,

I was that bewildered man
soaked in the sweat of my fear,
sunshine striking at my face
but blackness, darkness pushing all around . . . .

The Cry

In the third small hour
from our roof overhead
an almost human cry
of bird or animal.

I closed the window hard
against that unearthly scream,
then stood hard-rooted there
until the wail died, freeing
blood to run on again,
ears to rewind quietness.

So back to bed, finding
all too soon the sleep
'of the righteous
and the just',

while for all I knew
something up on that roof
still waited an answer
to its cry.

The Pouring

Porcelain-white
smooth jug
of your body

slowly lifted
then upturned,
spilling joy

on all the spent
aged grayness
of the day.

Killing a Bat

You don't get rid
of a bat by simply
flushing him swiftly
down the nearest toilet:

he'll swoop and swerve
through your head for days,
a torn-loose piece
of blackest night,

who was perfectly content
before being roused,
to rest on the curtains
of this upstairs room.

But a thing unclean,
unfit to live, to those
who swinging out wildly
with soaked towels, attempt

the one thing instinct
hammers in their heads,
kill him, kill:
while his wings fight the air

in a hopeless chance
to escape, stay alive.
But there's none, he dies,
and they die a little too.

Weeping Willow in Winter

Now that I've shattered
the ice riding bare-back
and crystal on your branches,

I try to push you upright,
bend you back from the snow,
my tree, my sleek beauty,

part way up, at least,
the rest I'll leave to you
and your mad desire
to climb and trap the sun
in your shiny branches,

to weave him a crown
of your lady-finger leaves.

Pomegranates in Studio One

In the TV studio the poet
has begun to read his poem
"The Pomegranates",
a good one, he hasn't written
too many better.
                        But someone
has placed four real (live?) pomegranates
in a bowl, and beside it another bowl
in which two more of the fruit
have been halved and quartered,
the whole thing sitting on a table now
with spotlights and cameras
on it.
        Strange how the eyes
cut off the words my ears strain to hear,
eyes pulling me away
from the poem and the poet,
all because of this radiant, natural fact.

131

Is it because we are tired
of too many words, even good ones,
or have we let the eyes
overpower the mind, leaving eyes
too undisciplined?
                    While I ponder this
and a poet exclaims on about pomegranates,
the whole barn of a building glows
from those fruited halves, those quarters,
blood-red on a table . . . .

Mavis Gallant

Born Mavis de Trafford in Montreal in 1922 and educated in a series of Quebec schools, Mrs. Gallant worked for a time as a journalist in Montreal. She now lives in Paris, and publishes much of her short fiction in the New Yorker. *Her first volume of short stories,* The Other Paris, *appeared in 1956, and was followed by two novels —* Green Water, Green Sky *(1959) and* A Fairly Good Time *(1970) — and a second collection of stories,* My Heart is Broken *(1964).*

Although Robert Weaver has anthologized her, Mrs. Gallant has received comparatively little attention from Canadian critics, partly because of her expatriate status and her apparent lack of interest in writing for Canadian publication. Edmund Wilson has called her "a brilliant example of the Canadian cosmopolitan,"[1] and Hugo McPherson suggests that "Henry James sounds distantly in Mavis Gallant's work. The world she creates is small, but within its bounds she is 'one of those upon whom nothing is lost'."[2] Her subject matter frequently reflects her Canadian origins; several of her stories are set in Quebec, and English-Canadian expatriates sometimes appear in her European stories. The heroine of A Fairly Good Time *is a Canadian married to a Frenchman in Paris. The title story from* My Heart is Broken, *reprinted here, has the sophisticated and ironic tone of much* New Yorker *fiction, yet in its treatment of the effect of a harsh and desolate environment upon an immature woman, it shows some affinities with the fiction of such Canadian Prairie writers as Sinclair Ross.*

Footnotes

[1] *Edmund Wilson,* O Canada: An American's Notes on Canadian Culture *(New York: 1964), p. 6.*
[2] *Hugo McPherson, "Fiction, 1940-1960," in* Literary History of Canada, *ed., C. F. Klinck et al. (Toronto: 1965), p. 721.*

My Heart Is Broken

"When that Jean Harlow died," Mrs. Thompson said to Jeannie, "I was on the 83 streetcar with a big, heavy paper parcel in my arms. I hadn't been married for very long, and when I used to visit my mother she'd give me a lot of canned stuff and preserves. I was standing up in the streetcar because nobody'd given me a seat. All the men were unemployed in those days, and they just sat down wherever they happened to be. You wouldn't remember what Montreal was like then. *You* weren't even on earth. To resume what I was saying to you, one of these men sitting down had an American paper — the *Daily News*, I guess it was — and I was sort of leaning over him, and I saw in big print 'JEAN HARLOW DEAD.' You can believe me or not, just as you want to, but that was the most terrible shock I ever had in my life. I never got over it."

Jeannie had nothing to say to that. She lay flat on her back across the bed, with her head toward Mrs. Thompson and her heels just touching the crate that did as a bedside table. Balanced on her flat stomach was an open bottle of coral-pink Cutex nail polish. She held her hands up over her head and with some difficulty applied the brush to the nails of her right hand. Her legs were brown and thin. She wore nothing but shorts and one of her husband's shirts. Her feet were bare.

Mrs. Thompson was the wife of the paymaster in a road-construction camp in northern Quebec. Jeannie's husband was an engineer working on the same project. The road was being pushed through country where nothing had existed until now except rocks and lakes and muskeg. The camp was established between a wild lake and the line of raw dirt that was the road. There were no towns between the camp and the railway spur, sixty miles distant.

Mrs. Thompson, a good deal older than Jeannie, had become her best friend. She was a nice, plain, fat, consoling sort of person, with varicosed legs, shoes unlaced and slit for comfort, blue flannel dressing gown worn at all hours, pudding-bowl haircut, and coarse gray hair. She might have been Jeannie's own mother, or her Auntie Pearl. She rocked her fat self in the rocking chair and went on with what she had to say: "What I was starting off to tell you is you remind me of her, of Jean Harlow. You've got the same teeny mouth, Jeannie, and I think your hair was a whole lot prettier before you started fooling around with it. That peroxide's no good. It splits the ends. I know you're going to tell me it isn't peroxide but something more modern, but the result is the same."

Vern's shirt was spotted with coral-pink that had dropped off the brush. Vern wouldn't mind; at least, he wouldn't say that he minded. If he hadn't objected to anything Jeannie did until now, he wouldn't start off by complaining about a shirt. The campsite outside the uncurtained window was silent and dark. The waning moon would not appear until dawn. A passage of thought made Mrs. Thompson say, "Winter soon."

Jeannie moved sharply and caught the bottle of polish before it spilled. Mrs. Thompson was crazy; it wasn't even September.

"Pretty soon," Mrs. Thompson admitted. "Pretty soon. That's a long season up

134

here, but I'm one person who doesn't complain. I've been up here or around here every winter of my married life, except for that one winter Pops was occupying Germany."

"I've been up here seventy-two days," said Jeannie, in her soft voice. "Tomorrow makes seventy-three."

"Is that right?" said Mrs. Thompson, jerking the rocker forward, suddenly snappish. "Is that a fact? Well, who asked you to come up here? Who asked you to come and start counting days like you was in some kind of jail? When you got married to Vern, you must of known where he'd be taking you. He told you, didn't he, that he liked road jobs, construction jobs, and that? Did he tell you, or didn't he?"

"Oh, he told me," said Jeannie.

"You know what, Jeannie?" said Mrs. Thompson. "If you'd of just listened to me, none of this would have happened. I told you that first day, the day you arrived here in your high-heeled shoes, I said, 'I know this cabin doesn't look much, but all the married men have the same sort of place.' You remember I said that? I said, 'You just get some curtains up and some carpets down and it'll be home.' I took you over and showed you my place, and you said you'd never seen anything so lovely."

"I meant it," said Jeannie. "Your cabin is just lovely. I don't know why, but I never managed to make this place look like yours."

Mrs. Thompson said, "That's plain enough." She looked at the cold grease spattered behind the stove, and the rag of towel over by the sink. "It's partly the experience," she said kindly. She and her husband knew exactly what to take with them when they went on a job, they had been doing it for so many years. They brought boxes for artificial flowers, a brass door knocker, a portable bar decorated with sea shells, a cardboard fireplace that looked real, and an electric fire that sent waves of light rippling over the ceiling and walls. A concealed gramophone played the records they loved and cherished — the good old tunes. They had comic records that dated back to the year I, and sad soprano records about shipwrecks and broken promises and babies' graves. The first time Jeannie heard one of the funny records, she was scared to death. She was paying a formal call, sitting straight in her chair, with her skirt pulled around her knees. Vern and Pops Thompson were talking about the Army.

"I wish to God I was back," said old Pops.

"Don't I?" said Vern. He was fifteen years older than Jeannie and had been through a lot.

At first there were only scratching and whispering noises, and then a mosquito orchestra started to play, and a dwarf's voice came into the room. "Little Johnnie Green, little Sallie Brown," squealed the dwarf, higher and faster than any human ever could. "Spooning in the park with the grass all around."

"Where is he?" Jeannie cried, while the Thompsons screamed with laughter and Vern smiled. The dwarf sang on: "And each little bird in the treetop high/Sang 'Oh you kid!' and winked his eye."

It was a record that had belonged to Pops Thompson's mother. He had been laughing at it all his life. The Thompsons loved living up north and didn't miss cities or company. Their cabin smelled of cocoa and toast. Over their beds were oval photographs of each other as children, and they had some Teddy bears and about a dozen dolls.

135

Jeannie capped the bottle of polish, taking care not to press it against her wet nails. She sat up with a single movement and set the bottle down on the bedside crate. Then she turned to face Mrs. Thompson. She sat cross-legged, with her hands outspread before her. Her face was serene.

"Not an ounce of fat on you," said Mrs. Thompson. "You know something? I'm sorry you're going. I really am. Tomorrow you'll be gone. You know that, don't you? You've been counting days, but you won't have to any more. I guess Vern'll take you back to Montreal. What do you think?"

Jeannie dropped her gaze, and began smoothing wrinkles on the bedspread. She muttered something Mrs. Thompson could not understand.

"Tomorrow you'll be gone," Mrs. Thompson continued. "I know it for a fact. Vern is at this moment getting his pay, and borrowing a jeep from Mr. Sherman, and a Polack driver to take you to the train. He sure is loyal to *you*. You know what I heard Mr. Sherman say? He said to Vern, 'If you want to send her off, Vern, you can always stay,' and Vern said, 'I can't very well do that, Mr. Sherman.' And Mr. Sherman said, 'This is the second time you've had to leave a job on account of her, isn't it?,' and then Mr. Sherman said, 'In my opinion, no man by his own self can rape a girl, so there were either two men or else she's invented the whole story.' Then he said, 'Vern, you're either a saint or a damn fool.' That was all I heard. I came straight over here, Jeannie, because I thought you might be needing me." Mrs. Thompson waited to hear she was needed. She stopped rocking and sat with her feet flat and wide apart. She struck her knees with her open palms and cried, "I *told* you to keep away from the men. I told you it would make trouble, all that being cute and dancing around. I said to you, I remember saying it, I said nothing makes trouble faster in a place like this than a grown woman behaving like a little girl. Don't you remember?"

"I only went out for a walk," said Jeannie. "Nobody'll believe me, but that's all. I went down the road for a walk."

"In high heels?" said Mrs. Thompson. "With a purse on your arm, and a hat on your head? You don't go taking a walk in the bush that way. There's no place to walk *to*. Where'd you think you were going? I could smell Evening in Paris a quarter mile away."

"There's no place to go," said Jeannie, "but what else is there to do? I just felt like dressing up and going out."

"You could have cleaned up your home a bit," said Mrs. Thompson. "There was always that to do. Just look at that sink. That basket of ironing's been under the bed since July. I know it gets boring around here, but you had the best of it. You had the summer. In winter it gets dark around three o'clock. Then the wives have a right to go crazy. I knew one used to sleep the clock around. When her Nembutal ran out, she took about a hundred aspirin. I knew another learned to distill her own liquor, just to kill time. Sometimes the men get so's they don't like the life, and that's death for the wives. But here you had a nice summer, and Vern liked the life."

"He likes it better than anything," said Jeannie. "He liked the Army, but this was his favorite life after that."

"There," said Mrs. Thompson. "You had every reason to be happy. What'd you do if he sent you off alone, now, like Mr. Sherman advised? You'd be alone and you'd

136

have to work. Women don't know when they're well off. Here you've got a good, sensible husband working for you and you don't appreciate it. You have to go and do a terrible thing."

"I only went for a walk," said Jeannie. "That's all I did."

"It's possible," said Mrs. Thompson, "but it's a terrible thing. It's about the worst thing that's ever happened around here. I don't know why you let it happen. A woman can always defend what's precious, even if she's attacked. I hope you remembered to think about bacteria."

"What d'you mean?"

"I mean Javel, or something."

Jeannie looked uncomprehending and then shook her head.

"I wonder what it must be like," said Mrs. Thompson after a time, looking at the dark window. "I mean, think of Berlin and them Russians and all. Think of some disgusting fellow you don't know. Never said hello to, even. Some girls ask for it, though. You can't always blame the man. The man loses his job, his wife if he's got one, everything, all because of a silly girl."

Jeannie frowned, absently. She pressed her nails together, testing the polish. She licked her lips and said, "I was more beaten up, Mrs. Thompson. It wasn't exactly what you think. It was only afterwards I thought to myself, Why, I was raped and everything."

Mrs. Thompson gasped, hearing the word from Jeannie. She said, "Have you got any marks?"

"On my arms. That's why I'm wearing this shirt. The first thing I did was change my clothes."

Mrs. Thompson thought this over, and went on to another thing: "Do you ever think about your mother?"

"Sure."

"Do you pray? If this goes on at nineteen — "

"I'm twenty."

" — what'll you be by the time you're thirty? You've already got a terrible, terrible memory to haunt you all your life."

"I already can't remember it," said Jeannie. "Afterwards I started walking back to camp, but I was walking the wrong way. I met Mr. Sherman. The back of his car was full of coffee, flour, all that. I guess he'd been picking up supplies. He said, 'Well, get in.' He didn't ask any questions at first. I couldn't talk anyway."

"Shock," said Mrs. Thompson wisely.

"You know, I'd have to see it happening to know what happened. All I remember is that first we were only talking . . . "

"You and Mr. Sherman?"

"No, no, before. When I was taking my walk."

"Don't say who it was," said Mrs. Thompson. "We don't any of us need to know."

"We were just talking, and he got sore all of a sudden and grabbed my arm."

"Don't say the name!" Mrs. Thompson cried.

"Like when I was little, there was this Lana Turner movie. She had two twins. She was just there and then a nurse brought her in the two twins. I hadn't been married or anything, and I didn't know anything, and I used to think if I just kept on seeing the movie I'd know how she got the two twins, you know, and I went, oh, I must have seen it six times, the movie, but in the end I never knew any more. They just brought her the two twins."

Mrs. Thompson sat quite still, trying to make sense of this. "Taking advantage of a woman is a criminal offense," she observed. "I heard Mr. Sherman say another thing, Jeannie. He said, 'If your wife wants to press a charge and talk to some lawyer, let me tell you,' he said, 'you'll never work again anywhere,' he said. Vern said, 'I know that, Mr. Sherman.' And Mr. Sherman said, 'Let me tell you, if any reporters or any investigators start coming around here, they'll get their . . . they'll never . . . ' Oh, he was mad. And Vern said, 'I came over to tell you I was quitting, Mr. Sherman.' " Mrs. Thompson had been acting this with spirit, using a quiet voice when she spoke for Vern and a blustering tone for Mr. Sherman. In her own voice, she said, "If you're wondering how I came to hear all this, I was strolling by Mr. Sherman's office window – his bungalow, that is. I had Maureen out in her pram." Maureen was the Thompsons' youngest doll.

Jeannie might not have been listening. She started to tell something else: "You know, where we were before, on Vern's last job, we weren't in a camp. He was away a lot, and he left me in Amos, in a hotel. I liked it. Amos isn't all that big, but it's better than here. There was this German in the hotel. He was selling cars. He'd drive me around if I wanted to go to a movie or anything. Vern didn't like him, so we left. It wasn't anybody's fault."

"So he's given up two jobs," said Mrs. Thompson. "One because he couldn't leave you alone, and now this one. Two jobs, and you haven't been married five months. Why should another man be thrown out of work? We don't need to know a thing. I'll be sorry if it was Jimmy Quinn," she went on, slowly. "I like that boy. Don't say the name, dear. There's Evans. Susini. Palmer. But it might have been anybody, because you had them all on the boil. So it might have been Jimmy Quinn – let's say – and it could have been anyone else, too. Well, now let's hope they can get their minds back on the job."

"I thought they all liked me," said Jeannie sadly. "I get along with people. Vern never fights with me."

"Vern never fights with anyone. But he ought to have thrashed *you*."

"If he . . . you know. I won't say the name. If he'd liked me, I wouldn't have minded. If he'd been friendly. I really mean that. I wouldn't have gone wandering up the road, making all this fuss."

"Jeannie," said Mrs. Thompson, "you don't even know what you're saying."

"He could at least have liked me," said Jeannie. "He wasn't even friendly. It's the first time in my life somebody hasn't liked me. My heart is broken, Mrs. Thompson. My heart is just broken."

She has to cry, Mrs. Thompson thought. She has to have it out. She rocked slowly, tapping her foot, trying to remember how she'd felt about things when she was twenty, wondering if her heart had ever been broken, too.

Eli Mandel

Born in Estevan, Saskatchewan in 1922, Eli Mandel served in the Army Medical Corps during the Second World War. Later he took an M.A. at the University of Saskatchewan. In 1957 he received a doctorate in English from the University of Toronto; his thesis was on Christopher Smart. He has taught English at the College Militaire de Saint-Jean and at York University; he is now teaching at the University of Alberta. In 1966 Mandel did a series of talks for the CBC; these were published as Criticism: The Silent-Speaking Words *(1966). In 1969 he published a book on Irving Layton. His most recent book of poetry,* An Idiot Joy *(1967), won a Governor-General's Award.*

Mandel's first collection of poems was in Trio *(1954), a Contact Press volume which he shared with Gael Turnbull and Phyllis Webb. His poetic practice here, especially in the sequence "Minotaur Poems," reflects the interest of the mythopoeic poets in the use of myth and archetype as a way of commenting on contemporary experience. In his later poetry he has moved toward a more personal, sometimes fragmentary style; at the same time, his interest in the unconscious sometimes leads him to bizarre and macabre imagery. John Ower suggests that "in Mandel's poetry even the commonplace and insignificant become charged with a strange and sometimes terrible* mana,*"[1] or spiritual force. The poet is therefore a "black and secret man" exploring the underside of consciousness; like Houdini, he deliberately chooses to be bound in darkness in order that art may emerge from his struggle to escape.*

Footnotes

[1] *John Ower, "Black and Secret Poet,"* Canadian Literature, 42 *(Autumn, 1969), 16.*

Estevan Saskatchewan

A small town bears the mark of Cain,
Or the oldest brother with the dead king's wife
In a foul relation as viewed by sons,
Lies on the land, squat, producing
Love's queer offspring only,
Which issue drives the young
To feign a summer madness, consort with skulls,
While the farmer's chorus, a Greek harbinger,
Forecasts by frost or rings about the moon
How ill and black the seeds will grow.

This goodly frame, the earth, each of its sons,
With nature as a text, and common theme
The death of fathers, anguished in betrayal
From the first family returns a sacrifice
Of blood's brother, a splintered eyeball
Groined in the fields, scarecrow to crows.
This warns Ophelia to her morning song,
Bawdy as a lyric in a pretty brain gone bad,
While on those fields the stupid harvest lies

IV (from Minotaur poems)

Now I am dressed in a multitude of rooms
like a Chinese box, and slip from covers
into covers   Dawn will not help me nor
the day's exposure   I am a prodigious pun
to hide and show myself between these walls
this otherwise where sunlight
dressed in a tweed suit pursues me
or a stranger in the rooms
        and footfalls on the stairs
and eyes   and over all
    the whispering and chattering of the walls
        the pipes and hammered arteries of the place.

140

Is that a revelation in a field of light
competing with a shadow on the rock?
A bird's shadow seen from here?
Or a cloud between the sky and land
footed and patterned into phrases?

It is hours since I have been in here.
If I had once seen anything
except birds,
rocks, land, and all winter long
                    the ice and snow

A Castle and Two Inhabitants

1

The several stories of the castle
Placed rickety like box on box
Or like those Chinese puzzles
That are whole outside but inside
Piece in piece, were carpentered
A while ago. The builder is inside.
We think he must be, for we never
Saw him leave it, or indeed go in.

It simply stands there, stands,
Though how it stands no one explains,
Nor how to go from room to room,
Nor why the king has chosen it
Upon a dreadful plane of space
To live in, there to hold his court.

2

There is a hunchback in the court
Who loves his daughter and who serves
The king with stories of a hunchback love.
The crooked ways are best, he says,
The only way a cripple learns to move,
And love is crooked and the twist is this:
My hunchback proves it.

                      Like the sun at noon
Hunched over earth that splendid hump
Curls round his body, like a swollen pear
Hung from a leafless tree, like the earth
On Atlas as he sways beneath its load.

He lumps it in our faces and he leers
About our daughters and he loves his own
And monthly serves the king a wreath,
The queen's own hair upon a horn.

3

There is a wizard also in our court
Who is both man and woman and who knows
How women love, who says the hunchback
Lied to us. Love is triangular, he cries,
And shining algebras fall from his cap
Made out of crystals shivered from a frost
Of passion.

            Sculpt from a crust of sky
An ice-cold man is propped on snowy stalks
Of dogma, double-eyed with embered coals.

Here generation ends. This simple love,
The wizard says, endures the rollick
Lust and summer of a hunchback sun.

Notes from the Underground

A woman built herself a cave
    and furnished it with torn machines
    and tree-shaped trunks and dictionaries.
Out of the town where she sprang
    to her cave of rusting texts and springs
    rushed fables of indifferent rape
    and children slain indifferently
    and daily blood.

Would you believe how free I have become
    with lusting after her?
               That I have become
    a melodramatist, my friends ashamed?

I have seen by the light of her burning texts
    how the indifferent blood drips
    from the brass mouths of my friends,
    and how at the same table I have supped
    and grown fat.

Her breasts are planets in a reedy slough.
Lie down beside that slough awhile
    and taste the bitter reeds.

Read in the water how a drowning man
    sings of a free green life.

Black and Secret Man

These are the pictures that I took: you see
The garden here outside my home. You see
The roots which hung my father, mother's
Tangled hedge, this runnelled creeper vine.
Here is the tree where in the summer hung
The guest of summer, temple-haunting martlet.
And here the tree with twenty mortal murders
On its crown.
             Now face the faces in the tree,
The snarling wood, the years of treedom.
Why, once when brains were out a man would die
But now like maggot-pies and choughs and rooks
A black and secret man of blood walks
In the garden.
             I never go there now.

But go there, go there, go there,
Snaps the hanging snapshot bird.

Day of Atonement: Standing

My lord, how stands it with me now
Who, standing here before you
(who, fierce as you are, are also just),
Cannot bow down. You order this.
Why, therefore, I must break
If bend I will not, yet bend I must.

But I address myself to you thus,
Covered and alert, and will not bare
My self. Then I must bear you,
Heavy as you are.
             This is the time
The bare tree bends in the fierce wind
And stripped, my God, springs to the sky.

144

Houdini

I suspect he knew that trunks are metaphors,
could distinguish between the finest rhythms
unrolled on rope or singing in a chain
and knew the metrics of the deepest pools

I think of him listening to the words
spoken by manacles, cells, handcuffs,
chests, hampers, roll-top desks, vaults,
especially the deep words spoken by coffins

escape, escape: quaint Harry in his suit
his chains, his desk, attached to all attachments
how he'd sweat in that precise struggle
with those binding words, wrapped around him
like that mannered style, his formal suit

and spoken when? by whom? What thing first said
"there's no way out"?; so that he'd free himself,
leap, squirm, no matter how, to chain himself again,
once more jump out of the deep alive
with all his chains singing around his feet
like the bound crowds who sigh, who sigh.

Pictures in an Institution

1

Notice: all mirrors will be covered
          the mailman is forbidden to speak
          professors are confined to their offices
          faculties no longer exist

2

I speak of what I know,
how uncle Asher, spittle on his lips,
first typed with harvest hands the fox
across a fence and showing all good men
come to their country's aid rushed off to Israel
there to brutalize his wife and son

how step-grandfather Barak wiped
sour curds out of his curly beard
before he roared the Sabbath in my ears
what Sara, long his widow, dreamed
the night she cried: God, let him die at last,
thinking perhaps of Josef who had lost
jewels in Russia where the cossack rode
but coughed his stomach out in Winnipeg

Your boredom does not matter. I take,
brutal to my thoughts, these lives, defy
your taste in metaphor; the wind-break
on the farm that Barak plowed to dust
makes images would ruin public poetry.

The rites of love I knew:
how father cheated brother, uncle, son,
and bankrupt-grocer, that we might eat
wrote doggerel verse, later took his wife,
my mother, in the English way beside my bed.
Why would he put his Jewishness aside?
Because there was no bread?
                     Or out of spite
that doctors sliced his double rupture,
fingered spleen, and healed his bowel's ache?

146

Lovers lie down in glades, are glad.
These, now in graves, their headstones sunk,
knew nothing of such marvels, only God, his ways,
owning no texts of Greek or anthropology.

3

Notice: the library is closed to all who read
        any student carrying a gun
        registers first, exempt from fines,
        is given thirteen books per month,
        one course in science, one in math,
        two options
                    campus police
        will see to co-eds' underwear

4

These names I rehearse:
                    Eva, Isaac,
Charley, Yetta, Max
                    now dead
or dying or beyond my lies

till I reeling with messages
and sick to hold again their bitter lives
put them, with shame, into my poetry.

5

Notice: there will be no further communication
        lectures are cancelled
        all students are expelled
        the reading of poetry is declared a public
                                        crime

Milton Acorn

Milton Acorn was born in Charlottetown, P.E.I., in 1925. He served in the Canadian army during World War II and then became a carpenter. He gave up this trade to write poetry. Since 1958 he has lived in Montreal, Toronto, and Vancouver; he has now returned to Charlottetown. In Montreal and Toronto in the early sixties, aided at various times by Al Purdy and Gwendolyn MacEwen, he edited a mimeographed poetry magazine Moment; *while in Vancouver he helped found the* Georgia Strait. *Since 1956 he has published several collections of poetry, and in 1963* Fiddlehead *devoted an issue to his work. A selection of his poems,* I've Tasted my Blood, *was edited by Purdy in 1969.*

Acorn's poetic ability has been acknowledged by several poets, including Purdy, Dorothy Livesay, and, lately, George Bowering. But he has been slower to win recognition from academic critics, partly because, as Purdy says, "Most litcrits . . . don't really want poets to express political opinions or write nasty polemics about injustice that name names and label phonies."[1] *Dorothy Livesay sees him as heir to both the social idealism and the Imagist techniques of the thirties.*[2] *Acorn himself acknowledges that he is "a 'Revolutionary Poet' — that is, revolutionary in the political sense, not the poetic sense."*[3] *This does not mean, however, that his poetry is simply versified Marxism; he is too much a poet to be confined within the rigidity of dogma. He is, nevertheless, the most outspokenly political poet represented in this collection. "I Shout Love," with its prophetic tone and long, flexible, Whitmanesque lines, is a good example of his political poetry. Acorn is also capable of pure Imagism, as in "Charlottetown Harbor," and lyrical expression of personal feeling, as in "Lyric."*

Footnotes

[1] *Al Purdy, "Introduction," to Milton Acorn,* I've Taste my Blood *(Toronto: 1969), p. xv.*
[2] *Dorothy Livesay, "Search for a Style: The Poetry of Milton Acorn,"* Canadian Literature, *40 (Spring, 1969), 33.*
[3] *Acorn, op. cit., p. ii.*

Charlottetown Harbor

An old docker with gutted cheeks,
time arrested in the used-up-knuckled hands
crossed on his lap, sits
in a spell of the glinting water.

He dreams of times in the cider sunlight
when masts stood up like stubble;
but now a gull cries, lights,
flounces its wings ornately, folds them,
and the waves slop among the weed-grown piles.

Lyric

If I said love that word
'd recreate me as love,
said love you that breath
'd drop me trembly on
your breasts, your breath.

Love's before you, before me;
nearest to god we know.
Utter his name truly then he
's possessor and law.
Listen, love, I say it.

I've Tasted My Blood

If this brain's over-tempered
consider that the fire was want
and the hammers were fists.
I've tasted my blood too much
to love what I was born to.

But my mother's look
was a field of brown oats, soft-bearded;
her voice rain and air rich with lilacs:
and I loved her too much to like
how she dragged her days like a sled over gravel.

Playmates? I remember where their skulls roll!
One died hungry, gnawing grey perch-planks;
one fell, and landed so hard he splashed;
and many and many
come up atom by atom
in the worm-casts of Europe.

My deep prayer a curse.
My deep prayer the promise that this won't be.
My deep prayer my cunning,
my love, my anger,
and often even my forgiveness
that this won't be and be.
I've tasted my blood too much
to abide what I was born to.

Poem with Fat Cats in the Background

Hungry men, their grins tight with embarrassment,
move by clever steps to intercept me
on the spit-grey downtown streets.
With my wrinkled shoes, my coat ill-used and borrowed,
I wonder how they know me.

One showed me his road-rough palms:
"Look, aren't these worker's hands?"
Oh many have tricks
to trap me — tired of rage and bored with pity,
into the pain of knowledge:
"This is real . . . This is a man!"

My worried arithmetic's blown out of my brain
and I give . . . a nickel, two dimes, a quarter.
Often they want to shake hands,
but I haven't done it yet
. . . Made a partner in Man's indignity
I ask for nothing but a curse.

Sky's Poem for Christmas

As from milky vapour, dust at atoms jostling like hornets,
a nebula swigs great swatches of itself into a new sun
raw with light, ravener to its parent mists, messenger
to far astronomers thirsty for the word, the word
that'll unlock them: I've never lost a faith
or wrenched my roots of eyes from the heart . . .
Each doom to joy and torment's nourished
within an old love, becomes a new focus
pulsing radiation, disrupting
the foggy smut of death about it;
while I still step to the blood's rhythm,
the soul's reason in those old stories
of kings and white-hot new stars, wonderful babes
like Jupiter's yowl making that Island cave boom like an organ,
born to laugh a challenge at the old cruel gods.

151

Surely at least once when a new star burst thru heaven
three old men forsook the stern fantasies
of mummy-clothes they'd wrapped around the world,
and surely they found at least one babe
who held great bear time by its short tail . . . .
For birth by birth the many-colored creatures of Earth
break ranks and dance apart calling their names and numbers
to reassemble with shoutings and elbow-digs
in formations first seen by the mindseye of a child.

Christmas I became that ho-ho-ho of a saint
to wind on a balky piebald disbelieving burro
along the wisemen's trail thru a desert of grown-up people
like cactus with its growth stalled in tormented poses:
til housed and run around by squirrels I found the boy Sky
with eyes hazel windows into outré dimensions
now looking out on wonder, now looking in
at wonder . . . I came not with gifts but
for a present of the universe made strange, tumbling
with odd fuzzy animals, blue of high heaven
siphoned down to tank up my brain,
for meteors he caught and sent sizzling past my ears:
and for myself made quaint, totemic
like a thick oak come wobbling, walking
grotesquely on its roots over patches of dark and sunlight.

Knowing I Live in a Dark Age

Knowing I live in a dark age before history,
I watch my wallet and
am less struck by gunfights in the avenues
than by the newsie with his dirty pink chapped face
calling a shabby poet back for his change.

The crows mobbing the blinking, sun-stupid owl;
wolves eating a hamstrung calf hindend first,
keeping their meat alive and fresh . . . these
are marks of foresight, beginnings of wit:
but Jesus wearing thorns and sunstroke
beating his life and death into words
to break the rods and blunt the axes of Rome:
this and like things followed.

Knowing that in this advertising rainbow
I live like a trapeze artist with a headache,
my poems are no aspirins . . . they show
pale bayonets of grass waving thin on dunes;
the paralytic and his lyric secrets;
my friend Al, union builder and cynic,
hesitating to believe his own delicate poems
lest he believe in something better than himself:
and history, which is yet to begin,
will exceed this, exalt this
as a poem erases and rewrites its poet.

I Shout Love

I shout Love in a land muttering slack damnation
as I would in a blizzard's blow,
staggering stung by snowfire in the numbing tongues of cold,
for my heart's a furry sharp-toothed thing
that charges out whimpering
even when pain cries the sign written on it.

I shout Love even tho it might deafen you
and never say that Love's a mild thing
for it's hard, a violation
of all laws for the shrinking of people.
I *shout* Love, counting on the hope
that you'll sing and not shatter in Love's vibration.

I shout Love . . . Love . . . It's a net
scooping us weltering, fighting for joy
hearts beating out new tempos against each other.

The wild centre life explodes from a seed
recreates me daily in your eyes' innocence
as a small ancient creature, Love's inventor,
listened to a rainbow of whispers.

I shout Love against the proverbs of the damned
which they pause between clubbings and treacheries
to quote with wise communicative nods . . . I know
they're lies, but know too
that if I declared a truce in this war
they'd turn into pronged truths and disembowel me.

By what grim structure in the skull
do you justify unloveliness? I tell you
this machine has masters
who play their contradiction of music on you.

I shout Love against my prison where unconscious joy
like a brown sparrow chirping hoppity zig-zag
seems my keeper . . . In his bright ignorant eye

154

I live a prisoner while masons plonk stone
to soak up sunlight meant for prisoners
each one a piece of my brain, fragment of my heart's muscle.

And prisoners with hunger aching like a tooth in the belly;
            All the robbed ones —
wonderless kids,
    strengthless men,
        women with no vision for their womb-thoughts.
How'll I escape? Clang shut my own cell door?

I shout Love for all the colors and shapes of men,
all their subleties
of blood and bone, thought and vision:
imagining for each
a destiny according to his particular beauty.

I shout Love for the womanflower, the manflower,
and don't too carefully tend them.
Inventing themselves moment by moment
out of joy, sorrow
and stark machinery of need,
what do they need of me before my truth?

I shout Love . . . which is just the beginning:
Truth . . . which is just the beginning:
Honor . . . which is just the beginning:
And sometimes turn from the long-fanged enemy
to eat the worm in my own heart.

Louis Riel, that man sad with wisdom
I Love . . . and his hope Canada:
for hopes are the taller parts of men,
my stilts and eyes' loving perspective,
hope my liver pumping the bile that is life.

Does anyone know where the corpse is buried?
Under whose stuffed seat? What dancer's foot?
Louis Riel I Love;
but the hangman drives to a Sunday picnic with his family
and whatever the martyr gained he claims.

Even I shout Love who aged ten thousand years
before my tenth birthday
in shame, wrath, and wickedness;
shout and grow young as cowards grow old;
Shout Love whom this world's paradoxical joy
makes stammer or keep silent between shoutings,
more held each hour by the wonder of it.

I shout You my Love in a springtime instant
when I wince half pain half joy to notes from an oriole
over balls of frost trapped in quickening roots,
and the tick-tock-tickle of warm rain
trickling into buds' eyes, plucking them open.

I shout Love into your pain when times change and you must change:
minutes seeming final as a judge's sentence
when skies crack and fall
like splinters of mirrors
and gauntle'd fingers, blued as a great rake,
pluck the balled yarn of your brain:

For Love's the spine holding me straight,
the eye in back of my shoulderblades
that sees and beats my heart for all thinkers,
and the touch all over and thru me
I've often called God.

The herring with his sperm makes milk of the wide wrinkling
        wriggling ocean
where snowy whales jump rolling among whitecaps
as I shout live your Love and the deeds of my words
pollinate the air you're breathing.
Since life's a dream garment hung singing or sighing on a bone tree
why shouldn't it be Love's adventure?

I shout Love between your knees that are my wings my Love,
when I ride like a dragon
blessing you fierce as curses.
Oh take me Love for I'm a storm of light
enwhorled with satanic darkness.

I whisper Love into the ear of a newborn girl,
breathing Love in her name.
May she grow up around her name singing inside her.

I shout Love against Death, that rattling, stinking harvest machine
that loves best the ripest and richest in Love.
I've seen their eyes bright with hunger
gorging on their last light;
and felt Love lurch sidling away
from the small help they wanted.

I shout Love and am no sentimentalist
but I rejoice in the deaths of rogues.

But Love life thrilling roots
like nerves digging and buried corpse,
the old fierce eye rotted and born new,
an enemy lost in a lover.

I shout Love wherever there's loveless silence;
in dumb rocks, in black iron lie oppressed minds
like parsecs of night between the stars,
where suns in tumultuous sleep toss eruptions about them
and I wake with a cry
spinning among the galaxies.

I shout Love to the young whose eyes are clouded with light
as their light clouds my eyes.
Only as beards of wheat swaying at the fingertips may I touch them
for they're born in the centre, are the centre,
and I shout Love, even tho
there's something of me they must destroy.

You to whom honor came so easily
in your darling girl world,
when your joy changed so quickly to defiance
you shocked us but
you made our hearts and brains beat one rhythm
and we followed you.

I shout Love at those grey-lipped men who trim life:
Shout Love into their dim ears, their shaking heads.

157

I Love the dawn, with a half-risen sun rosy like the head of God's
  phallus.

But what if I came shouting Love now
to you shivering in your blanket
unfed for forty-eight hours?
The liberals goggle over their cocktails
to talk patiently of feeding you,
but I shout Love and I mean business.

I shout Love in those four-letter words
contrived to smudge and put it in a harmless place,
for Love today's a curse and defiance.
Listen you money-plated bastards
puffing to blow back the rolling Earth with your propaganda
    bellows and oh-so-reasoned negations of Creation:
When I shout Love I mean your destruction.

Margaret Laurence

Margaret Wemyss was born in Neepawa, Manitoba in 1926 and spent her youth there. She studied English literature at United College, Winnipeg, and graduated with an Honours degree in 1948. She married Jack Laurence, a civil engineering graduate, in the same year. In 1949 they went to England, and the following year to Somaliland (now Somalia), where Mr. Laurence was in charge of a dam-building project. In 1952 they moved to the Gold Coast (now Ghana); in 1957 they returned to Canada and lived in Vancouver for five years. Mrs. Laurence now divides her time between a house in England and a cottage near Peterborough, Ontario. In 1969-70 she was Writer-in-Residence at the University of Toronto.

Mrs. Laurence is perhaps best known in Canada for her three novels set in this country — The Stone Angel (1964), A Jest of God (1966), and The Fire-Dwellers (1968). A Jest of God won a Governor-General's Award and became the basis of a film, Rachel, Rachel, directed by Paul Newman. A substantial part of her work, however, reflects her African experience; she has published translations of Somali folk tales, a history of Nigerian literature, a travel book about Somalia, The Prophet's Camel-Bell (1963), and a novel, This Side Jordan (1960), set in Ghana. The story reproduced here was first published in Queen's Quarterly in 1956 and reprinted in The Tomorrow-Tamer (1963), a collection of Mrs. Laurence's stories about Ghana.

Although it may seem incongruous to include a story set in Ghana as specifically Canadian, the recent publication of Dave Godfrey's The New Ancestors (1970) and David Knight's Farquharson's Physique and What it Did to His Mind (1971), novels set in West Africa, indicates that other Canadian writers besides Margaret Laurence have a special interest in Africa. While it is unlikely that Mrs. Laurence conciously intended a parallel between West African and Canadian society, "The Drummer of All the World" illustrates the possibilities of writing fiction about a nation emerging from colonialism, and provides an opportunity for a study of conflicts both between generations and between cultures. Though it may appear somewhat episodic and lacking in unity, it is unified by the consciousness of the narrator as he comes to the difficult awareness not only that he has been shut out of Eden but also that Eden itself was not as idyllic as he had imagined.

The Drummer of All the World

My father thought he was bringing Salvation to Africa. I, on the other hand, no longer know what salvation is. I am not sure that it lies in the future. And I know now that it is not to be found in the past.

The mission where I was born was in a fishing village between Accra and Takoradi, on Africa's salt-steaming west coast. I lived there all my early boyhood. A missionary — how difficult it was to live down my father's profession. I almost wish I had not tried.

A missionary had to have a genuine calling in those days. Nothing less would have withstood the nagging discomfort of the place. Our bungalow was mudbrick, dank and uncleanable. Our lights were unreliable hurricane lamps, which my father always forgot to fix until the sudden surging arrival of night. Our bath was a cement tub where grey lizards flattened themselves for coolness. A green fur of mould grew over everything, especially over my father's precious books, irritating him to the point of desperation. Diarrhoea was a commonplace, malaria and yellow fever only slightly less so.

I did not notice these things much. For me it was a world of wonder and half-pleasurable terror. Our garden was a jungle of ragged banana palms and those giant leaves called 'elephant's ears'. In front of the bungalow the canna lilies stood, piercingly scarlet in the strong sunlight. Sometimes the nights were suffocating, and the mosquito net over my bed showed scarcely a tremor of breeze. Every lizard nervously hunting for insects, every cockroach that scuttled across the floor, seemed to me the footsteps of *asamanfo*, the spirits of the dead. Then the rains would come, and at night the wooden shutters would slam against the house like untuned drums, and the wind would frighten me with its insane laughter.

The chief thing I remember about my mother is that she was always tired. She was very pale and thin, and often had malaria. In a sense, she even welcomed it.

'It is God's way of trying us, Matthew,' she would say to me. 'Remember Job.'

She never gave in. She went on, thumping the decayed hand-organ in the little mud church, chalking up the week's attendance, so many black souls for Jesus. I think she would have been happier if she had even once admitted that she hated Africa, hated the mild-eyed African women who displayed in public their ripe heavy breasts to suckle their babies, and the brown-skinned men with their slender fingers, their swaggering walk, their bare muscular thighs. I suppose she must have realized her hatred. Perhaps that is why she worked herself to death — trying to prove it was not so.

When I was young I had an African nurse. She was old Yaa, the wife of Kwaku, our cook. I don't suppose she was really old. Her second son, Kwabena, was my age, and the younger ones kept coming for years. But she seemed ancient as stone to me then, with her shrewd seamed face and her enormous body. It was Yaa and Kwabena who taught me Twi, taught it to me so thoroughly that by the time I was six I could speak it better than English.

Kwabena and I used to run, whooping and yelling, beside Yaa as she walked back from the market, her great hips swaying under the thick folds of her best green and mauve cloth, and her wide brass headpan piled high with mangoes and paw-paw, yams and red peppers.

'Ei ei!' she would cry, as the goats and chickens scattered out of her way on the narrow street. 'Another week of this walk and I am finished! The bottom of the hill — that would not have suited God, oh no! If the master had less worry about my soul and more about my feet — '

When Kwabena and I stole eggs to give to the fetish, she whipped us. I would have died rather than tell my father — not for shame, but for love of her.

'A hen treads on her chicks,' she would tell us the old proverb, 'but not to kill them.'

In the rains I used to lie awake, listening to the thunder that seemed to split the sky, and thinking of Sasabonsam, the red-furred Great Devil, perched on his *odum* tree with those weird folk of witchery, the *mmoatia* who talked in whistles. Then I would hear the soft slapping of Yaa's footsteps in the passage, and she would come in and rock me in her arms.

'Do they think he is a man yet?' she would demand angrily, of no one. 'Sleeping in a room by himself! Listen, little one, shall I tell you what the thunder is? In the beginning, when Odamankoma created all things — '

And soon I would be asleep.

I found out accidentally that Yaa had suckled me at her breast when I was a baby. My mother never knew.

'I asked what day I was born,' I told Kwabena. 'It was a Tuesday.'

His face lit up. 'Then we are brothers in one way — '

Kwabena's name was given to the Tuesday-born. Yaa laughed.

'You are brothers anyway,' she said.

And then she told me. I do not know why that should make a difference to me, even yet, when I think of her. Perhaps because her love, like her milk, was plentiful. She had enough to spare for me.

My father was an idol-breaker of the old school. He hated only one thing more than the heathen gods and that was the Roman Catholic Church.

'Formalism, Latin — all learned by rote,' he would say. 'They have no spontaneity. None at all.'

Spontaneity to my father meant drilling the Mission Boys' Fife and Drum Band to play 'Nearer My God to Thee' until their mouths were sore and puckered with blowing and their heads spinning with the uncomprehended tune.

The mission had a school. My father taught the boys to read and write; and who knows, in the eternal scheme of things perhaps that is all he was meant to do. But he was not a very patient man. Once when a family of rats died in the well, and the merchant cheated him on the price of cement for a new one, he beat six boys in a single afternoon. I cannot say that I blame him. He worked hard and had so pathetically little to show for his toil and his poverty. He would have been superhuman if the light of holiness had not flickered low from time to time.

For twenty years he tried to force, frighten or cajole his flock away from drumming

161

and dancing, the accompaniments of the old religion. He forbade the making of wooden figures. I suppose we have to thank men like my father for the sad fact that there are so few carvers of any merit left in West Africa.

He broke idols literally as well as symbolically. Perhaps it was necessary. I do not know. I heard the story of Moses and the Golden Calf so often that after a few years of almost tasting the powdered gold harsh against my throat, I passed into the stage of boredom.

'I have discovered another fetish hut,' my father announced importantly one day.

I nearly betrayed myself and the whole village by asking which one.

'Where?'

'On the shore, between the palm grove and the fishing beach. I am going to break into it.'

I knew the one. The *obosom* there was a powerful one, Kwabena had told me. I stared at him with wide eyes. My father probably thought I was full of admiration for his zeal. In fact, I was wildly curious.

'He will — of course — die,' Kwabena said when I told him.

My father did break into the fetish hut, and he did not die. He did not even have indigestion or a fever. The fetish inside the little hive of woven palm leaves was part of the vertebrae of an enormous sea creature, possibly a whale. It was very old, and crumbled when he kicked it. I suppose it was a blow for truth. But I was ashamed.

I still am. Moses broke the idols of his own people.

The parades were something my parents organized and bore with, but never liked. They took place on saints' days or whenever the attendance of the Band of Jesus was falling off.

'If only the girls would just walk along,' my mother would complain, 'instead of — what they do. And to the hymns, too.'

'I know,' my father soothed her. 'But it's necessary. We will just have to keep impressing them with the desirability of dignity. But we can't cut out the parades. Remember, they're like children, these people. In order to be drawn to the church, they must have the pageantry, the music — it's better than their own heathen dancing, anyway. Besides, the Roman Catholics have parades.'

My father marched with the parade only once, and that time the District Commissioner's wife happened to see him. He was so humiliated he never went again. I can still see those parades, headed by the mission banner in purple and yellow silk. I wish you could have heard the Mission Boys' Fife and Drum Band playing 'Onward, Christian Soldiers' with a syncopated jazz beat, hot as the forest's pulse. The words, badly translated in Twi, were chanted by the snaking line of girls, their hands outstretched, their shoulders lifting to the off-beat, their whole bodies giving back the rhythm. Dignity! They could no more stop themselves from dancing than they could from breathing. Every sinew, every bone, in their bodies responded to rhythm as to a lover's touch.

One Easter my father discovered that I had gone with Kwabena, as always, and joined the parade at a distance from the church.

162

'I can't understand,' my father began, more in sorrow than anger, 'why Kofi let you stay. I've told him — '

Kofi was one of the monitors, one of the very few of his flock whom my father trusted.

'He didn't see me,' I replied abruptly.

He could hardly have missed seeing me, turning cartwheels with Kwabena at the head of the parade. But Kofi was the last person who would have tattled. Fortunately for my father, he never found out, as I had done, that Kofi was one of the most renowned fetish priests along the coast.

'We have explained it all to you, Matthew,' my father went on. 'The parades are not — proper — for you in the practice of your faith.'

'Why not?' I was still excited. 'It was fun — why shouldn't I go?'

'Religion is not fun,' thundered my father. 'It is serving God.'

How can I describe Kwabena, who was my first and for many years my only real friend? I cannot think of him as he is now. The reality of him is the little boy I remember, slighter than I but more wiry, braver but less far-sighted. Until my mother objected, he used to run naked, his brown body paled with dust. He had Yaa's aggressive spirit and his laughter was like hers, irreverent, deep, flooded with life. He was totally unlike the charming, indolent Kwaku, his father.

I used to go with him into the village, although may parents had forbidden it, into the mudbrick huts thatched with dried palm leaves, the fusty little dwellings stinking of goats and refuse and yellow spicy palm oil. The filth and the sorrow — I hardly noticed them. I was shown a girl child who had died of malaria, the belly bloated, the limbs twisted with the fever. And what interested me most was that they had left her gold earrings on. Avariciously, I longed to steal those thin bright circles before they were wasted in the earth.

I do not know when Kwabena began to notice suffering. Perhaps the knowledge of it was born in him.

When I was with Kwabena, the world of the mission and Band of Jesus did not exist for me. However powerfully my father preached, he could not stop the drums playing in the evenings. Kwabena and I would sit under the casuarina tree in our garden and listen to the thudding rhythm, the tempo building up and up until you knew the drummer was hypnotized with the sound.

'Ei! That one! It is almost like the voice of Drum himself,' Kwabena would say.

And I would imagine the vast-bellied giant, the Drummer of all the world, drumming on himself, the Drum of drums. For years I thought of the great grinning mask each time the drums pulsed in the moon-grey night, seeming to shiver even the ribboned leaves of the banana palms.

The casuarina tree was a special meeting-place for Kwabena and me. It was there that the wind spoke to us, whispering through the feather fans of the branches like the warning voices of the ancestors themselves. It was there that Kwabena used to tell me stories about Ananse Kokuroko, Ananse the gigantic spider, who desired greedily all power and all wealth, and who wove his web of cunning to ensnare the stupid and the guileless. Whenever I saw a spider I always sidestepped it, out of respect for the Father of Spiders, and for a time I half believed they could understand what I was saying. .

There was a deserted palm hut on the shore, a mile from the village. Kwabena said it was where Death lived. We always walked far to the side of it and never looked at it directly. Kwabena was especially mindful of taboos, for he wanted to be a fetish priest when he became a man.

In the sweltering afternoons Kwabena and I would steal away from the bungalow and go to the lagoon. The sea was nearby and clean, and we were allowed to swim there. I suppose that is why we preferred the lagoon. Kwabena would peel off his scanty garb.

'I can dive better than you, Matthew!'

Often I hesitated, some deep English fear of unclean water stirring within me.

'It is forbidden — '

Kwabena would spout brown water from his mouth like a whale.

'You are afraid! If I had such fear I would go and hide myself in the forest, for shame!'

So I would strip also, indignantly, and jump in. I never got bilharzia — some kindly spirit must protect the very foolish.

The shore was ours, with its twisted seashells and moss-hair rocks and stretches of pale sand where transparent crabs scurried like tiny crustaceous ghosts. Ours the thin-prowed fishing boats that impertinently dared the angry surf each day. Ours the groves of slender palms, curved into the wind, and the bush paths with their tangled vines and tree roots torn from the red earth by storms. Ours was the village, too, with its baked mud streets where old gossiping men squatted and children slept and big-breasted women walked with babies slung on their backs and laden brass trays balanced on their heads.

This was my Africa, in the days of my childhood, before I knew how little I knew.

I was ten when I first saw Afua. She was Yaa's niece, and when her mother died she came to live with Yaa and Kwaku. She was a thin and bony little girl, and as though she sensed her ugliness she was very shy. No one ever noticed her except Yaa, who would chatter away encouragingly as the two of them pounded fu-fu in the shade of the mango tree.

'I know — you are a little owl now, but it will not always be so. There is beauty in you. You will fatten and grow tall, and one day all the young men will want you. You will not have to marry a poor man.'

And the child would look at her gravely, not believing.

Afua had been living in our compound for nearly two years before I really saw her. She had changed in that time, without my realizing it. Perhaps I, too, had changed. My childhood was nearly over, although I did not know it then and still longed for the slow years to pass.

It was afternoon and the sun filled the street with its hot orange light, making vividly dark the shadows on the earth and walls. Afua had been carrying a basket of melons home from the market. Now the basket lay forgotten in the festering gutter.

Afua was dancing with her shadow. Slowly, lightly, then faster, until she was

164

whirling in the deserted street, her hands clapping, her hips swaying with a sudden knowledge of her womanhood. I had to stop and watch her. For the first time I saw her ripening breasts under her faded cotton cloth, and the beauty given to her face by her strong fine-shaped bones. When I saw Kwabena coming along the street behind me, I did something totally strange to me. I turned and went to meet him, and led him back the other way, so he should not see her.

My father had forbidden me to take part in the mission parades, and I never went again. I wondered afterwards what he would have thought if he had known what I did instead. When the talking drums sounded in the evening, I got Kwaku to tell me any of their invocations which he understood, or the proverbs and parables which they drummed forth.

> Odamankoma created the Thing,
> The Carver, He hewed out the Thing —

I learned some of the other names of Nyame — the Shining One, Giver of Rain, Giver of Sun. Once for a whole year I called God by the name of Nyame in my silent prayers. I tried to find out from Kwaku — and was laughed at — the meaning of the saying 'Odamankoma created Death, and Death killed Him'. When my mother was ill for the last time, I invoked Nyankopon's strong name, Obommubuwafre, not for love of her but as a duty.

God of my fathers, I cannot think You minded too much. If anything, I think You might have smiled a little at my seriousness, smiled as Kwaku did, with mild mockery, at the boy who thought Africa was his.

The year after my mother died, I went back to England to school. It was not until I was seventeen that I returned to Africa on a visit. I had grown very like my father, tall and big-shouldered, and I did not have much difficulty in working my passage out as deckhand on a cargo boat.

Kwabena was at school in Takoradi, but he came home several times to see me. He had grown taller, although he was still a head shorter than I, and his lank child's body had filled in and become stocky. Apart from that, to my unobservant eyes he was the same. I wonder now how I could have thought so. The indications were plain enough, had I not wanted to ignore them. I asked him to come with me to the palm grove one day, to look at the fetish huts. His face became guarded.

'I do not go there any more,' he said.

We passed a man planting cassava in a little field.

'They pour libation to make the crops good,' Kwabena commented, 'and then work the land like that, by hand, with a hoe.'

We saw the District Commissioner one afternoon, his white topee gleaming. He was holding a formal palaver with the local chief.

'We will not always be slaves of the English,' Kwabena said.

'That's stupid,' I replied. 'You're not slaves now.'

'If they own us or own our country, where is the difference?'

165

'So they will have to go?'

'Yes,' he answered firmly. 'They will have to go.'

'Splendid,' I said ironically. 'And I with them? If I were here in government?'

He did not reply for a moment.

'Perhaps I would not wish it,' he said finally, carefully. 'But there is a saying – follow your heart, and you perish.'

We did not talk of it again, and after a while I forgot.

Afua still lived with Yaa and Kwaku. I thought she had changed more than anyone. I see now that she had changed less than Kwabena, for the difference in her was one that life had brought about, easily, of itself. Her body gave the impression of incredible softness and at the same time a maternal strength. She belonged to earth, to her body's love, to toil, to her unborn children. One evening, after Kwabena had gone back to Takoradi, I fulfilled the promise to myself and went to the palm grove. It was deserted, and the wind ruffled the tops of the trees like fingers through unruly hair. Afua walked quietly, and I did not hear her until she was very close. But she did not enter the grove.

'Why do you stand there?' she asked.

'I don't know. Perhaps to hear the ancestors' voices.'

'You must not.'

'Why?'

'Because it is a sacred place,' she answered simply, 'and I am afraid.'

The beach was only a few yards away. We walked down there.

'You have grown very tall,' she smiled, and she placed one of her hands lightly on my wrist. Then she hesitated. 'Are – are Englishmen like other men?'

I could not help laughing at that, and she laughed too, without self-consciousness or shame. Then, clumsily, I took her in my arms.

She was more experienced than I. I would not have blamed her if she had mocked me. But she did not. For her, it answered a question. Quite probably that is all. But for me it was something else. Possessing her, I possessed all earth. Afterwards, I told her that I had to go back to England soon. Perhaps I expected her to say she would be broken-hearted.

'Yes, it is right that you should return to your own land,' Afua said.

I was about to tell her that I would come back here, that I would see her again. But something stopped me.

It was the sudden memory of what Kwabena had said. 'Follow your heart, and you perish.'

Of course I did go back to Africa after all, but not for another ten years. Africa had changed. The flame trees still scattered their embers of blossoms upon the hard earth. The surf boats still hurtled through the big waves. The market women's mammy-cloths were as gaudy, their talk as ribald as ever. Yet nothing was the same.

The country was to have its independence the following year, but the quality of change was more than political. It was so many things. It was an old chieftain in a greasy and threadbare robe, with no retinue – only a small boy carrying aloft the red

166

umbrella, ancient mark of aristocracy. It was an African nightclub called 'Weekend in Wyoming', and a mahogany-skinned girl wearing white face powder. It was parades of a new sort, buxom market women chanting 'Free — dom!' It was the endless palaver of newborn trade unions, the mushroom sprouting of a dozen hand-set newspapers. It was an innuendo in the slogans painted on mammy-lorries — The Day Will Come, Life Is Needed, Authority Is Never Loved. It was the names of highlife bands — The Majestic Atoms, Scorpion Ansah And His Jet Boys. It was the advertisements in newspapers — 'Take Tiger Liver Tonic for fitness, and see how fast you will be promoted at work.' It was the etiquette and lovelorn columns — 'Is it proper for a young lady to wear high heels with traditional African dress?' or 'I am engaged to a girl whose illiteracy is causing me great embarrassment — can you advise?'

The old Africa was dying, and I felt suddenly rootless, a stranger in the only land I could call home.

I drove up the coast to our old village one day to see Afua. I ought to have known better, but I did not. Afua is married to a fisherman, and they have so far four living children. Two died. Afua must have married very young. Her face is still handsome. Nothing could alter the beauty of those strong sweet bones — they will be the same when she is eighty. Yes, her face is beautiful. But that is all. Her body is old from work and child-bearing. African women suckle their children for a long time. Her breasts are old, ponderous, hanging. I suppose they are always full of milk. I did not mind that so much. That is the way of life here. No, I am wrong. I did mind. But that was not what I minded the most.

She came to the door of the hut, a slow smile on her lips. She looked questioningly at my car, then at me. When she saw who it was, she stopped smiling. Around her, the children nuzzled like little goats, and flies clung to the eyelids of the sleeping baby on her back. The hot still air was clogged with latrine stench and the heavy pungency of frying plantains.

'I greet you — master,' Afua said.

And in her eyes was the hatred, the mockery of all time.

I met Kwabena accidentally on the street in Accra. He had grown thinner and was dressed very neatly now in white shirt and grey flannels. He looked disconcertingly serious, but when he smiled it was the same grin and for a moment I thought it was going to be all right. But when I gave him the Twi greeting, he did not reply to it.

'So you have come back after all, Matthew,' he said finally.

'Yes, I've come back.' Perhaps my voice was more emphatic than I had intended. 'This is where I belong.'

'I see.'

'Or perhaps you don't think so — '

Kwabena laughed. Africans quite often laugh when they are not amused.

'What I think,' he commented, 'should not matter to you.'

'For heaven's sake, Kwabena,' I demanded, 'what's wrong?'

'Nothing is wrong,' he replied vaguely. Then, with a show of interest, 'Well, are you with government, as you used to say you would be?'

'Yes. Administration. They're not taking on new European staff any more — I only managed it because I speak Twi. And you?'

'Oh, I am a medical orderly.' His voice was bitter. 'An elevated post.'

'Surely you could do better than that?'

'I have not your opportunities. It is the closest I can get now to real medical work. I'm trying to get a scholarship to England. We will see.'

'You want to be a doctor?'

'Yes — ' He laughed in an oddly self-conscious way. 'Not a ju-ju man, you understand.'

Suddenly, I thought I did understand. With me, he could never outgrow his past, the time when he had wanted to be another kind of doctor — a doctor who dealt in charms and amulets, in dried roots and yellow bones and bits of python skin. He knew I would remember. How he must have regretted betraying himself to me when we were both young.

I wanted to tell him that I knew how far he had travelled from the palm hut. But I did not dare. He would have thought it condescension.

He was talking about his parents. Kwaku, he said, was working in Takoradi. He was getting old for domestic work, but he could not afford to retire. None of the sons or daughters had made or married money.

'And your mother?' I asked him.

'She died three years ago. She had hookworm for years. She was a Christian, as you know, but she still bought bush medicine and charms instead of going to a doctor. I couldn't persuade her. She became very weak. When she got typhoid she didn't have much chance.'

For a moment I could not speak, could not believe that Yaa was really dead. It seemed wrong that I should learn of it this way, so long afterwards. And wrong, too, that I had thought of her these past years as unchanged, as though I had believed she would keep on during all my lifetime, shouting her flamboyant abuse to the sellers in the market, and gathering each successive generation of children into her arms.

'I — I didn't know,' I stumbled. 'No one told me — '

'Why should they tell you' — he smiled wryly — 'if an old African woman dies?'

Pain and anger spread like a bloodstain over my whole mind.

'You know as well as I do,' I replied harshly, 'that she was more mother to me than my own mother.'

Kwabena looked at me as though he hated me.

'Yes,' he said. 'I shared my mother with you, in exchange for your cast-off khaki shorts.'

There was something in it that shocked both of us, and we were uncomfortably silent.

'I did not mean to say that,' Kwabena said finally, and there was shame in his voice, but no withdrawal.

I could not help thinking of the two boys who had both been born on a Tuesday, and of the woman, immense, bad-tempered, infinitely gentle, who had said, 'You are brothers anyway.' I found I was not angry at Kwabena any more. It was no one's fault that life had allowed us a time of illusion, and that the time was now past.

168

'Never mind.' I felt very tired. 'It doesn't matter.'

'What do you think of the country' — he seized on the first topic to hand, as Englishmen seize on the weather — 'now that you're back?'

'Mixed feelings,' I said. 'Independence is the new fetish, and political parties are the new chieftains. I'm not sure that much is gained.'

'A chieftain in a Kente cloth — you prefer that to a politician in a business suit?'

Whatever subject we touched seemed to be wrong. But I no longer cared.

'Quite frankly, yes. I think it's more genuine. I don't see anything very clever in all this cheap copying of western ways.'

'So — ' Kwabena said thoughtfully. 'You would like us to remain forever living in thatch huts, pounding our drums and telling pretty stories about big spiders.'

I stared at him, hardly able to comprehend what he had said.

'You forget,' he went on, 'that the huts were rotten with sickness, and the tales made us forget an empty belly, and the drums told of our fear — always there was fear, fear, fear — making us pay out more and more to the fetish priest — '

He broke off and looked away. When he spoke again, it was calmly, almost coldly.

'That was one thing about your father. He did not like us — that is true. He did not understand us. And we did not like or understand him. Nearly everything he did was wrong. But at least he did not want us to stand still.'

'As I do?' The words dried my throat, for I had meant them as irony, but they had not come out that way.

Kwabena did not reply. Instead he looked elaborately at his watch, like a doctor dismissing a demanding patient.

'I must not keep you any longer,' he concluded. 'Also, I have to be back at work by one o'clock.'

I did not see him again.

Since then very little has happened to me. I do my job adequately but not brilliantly. My post is to be given to an African soon.

I married on my last leave. My wife is slight and fair, quite good-looking. She does not like Africa much, and she is always telling me that the servants have no idea of cleanliness. I do not argue with her. Quite probably she is right. She is looking forward to the day when we will have a semi-detached house in England's green and pleasant land.

And I? I thought of Kwabena's words for a long time. He was right about me, I suppose. But I wonder if I can ever forgive him for it. No man wants to know that the love in him is sterile.

To reject the way of a lifetime is not easy. It must have been hard for Kwabena, and now in another way it is hard for me. But at last I know, although I shall never be able to admit it to him. It was only I who could afford to love the old Africa. Its enchantment had touched me, its suffering — never. Even my fright had stopped this side of pain. I had always been the dreamer who knew he could waken at will, the tourist who wanted antique quaintness to remain unchanged.

We were conquerors in Africa, we Europeans. Some despised her, that bedraggled

169

queen we had unthroned, and some loved her for her still-raging magnificence, her old wisdom. But all of us sought to force our will upon her.

My father thought he was bringing Salvation to Africa. I do not any longer know what salvation is. I only know that one man cannot find it for another man, and one land cannot bring it to another.

Africa, old withered bones, mouldy splendour under a red umbrella, you will dance again, this time to a new song.

But for me it is different. Now the wind in the casuarina trees is only a wind. The drums at night are only men pounding on skins stretched over wood. The Drummer of all the world is gone. He no longer drums himself, for me. A spider is only an insect, and not the child of Ananse. A deserted hut on the shore is only a heap of mud and dried palm leaves. Death no longer keeps such a simple establishment.

I shall be leaving soon. Leaving the surf that stretches up long white fingers to clutch the brown land. The fetid village enclosed and darkened by a green sky of overhanging palm trees. The giant heartbeat of the night drums. The flame tree whose beauty is suddenly splendid — and short-lived — like the beauty of African women. The little girl dancing with her shadow in the stifling streets. The child sleeping, unmindful, while flies caress his eyes and mouth with the small bright wings of decay. The squalor, the exultation, the pain. I shall be leaving it all.

But — oh Kwabena, do you think I will ever forget?

James Reaney

Born in 1926, James Reaney was raised on a farm near Stratford, Ontario. He attended the University of Toronto, receiving a B.A. in English Language and Literature in 1948, an M.A. in 1949, and a Ph.D. in 1959. His doctoral dissertation on the influence of Spenser on Yeats was directed by Northrop Frye, whose ideas were influential in shaping Reaney's interest in mythical patterns in poetry. Reaney taught English at the University of Manitoba during the nineteen-fifties; in 1960 he moved to the University of Western Ontario.

One of Reaney's major interests has been in presenting a local or particular experience so that the universal or mythical design which underlies it becomes apparent. His first book, The Red Heart *(1949), renders a child's growing awareness of his world.* A Suit of Nettles *(1958), modelled on Spenser's* Shepherd's Calendar, *is a sequence of pastoral poems based on life in an Ontario farmyard. The regional direction of his work was confirmed by his next two books of poetry,* Twelve Letters to a Small Town *(1962) and* The Dance of Death at London Ontario *(1963). He has also written short stories and critical essays and, since 1960, has edited a little magazine* Alphabet, *each issue of which is organized around a particular mythical figure.*

The following editorial from Alphabet *No. 4 (June, 1962) reflects Reaney's growing interest in working in a dramatic form. It also shows his beliefs that drama must be locally rooted and that "realism" on the stage is less important than the effort to free the imaginations of both actors and audience. These ideas are apparent in* One-Man Masque, *taken from* The Killdeer and Other Plays *(1962). This volume also contains two full-length plays and the libretto for a chamber opera for which John Beckwith composed music. Reaney has worked with local theatre groups in London, Ontario,[1] and has written several more plays. One of these,* Colours in the Dark, *was directed by John Hirsch at the Stratford Festival in 1967.*

Footnotes

[1] *James Reaney, "Ten Years at Play,"* Canadian Literature, *41 (Summer, 1969), 53-61.*

To the Avon River Above Stratford, Canada

What did the Indians call you?
For you do not flow
With English accents.
I hardly know
What I should call you
    Because before
I drank coffee or tea
    I drank you
    With my cupped hands
And you did not taste English to me
    And you do not sound
    Like Avon
    Or swans & bards
But rather like the sad wild fowl
    In prints drawn
    By Audubon
And like dear bad poets
    Who wrote
    Early in Canada
And never were of note.
You are the first river
    I crossed
And like the first whirlwind
    The first rainbow
    First snow, first
    Falling star I saw,
You, for other rivers are my law.
    These other rivers:
    The Red & the Thames
    Are never so sweet
To skate upon, swim in
    Or for baptism of sin.
    Silver and light
The sentence of your voice,
    With a soprano
Continuous cry you shall
    Always flow
    Through my heart.
The rain and the snow of my mind

Shall supply the spring of that river
        Forever.
Though not your name
Your coat of arms I know
        And motto:
A shield of reeds and cresses
        Sedges, crayfishes
The hermaphroditic leech
Minnows, muskrats and farmers' geese
And printed above this shield
One of my earliest wishes
'To flow like you.'

One-man Masque

Scene: *The curtain rises to reveal a collection of objects arranged in a circle. Starting on the left we have a cradle, a baby carriage, a child's chair, a big chair, a table, a bed, a rocking-chair and a coffin. This line of objects fills the extreme front of the stage.*

Now, starting near the coffin and circling back towards the cradle again we have another line of objects: a hall tree, a rain barrel, a section of stairs, a dresser with a mirror, a tree branch, a ladder, a spinning-wheel and a cardboard box. The cardboard box loops us back to the cradle again.

In the centre of the circle as an onstage audience there should be two mannequins sitting on false chairs, a man and a woman. Enter a live man with a closed umbrella.

Man

Ladies and gentlemen, life is extremely difficult to define. Ladies and gentlemen are extremely difficult to define. There is the life called life which is mysterious. There is the life called death which is unknown. You might say that life was a gentleman and death was a lady. The gentleman of life is made up of the following objects: simple objects that you'd find around any house.

173

One cradle, one small child's chair, one baby carriage, some adult chairs, one table not too profusely set although here we have one plate, one knife, one fork, one spoon, one cup and one saucer. Here is a bed and here is a rocking-chair. Here is a coffin. That's life for you.

Back here we have Lady Death. One old hall tree, one step-ladder, one spinning-wheel, one shoe-harp, one tree-branch, one ancient barrel, one large cardboard box, and a dresser with a mirror. That's Lady Death for you.

Come with me, listener and looker, through the worlds of life, of life and death.

He picks up the child's chair, puts it on his knee and talks to it.

And so you want to live? How does one breathe? At first it was not easy. Long ago our ancestors did not breathe. They simply were. They wered. But they dreamed of breathing. One day someone discovered that their lungs were filled with air. So everyone breathed out and there was lots of air for everybody so that everybody could breathe.

How does one live? Oh, you mix up time and space. Space? Space is when you reach into your head for the red ball you see there and it isn't there! It's out there — somewhere! Put on your eyes — you're blind without them.

Time? Time is when you see a thing out there and later on you don't see it out there. But you can only see it in here. So there's been a thing called time come along. What's that for? That's your head. Put it on. It keeps the sun off your body. Yes — after being ten miles high — it's going to be cramped being a baby. Is your body tied on you tight? Living is as easy as — opening an umbrella!

He opens the umbrella and skips round the circle of objects beginning with the hall tree and so on through the objects in the line of Death.

First there was the old hall tree. Second comes the ancient barrel. *This is spoken into the barrel as he leans into it and his voice changes into something wet and hollow and deeper.* Third there was the shoe-harp stairs. Fourth the grass came like a step-ladder. Fifth the flowers bloomed like straight ladders. Sixth the branches swarmed with leaves, seventh — cardboard swollen in the rain. Eighth — big as a spinning-wheel and ninth — to Mr. and Mrs. Everybody — a small chair. *He holds the chair aloft triumphantly.*

The Baby

Small babe, tell me
As you sat in your mother's cave
What did you build there,
Little baby mine?

Sir, I made the tooth
    I invented the eye
I played out hair on a comb harp
    I thought up the sigh.

174

I pounded the darkness to
    Guts, Heart and Head:
America, Eurasia and Africa
    I out of chaos led.

I fought the goblins
    For the heart;
'Twas a jewel they desired,
    But I held it.

I fought off the rats
    From the guts.
They nibbled but I
    Smashed the mutts.

I choked the bat so intent
    For the diamond of my mind;
I caught him in the ogre's cellar
    The tub of blood behind.

And the darkness gave me
    Two boneless wands or swords:
I knew not their meaning then
    Whether traps or rewards.

One was the vorpal phallus
    Filled with jostling army,
Henhouse and palace
    Street crowds and history.

Two was the magic tongue
    Stuffed with names and numbers,
The string of song,
    The waker from fallen slumbers.

My mother opened her grave,
    I sprang out a giant
Into another cave
    Where I was a seed again.

Hapless and wriggly small
    As in my father's groin:
My Shakespeare's tongue a wawl
    And impotent my loin.

The sun-egg I must reach
    Was steeples far away,
The world that I must name
    Was shapeless, sneaky gray.

Is it wonder then I rage
    An old man one hour old,
A bridegroom come to a bride
    Careless, unready and cold.

My wedding cake's still in the field;
    My bride is ninety and maggoty;
My groomsmen glaring hangmen;
    My bridal bed bouldery.

Small babe, tell me
    As you sit in your mother's cave
What do you build there,
    Little baby mine?

    He picks up the cradle, carries it across the stage and puts it in the coffin.

Childhood

    to the small chair
So you've learnt to walk. Now learn to talk. You can only walk as well as you can talk.
People who talk well walk well. Repeat after me: Bare Subject! Bare Predicate! Bare
Object! Barest Subject! Barest Predicate! Barest Object!
    Using a child's voice that slowly changes from four years old to twelve years old.
Does the moon ever go under a cloud being above the moon then?
Where should I put the paste? On the scrapbook or the back of the picture?
Was that a lady playing those bagpipes?
I'm frightened. There's a lady walking down the street in a long black dress. There's a
man with no legs. Look at those two little boys — exactly alike!

Don't you wish that you could have seen a great auk or a dodo? Perhaps when I grow up I shall sail to a place where they still are — around the corner of a cliff — the great auk, over the low sandy hill — on the desolate beach — two dodos.

It's raining outside. So we can't go out and play.

Did you see that lady open her umbrella when she came out of the store and found that there was a rain shower?

When I wake up in the morning I sometimes just like to lie and think.

What do you think about?

Nothing. I just think.

Adolescence

The speaker who has been slowly raising the small chair to indicate growth, lets it down and then puts on a top hat. He moves to behind the table.

I am the Principal of Prince Rupert School. A private academy where the young brat is moulded into the youthful rat.

Good morning, Miss Flume. Do bring in the correspondence and the steaming kettle. Which are the outgoing letters and which have come in? Ah yes.

A letter from the Latin master to his mother.

A letter from the Greek master to his friend.

A letter from the French master to his niece.

A letter from the German mistress to Adolf Hitler.

A letter from the Mathematics master to his estranged wife.

A letter from the Art master to his pet in quarantine with gingivitis.

Ah yes — and here are the poison pen letters. Quite the usual batch. Not much I didn't know there, Miss Flume. Do seal them up again. The usual acrid descriptions of yours truly. Sometimes I think they know I read their letters. Well . . .

The speaker rattles the rattle, then puts a cup to his ear for the telephone receiver.

Ah yes, Foxy. Where are you phoning from? The pay phone at the store in the village. Oh good-o! Well tell me — all that went on in the dormitory last night.

What! Little Fledge still refuses to undress while anybody is watching. Well I do trust that he climbs into his nightgown somehow or other sometime. Mr. Prout sees to that I trust.

Oh. You mean the rest of the lads pull his clothes off him.

Oh — what a jolly sport!

I see.

Chuggy kept the whole dormitory spellbound with stories his aunt told him about her years as a ward aide at one of the biggest lying-in hospitals in Europe. Really — a baby with a horse's head. Yes. I think it's probably very true, Foxy, dear boy. It might very likely have been hers.

And Mr. Prout still leaves the door of his room open while he is dressing in the morning? Prancing about without his clothes on? What is he playing on the gramophone these days? Wagner and Chausson? Hmh. Well, well, well. Continue.

Smith is forming a evangelical circle that meets in the ravine secretly and holds prayer

177

meetings! In the ravine behind our chapel — dedicated by the Lieutenant-Governor! I'll get that little troublemaker. Join that circle right away, Foxy. We'll root that little religious awakening out.

And — Rook is drawing an obscene drawing in the back of his Vocational Guidance text book. Oh describe it to me! *pause* It's not finished yet, Foxy. Foxy — suppose we leave it alone for a few days and let it — ripen into something really culpable. Good Boy! Good Boy Foxy! Goodbye. *He puts down the cup.* Oh Miss Flume — what a dear little sneak it is. Remind me to expel him before he gets delusions of grandeur. *The rattle goes again and he lifts cup to his ear.*

Madam! You say there's a peeping Tom emanating from the academy who's terrorizing all you ladies in the village? Well — I wonder who it could be. Madam — do you really want to know who it is — yes? You really do? *laughing fiendishly* Well — it's me. Me, the Principal of Prince Rupert Hall.

A St. Hilda's Girl

The speaker picks up a Kresge artificial flower from the table and holds it in front of him.

After attending Harbord Collegiate — Lower School, Middle School and Upper School — I went to St. Hilda's College where my sister had been head girl some years before. At St. Hilda's the social year began with three receptions given for the men at Trinity College. Out of this might grow an invitation to the Athletic Dance at Trinity in November. In December you might invite a man to the St. Hilda's Formal. And then *perhaps* he invited you to the Conversat at Trinity in January. There were two more dances at St. Hilda's and then the Valentine Dance at Trinity and then there was Lent and then you got engaged to whatever came to the surface out of all this. Well, I invited a young man to the St. Hilda's Formal but he didn't invite me to the Conversat. I had a friend who said two days before the Conversat: "I haven't got an invitation to the Conversat yet and it's two days to go, but I'm going to get one.' And she did. I often wonder how she did it.

Rachel

When I was a young young man
   In passing the city dump
Out of smoking rubbish I heard
   A small and rusty wail:

Naked without any clothes
   Unwashed from the caul
   Thy navel string uncut
A crusted, besmattered and loathsome thing.

I ruined my clothes and stank for a week
    But I brought you to my house.
I found that your mother was a gipsy
    Your father an Indian.

Live, I said, and you lived.
    You grew like a flax field
Your hair gold as the Sun
    Your breasts were blossoms.

I passed your foster house,
    It was the time of love.
I rewarded your music teacher
    For the pearly runs in your Scarlatti.

It was the time of love.
I was so afraid you might say no.
    My heart beat like giant steps
    I felt agony in your garden.

    Then you came to my house.
I was ashamed to ask you so often.
    I gave you a golden ring
    I gave you a glass pen.

    You dressed in silk
    You bathed in milk
But on your shoulder as we
Embraced I saw the red speck.

It had never washed off
    But I went unto you
    With all the more love:
You prospered into a kingdom.

I must go away to abroad:
    When I returned uptown
I met you and you knew me not,
    Your hair like flax tow

Crimped like an eggbeater, your
Mouth like a cannibal's — bloody,
Your eyelids — massive with blue mud;
    And a handmuff made of bats' fur.

I found out about your carryings on,
    Your lovers and infidelities.
My child you had sold to a brothel,
    You had to pay for your men.

In pity I bribed men to go to you,
    But your two biggest lovers,
Lord Dragon and Count Dino,
    I whispered your triple crossings.

They gathered their devils and mobs.
In the name of virtue they attacked
    Your tall town house:
You bore then your seven month bastard.

They brought you out on your balcony,
    Your house devoured with flame,
    Out they threw you and the dogs
        Licked your blood up.

Then from your hand I took
    My ring: from the hag's claw
    I took my golden ring,
Her breasts like pigsties.

    I found her child and I
    Washed you in my tears.
    Still there is the spot
Red on your shoulder — a speck.

I wash you with my tears
    And still the speck remains,
    My darling, it is my fault —
        I have not tears enough.

Eaton's Catalogue

The speaker takes a copy of the current issue, lolls on the bed and reads ecstatically the descriptions of wedding gowns.

The Telephone

The speaker uses an older voice, cup and saucer for telephone and stands at the end of the bed near the rocking chairs.

Hello Eric. Just back from graduate school? And you've just gotten over a nervous breakdown? Oh — I see. It hasn't come yet. You think you're going to have a nervous breakdown. Well — when can we see you? We're just dying to see you. When can you come over?

No, Eric. Sorry — not Friday night. We have something on.

No, not Saturday. My wife's having people in.

On Sunday — no we're going to the car show.

On Monday — no — our parents are coming to see us.

Of course Tuesday would be no good for you. Yeah. Yeah.

Shrove Tuesday? No — we're too busy with our pancakes.

Ash Wednesday? No, that day and all through Lent is out which means Good Friday, Good Saturday, Easter Sunday and Monday.

Ascension Day — no, we're ballooning.

May Day — there's the fertility rite club. We couldn't miss that.

July First? We're gathering maple leaves.

July Fourth. Our cousins from Buffalo.

St. Swithin's Day — too nerve-wracking.

Lammas Eve — we're baking bread.

Michaelmas — we're basting our son for college.

St. Lucy's Day? Too dark to go out. You're afraid of the dark anyhow, Eric.

Christmas Eve? No — there's a funny old man comes to see us.

How about a Leap Year? You mean February 29? Good! Heavens no though! That's our wedding anniversary. Yeah.

Doomsday! Well now Eric, you're talking. Wait a minute, wait a minute. My wife's quite a good friend of the Whore of Babylon. Yeah. Their sorority chapter is having a picnic that afternoon. And they're never back very early. So how about the day before Doomsday? The day the Sixth Seal is opened? You mean the day the star that calls itself Wormwood comes down? And the skies rain blood? Round about that time. Well, for a minute *pause* for a minute I was going to say you couldn't come and see me, Eric, and that is true as on the Sixth Day the Sixth Seal is opened and all those angels pour out their vials. Because as a matter of fact our house is going to be in considerable disorder. We're going to completely redecorate in honour of the Second Coming. BUT — Yeah, y'know what? I can come over to your place for an hour on that evening. We might even have time for half a game of chess. Very well then. Fine. And it's nice to hear the sound of your voice Eric. And we've looked forward to seeing you again.

181

Rocking-Chairs

The speaker sits down in a rocking-chair and assumes the various old voices indicated.

In 1910 I went down to apply for entry into — the University of Colorado. With my Ontario Upper School they allowed me to enter the third year of their course there. I had been educated by the nuns at a convent in Oshawa — Anglican nuns, of course. In 1913 we toured the Continent. I remember seeing Henry James's house at Rye although at that time I don't believe he was in it.

I can remember when there was a boy in our village who had the peeping Tom disease. Used to run around looking in people's windows. They finally sent him away. Percy Smith had T.B. of the skin. The only treatment he could take was to strip and lie in the sun.

There's five hundred yaller boys in the cellar somewhere, child, if I could only remember under which one of them five hundred flagstones in the cellar . . . they are.

I can remember when there was nothing, absolutely nothing above College St. It was all below College St. then.

My grandfather attained a great age. He was 109 years old when, I remember, I was a small boy of seven and I would get up at night, in the middle of the night to light his pipe for him.

Granny Crack

I was a leather skinned harridan
I wandered the county's roads
Trading and begging and fighting
With the sun for hat and the road for shoes.

You played a pigsty Venus
When you were young, old dame,
In the graveyard or behind the tavern.
The burdock girl was your name.

She talked vilely it is remembered,
Was a moving and walking dictionary
Of slang and unconventional language
The detail of her insults was extraordinary.

We dozen scoundrels laid you
For a quarter each in the ditch
To each you gave the sensation
That we were the exploited bitch.

You saw me freckled and spotted
My face like a killdeer's egg
When, berry-picking kids, you ran from me
Frightened down the lane by the wood.

They saw her as an incredible crone
The spirit of neglected fence corners,
Of the curious wisdom of brambles
And weeds, of ruts, of stumps and of things despised.

I was the mother of your sun
I was the sister of your moon
My veins are your paths and roads
On my head I bear steeples and turrets
I am the darling of your god.

The Scavenger

*The speaker puts on a long unravelled scarf, a cap and starts wheeling the baby
carriage about, picking up empty pop bottles and throwing them into the carriage.*
They give you two cents a bottle. I've sold my corpse to the medical school.
*He comes to the coffin in which he scrummages out a skull. This he puts into the
carriage.*
I get all the State allows and if I can collect one hundred pop bottles a day — I collect
them in all the places, squares, alleys, beaches, parks, avenue, crescents . . . I can just
get by.
*In pulling at something in the coffin he falls forward into it; his cap is thrown up
but he has disappeared into the coffin and does not reappear. Eventually out of the
coffin comes the speaker wearing dark glasses and carrying a flashlight wrapped in a
swath of blue cellophane. He finds his way more by listening and smelling than by
any other way. In the world of werewolves and ghosts he seems never at a loss.*

Death's World

*The speaker has announced this through a megaphone and now makes wind noises
with it.*
Who is that walking beneath the trees there? Is it a man looking at his watch? I've seen
that face before. It's an unusual watch he has in his hand. It's an acorn nut. He tells
time by looking at the dial of its dark decaying husk.
*The speaker stands in front of the rain barrel, draws on huge brown furry motoring
gloves and says:*

183

The Ghost

The evening waddles over the fields like a turkey.
I lurk,
Where my knowledge was chopped from my power.
All knowledge waits for you at the corner here so murky.

The awkward doltish low I.Q. farmboy shambles down the steps,
The empty echoing pitcher in his hand:
I am!
Ha ha! And his hair stands straight up like brambles.

Everything — Egyptian hieroglyphs and crystallography,
Diary of shadows,
Vast God and the interiors of tree trunks, snowflakes
All spin like a fiery corkscrew into his psychology.

For I know everything now having passed into source,
Even
Through me he knows himself — a kidnapped prince.
It is too much for him — he falls down — hoarse
As they shriek and lift him up — I am not.

The evening waddles over the fields like a turkey.
I lurk,
Where my knowledge was severed from my power.
All knowledge waits for you at the corner here so murky.
    *The speaker takes off the gloves and sails to the top of the stairs. He runs down
    them and says:*
Sister Cecilia, the figure in the convent orchard has been seen again. Digging where
the abandoned well is under the old tree.

The Executioner of Mary Stuart

There was a jolly headman once
Attached to an ancient castle
They chose him specially for his task
To murder other rascals

For example I have often felt
My analogy might be
A rat trap made from the bones of rats
And that was simple old me.

184

So my life was ruined but I
Was given a sort of reward:
The clothes of the executed
Often some astonishingly rich brocade.

One day I caught in my jaws
A woman who dazzled the sun
I chopped off her head as my task
And took what was left for my fun

Annunciation to the Mud
In the beginning was the Dark
Bridegroom to a headless Queen
Far off I hear the hell dogs bark.

The speaker now stands in front of the dresser and yells through the megaphone.

Doomsday

Red Sky
Morning
Shaking like a scarlet head
Doomsday
Rise Up
Spring your lids, you dead

Scrape out
Coffins
Put yourself together
Pat that dust
Find that bust
This is the last weather

Trumpet
Drummer
Thunder
Vomit you cannibals
Shake out those
Those old flesh dresses
For the resurrection parties and balls.

185

Here comes St. Sebastian with a handful
Of arrows
The big threshing woodpecker is
Beating on the green drum
Here comes the poor boy who got caught in
The harrows
Here comes St. Bartholemew with his skin:
Scroll away
Hell this way
Heaven that
Rat a tat tat
There goes Death and there goes Sin
Here come Cain and Abel
Hand in hand
Here come horizontals turning into slopes.
Here comes a table
Changing back to a tree and
Here come the hanged people skipping
With their ropes.

Red sky
Morning
Shaking like a scarlet head
Doomsday!
Rise up!

Spring your lids, you dead!
Scrape out
Coffins!
Put yourself together!
Pat that dust
Find that bust
This is the last weather!

Trumpet!
Drummer!
Thunder!
Vomit you cannibals!
Shake out those,
Those old flesh dresses
For the resurrection parties and balls!

The speaker now stands close to the cardboard box and hunches over for

The Dwarf

Six inches of my six foot pa
Compressed my height to these three feet.
On Sabbath day he sold me to
The castle of the starry street.

There I sleep in a cradle and amuse
The castle with my minority.
No, I am not someone far away.
Reach out and touch me.

I plucked a berry for the young queen
Such fruit as drove her mad.
She haunts the stables and the mews,
Is serviced by the coachman's lad.

I stole the tall crown prince's toy
And put it in his brother's chest.
He knocked his brother out of life
With father's curse he fled to east.

The servants swore that they saw angels;
I said that they must grovel,
I sneered and laughed at all their visions.
Now they see only hovel.

The swineherd was a noble man,
More noble than my lord.
With a whicker-whack I tripped him up.
His brow now levels swineward.

'Twas I who hid beneath the bed
When the princess planned elopement.
They got as far as the Scarlet Sea
When my lord's riders they met.

I filled their hearts with maddening lust,
I made three eyes unfashionable,
I filled their hearts with maddening chastity,
I split them into sexual.

Lady Air and Sir Earth,
Alderman Water and the Earl of Fire,
Yeoman Quintessence and Miss Light
I set at jar and gyre and ire.

From this casement look ye out
At rotting sheep and mildewed crop.
There's the minstrel limping off
I bade them yesterday his tongue lop.

The castle's empty, wonder none —
I bade them rebuild inside out.
Their fire flew up into the sun,
Their cistern rolled into a moon.

In a great battle my dear lord
Killed and was killed by the crown prince.
I've holed up here among the ruins
The compressed cause of everything.

The only thing I know to do
Is crawl into this manger.
I'll prop the dead queen's body up,
Perhaps 'twill fool a stranger.

Come here shepherds. Here's the way.
Bah bah bah for an incarnation.
This way aristocratic intelligence.
Meow meow for a new sensation!

To the curious observant baby
The humble and the royal bow.
Hush a bye my baby do, for see —
The spider on your mother's brow.

*The speaker stands just behind where the cradle used to be. As he gets going he
spreads his arms and flies over the stage like Milton's Holy Ghost bird with wings
'vast and outspread' moving over the waters. He has by now discarded the
flashlight and the dark glasses.*

188

The Lost Child

Long have I looked for my lost child.
I hear him shake his rattle
Slyly in the winter wind
In the ditch that's filled with snow.

He pinched and shrieked and ran away
At the edge of the November forest.
The hungry old burdock stood
By the dead dry ferns.

Hear him thud that ball!
The acorns fall by the fence.
See him loll in the St. Lucy sun,
The abandoned sheaf in the wire.

Oh life in Death! my bonny nursling
Merry drummer in the nut brown coffin,
With vast wings outspread I float
Looking and looking over the empty sea

> *He finds the cradle by the coffin and rescues it, saying the last lines kneeling like*
> *a shepherd at Christ's Cradle.*

And there! in the — on the rolling death
Rattling a dried out gourd
Floated the mysterious cradle
Filled with a source.

I push the shore and kingdom to you,
O winter walk with seed pod ditch:
I touch them to the floating child
And lo! Cities and gardens, shepherds and smiths.

> *After the speaker has placed the cradle back where it used to be again he is*
> *handed a tray of lighted candles which he holds out in front of him. He advances*
> *towards the audience saying,*

Ladies and gentlemen, Life and Death are indeed difficult to define.

> *The speaker lifts the tray of lighted candles up and puts them on his head. The two*
> *mannequins float up and disappear.*

189

Editorial

In an issue devoted to flying bodies that fall (with one divine exception mentioned on page 36ff), it seemed natural to write an editorial on Canadian drama. One venture dedicated to the cause has just wound up with that fine old native drama *L'Année Dernière à Marienbad*. I seem to hear voices at this point, mocking voices saying "What do we need a native drama for? Why all this absurd nationalism?" Because I don't believe you can really be world, or unprovincial or whatever until you've sunk your claws into a very locally coloured tree trunk and scratched your way through to universality.

We do not know if we understand the plays from abroad that are our dramatic fare until we have "stood" works equivalent in intensity from our own environment. If Eliot's verse plays had been premiered incognito in the forties one wonders what audiences would have done. Would they have stood for it at all? Given the proper clues (Anglican poet, English sounding) and the same audience laps up libation scenes and birthday candle rituals it would never take from a local poet. What a maddening situation for the artist! Always this feeling of circumference for the native artist, centre for everyone else!

How can those interested in making life better in this country help our drama? There should be a club that does nothing but seasons of plays by Canadians. It should do them in a bare, long room up above a store, probably infested by Odd Fellows or Orangemen on easily avoidable nights. Nobody should have any truck with that grand Bugaboo — Lighting. Five two hundred Mazda watters always turned on will do for any play that lights its own way, as a play should. One thing we don't need right now is "spectacle", often hiding the play's barrenness — I'm thinking of last summer's Stratford *Barricade* — or just hiding it. And ask people to write plays for you, if you can't stand what has been done.

What is most of all needed is not money, but a simple, austere idea. Then, eventually, the money may have something to follow. I have a friend who while acting in one of our folk dramas (Gwen Ringwood) got stuck with his milk pail in a door. Well, loosen him!

London, Ontario, June 1962.

from *Alphabet,* # 4, June 1962

Hugh Hood

Born in Toronto in 1928 of an English-speaking father from Nova Scotia and a French-speaking mother, Hugh John Blagdon Hood was educated at the University of Toronto. He received a doctorate in English from that institution in 1955, with a dissertation on theories of the imagination in English thinkers of the eighteenth century. He now lives in Montreal, where he teaches English at the University of Montreal. He has published sketches of Montreal life, short stories, and three novels — White Figure, White Ground *(1964),* The Camera Always Lies *(1967), and* A Game of Touch *(1970).*

The characters of Hood's short stories, in contrast to Garner's, tend to be from the urban middle class. He is not concerned, however, with society so much as with delineating states of individual consciousness. The plot of "Flying a Red Kite"[1] is loosely conceived; what is important is the point of view of the main character, Fred, whose sense of spiritual unease is externally so undramatic that it manifests itself only in a minor disagreement with his wife over the meaning of the term "spoiled priest." The carefully described urban setting reflects Fred's state of mind. The red kite, the central image of the story, is a "natural symbol," and Fred's success in getting it to fly suggests his overcoming of the despair brought on by his ordinary circumstances and the conversation of the men on the bus.

Footnotes

[1] *There is a National Film Board short film, "The Red Kite," based on this story.*

Flying a Red Kite

The ride home began badly. Still almost a stranger to the city, tired, hot and dirty, and inattentive to his surroundings, Fred stood for ten minutes, shifting his parcels from arm to arm and his weight from one leg to the other, in a sweaty bath of shimmering glare from the sidewalk, next to a grimy yellow-and-black bus stop. To his left a line of murmuring would-be passengers lengthened until there were enough to fill any vehicle that might come for them. Finally an obese brown bus waddled up like an indecent old cow and stopped with an expiring moo at the head of the line. Fred was glad to be first in line, as there didn't seem to be room for more than a few to embus.

But as he stepped up he noticed a sign in the window which said *Côte des Neiges-Boulevard* and he recoiled as though bitten, trampling the toes of the woman behind him and making her squeal. It was a Sixty-six bus, not the Sixty-five that he wanted. The woman pushed furiously past him while the remainder of the line clamoured in the rear. He stared at the number on the bus stop: Sixty-six, not his stop at all. Out of the corner of his eye he saw another coach pulling away from the stop on the northeast corner, the right stop, the Sixty-five, and the one he should have been standing under all this time. Giving his characteristic weary put-upon sigh, which he used before breakfast to annoy Naomi, he adjusted his parcels in both arms, feeling sweat run around his neck and down his collar between his shoulders, and crossed Saint Catherine against the light, drawing a Gallic sneer from a policeman, to stand for several more minutes at the head of a new queue, under the right sign. It was nearly four-thirty and the Saturday shopping crowds wanted to get home, out of the summer dust and heat, out of the jitter of the big July holiday weekend. They would all go home and sit on their balconies. All over the suburbs in duplexes and fourplexes, families would be enjoying cold suppers in the open air on their balconies; but the Calverts' apartment had none. Fred and Naomi had been ignorant of the meaning of the custom when they were apartment hunting. They had thought of Montreal as a city of the Sub-Arctic and in the summers they would have leisure to repent the misjudgment.

He had been shopping along the length of Saint Catherine between Peel and Guy, feeling guilty because he had heard for years that this was where all those pretty Montreal women made their promenade; he had wanted to watch without familial encumbrances. There had been girls enough but nothing outrageously special so he had beguiled the scorching afternoon making a great many small idle purchases, of the kind one does when trapped in a Woolworth's. A ball-point pen and a note-pad for Naomi, who was always stealing his and leaving it in the kitchen with long, wildly-optimistic, grocery lists scribbled in it. Six packages of cigarettes, some legal-size envelopes, two Dinky-toys, a long-playing record, two parcels of second-hand books, and the lightest of his burdens and the unhandiest, the kite he had bought for Deedee, two flimsy wooden sticks rolled up in red plastic film, and a ball of cheap thin string — not enough, by the look of it, if he should ever get the thing into the air.

When he'd gone fishing, as a boy, he'd never caught any fish; when playing hockey he had never been able to put the puck in the net. One by one the wholesome outdoor

192

sports and games had defeated him. But he had gone on believing in them, in their curative moral values, and now he hoped that Deedee, though a girl, might sometime catch a fish; and though she obviously wouldn't play hockey, she might ski, or toboggan on the mountain. He had noticed that people treated kites and kite-flying as somehow holy. They were a natural symbol, thought Fred, and he felt uneasily sure that he would have trouble getting this one to fly.

The inside of the bus was shaped like a box-car with windows, but the windows were useless. You might have peeled off the bus as you'd peel the paper off a pound of butter, leaving an oblong yellow lump of thick solid heat, with the passengers embedded in it like hopeless breadcrumbs.

He elbowed and wriggled his way along the aisle, feeling a momentary sliver of pleasure as his palm rubbed accidentally along the back of a girl's skirt — once, a philosopher — the sort of thing you couldn't be charged with. But you couldn't get away with it twice and anyway the girl either didn't feel it, or had no idea who had caressed her. There were vacant seats towards the rear, which was odd because the bus was otherwise full, and he struggled towards them, trying not to break the wooden struts which might be persuaded to fly. The bus lurched forward and his feet moved with the floor, causing him to pop suddenly out of the crowd by the exit, into a square well of space next to the heat and stink of the engine. He swayed around and aimed himself at a narrow vacant seat, nearly dropping a parcel of books as he lowered himself precipitately into it.

The bus crossed Sherbrooke Street and began, intolerably slowly, to crawl up Côte des Neiges and around the western spur of the mountain. His ears began to pick up the usual melange of French and English and to sort it out; he was proud of his French and pleased that most of the people on the streets spoke a less correct, though more fluent, version than his own. He had found that he could make his customers understand him perfectly — he was a book salesman — but that people on the street were happier when he addressed them in English.

The chatter in the bus grew clearer and more interesting and he began to listen, grasping all at once why he had found a seat back here. He was sitting next to a couple of drunks who emitted an almost overpowering smell of beer. They were cheerfully exchanging indecencies and obscure jokes and in a minute they would speak to him. They always did, drunks and panhandlers, finding some soft fearfulness in his face which exposed him as a shrinking easy mark. Once in a railroad station he had been approached three times in twenty minutes by the same panhandler on his rounds. Each time he had given the man something, despising himself with each new weakness.

The cheerful pair sitting at right-angles to him grew louder and more blunt and the women within earshot grew glum. There was no harm in it; there never is. But you avoid your neighbour's eye, afraid of smiling awkwardly, or of looking offended and a prude.

"Now this Pearson," said one of the revellers, "he's just a little short-ass. He's just a little fellow without any brains. Why, some of the speeches he makes . . . I could make them myself. I'm an old Tory myself, an old Tory."

"I'm an old Blue," said the other.

"Is that so, now? That's fine, a fine thing." Fred was sure he didn't know what a Blue was.

"I'm a Balliol man. Whoops!" They began to make monkey-like noises to annoy the passengers and amuse themselves. "Whoops," said the Oxford man again, "hoo, hoo, there's one now, there's one for you." He was talking about a girl on the sidewalk.

"She's a one, now, isn't she? Look at the legs on her, oh, look at them now, isn't that something?" There was a noisy clearing of throats and the same voice said something that sounded like "Shaoil-na-baig."

"Oh, good, good!" said the Balliol man.

"Shaoil-na-baig," said the other loudly, "I've not forgotten my Gaelic, do you see, shaoil-na-baig," he said it loudly, and a woman up the aisle reddened and looked away. It sounded like a dirty phrase to Fred, delivered as though the speaker had forgotten all his Gaelic but the words for sexual intercourse.

"And how is your French, Father?" asked the Balliol man, and the title made Fred start in his seat. He pretended to drop a parcel and craned his head quickly sideways. The older of the two drunks, the one sitting by the window, examining the passing legs and skirts with the same impulse that Fred had felt on Saint Catherine Street, was indeed a priest, and couldn't possibly be an impostor. His clerical suit was too well-worn, egg-stained and blemished with candle-droppings, and fit its wearer too well, for it to be an assumed costume. The face was unmistakably a southern Irishman's. The priest darted a quick peek into Fred's eyes before he could turn them away, giving a monkey-like grimace that might have been a mixture of embarrassment and shame but probably wasn't.

He was a little gray-haired bucko of close to sixty, with a triangular sly mottled crimson face and uneven yellow teeth. His hands moved jerkily and expressively in his lap, in counterpoint to the lively intelligent movements of his face.

The other chap, the Balliol man, was a perfect type of English-speaking Montrealer, perhaps a bond salesman or minor functionary in a brokerage house on Saint James Street. He was about fifty with a round domed head, red hair beginning to go slightly white at the neck and ears, pink porcine skin, very neatly barbered and combed. He wore an expensive white shirt with a fine blue stripe and there was some sort of ring around his tie. He had his hands folded fatly on the knob of a stick, round face with deep laugh-lines in the cheeks, and a pair of cheerfully darting little blue-bloodshot eyes. Where could the pair have run into each other?

"I've forgotten my French years ago," said the priest carelessly. "I was down in New Brunswick for many years and I'd no use for it, the work I was doing. I'm Irish, you know."

"I'm an old Blue."

"That's right," said the priest, "John's the boy. Oh, he's a sharp lad is John. He'll let them all get off, do you see, to Manitoba for the summer, and bang, BANG!" All the bus jumped. "He'll call an election on them and then they'll run." Something caught his eye and he turned to gaze out the window. The bus was moving slowly past the cemetery of Notre Dame des Neiges and the priest stared, half-sober, at the graves stretched up the mountainside in the sun.

"I'm not in there," he said involuntarily.

"Indeed you're not," said his companion, "lots of life in you yet, eh, Father?"

"Oh," he said, "oh, I don't think I'd know what to do with a girl if I fell over one."

He looked out at the cemetery for several moments. "It's all a sham," he said, half under his breath, "they're in there for good." He swung around and looked innocently at Fred. "Are you going fishing, lad?"

"It's a kite that I bought for my little girl," said Fred, more cheerfully than he felt.

"She'll enjoy that, she will," said the priest, "for it's grand sport."

"Go fly a kite!" said the Oxford man hilariously. It amused him and he said it again. "Go fly a kite!" He and the priest began to chant together, "Hoo, hoo, whoops," and they laughed and in a moment, clearly, would begin to sing.

The bus turned lumberingly onto Queen Mary Road. Fred stood up confusedly and began to push his way towards the rear door. As he turned away, the priest grinned too embarrassed to answer but he smiled uncertainly and fled. He heard them take up their chant anew.

"Hoo, there's a one for you, hoo. Shaoil-na-baig. Whoops!" Their laughter died out as the bus rolled heavily away.

He had heard about such men, naturally, and knew that they existed; but it was the first time in Fred's life that he had ever seen a priest misbehave himself publicly. There are so many priests in the city, he thought, that the number of bum ones must be in proportion. The explanation satisfied him but the incident left a disagreeable impression in his mind.

Safely home he took his shirt off and poured himself a Coke. Then he allowed Deedee, who was dancing around him with her terrible energy, to open the parcels.

"Give your Mummy the pad and pencil, sweetie," he directed. She crossed obediently to Naomi's chair and handed her the cheap plastic case.

"Let me see you make a note in it," he said, "make a list of something, for God's sake, so you'll remember it's yours. And the one on the desk is mine. Got that?" He spoke without rancour or much interest; it was a rather overworked joke between them.

"What's this?" said Deedee, holding up the kite and allowing the ball of string to roll down the hall. He resisted a compulsive wish to get up and re-wind the string.

"It's for you. Don't you know what it is?"

"It's a red kite," she said. She had wanted one for weeks but spoke now as if she weren't interested. Then all at once she grew very excited and eager. "Can you put it together right now?" she begged.

"I think we'll wait till after supper, sweetheart," he said, feeling mean. You raised their hopes and then dashed them; there was no real reason why they shouldn't put it together now, except his fatigue. He looked pleadingly at Naomi.

"Daddy's tired, Deedee," she said obligingly, "he's had a long hot afternoon."

"But I want to see it," said Deedee, fiddling with the flimsy red film and nearly puncturing it.

Fred was sorry he'd drunk a Coke; it bloated him and upset his stomach and had no true cooling effect.

"We'll have something to eat," he said cajolingly, "and then Mummy can put it together for you." He turned to his wife. "You don't mind, do you? I'd only spoil the thing." Threading a needle or hanging a picture made the normal slight tremor of his hands accentuate itself almost embarrassingly.

"Of course not," she said, smiling wryly. They had long ago worked out their areas of uselessness.

"There's a picture on it, and directions."

"Yes. Well, we'll get it together somehow. Flying it . . . that's something else again." She got up, holding the notepad, and went into the kitchen to put the supper on.

It was a good hot-weather supper, tossed greens with the correct proportions of vinegar and oil, croissants and butter, and cold sliced ham. As he ate, his spirits began to percolate a bit, and he gave Naomi a graphic sketch of the incident on the bus. "It depressed me," he told her. This came as no surprise to her; almost anything unusual, which he couldn't do anything to alter or relieve, depressed Fred nowadays. "He must have been sixty. Oh, quite sixty, I should think, and you could tell that everything had come to pieces for him."

"It's a standard story," she said, "and aren't you sentimentalizing i ?"

"In what way?"

"The 'spoiled priest' business, the empty man, the man without a calling. They all write about that. Graham Greene made his whole career out of that."

"That isn't what the phrase means," said Fred laboriously. "It doesn't refer to a man who actually *is* a priest, though without a vocation."

"No?" She lifted an eyebrow; she was better educated than he.

"No, it doesn't. It means somebody who never became a priest at all. The point is that you *had* a vocation but ignored it. That's what a spoiled priest is. It's an Irish phrase, and usually refers to somebody who is a failure and who drinks too much." He laughed shortly. "I don't qualify, on the second count."

"You're not a failure."

"No, I'm too young. Give me time!" There was no reason for him to talk like this; he was a very productive salesman.

"You certainly never wanted to be a priest," she said positively, looking down at her breasts and laughing, thinking of some secret. "I'll bet you never considered it, not with your habits." She meant his bedroom habits, which were ardent, and in which she ardently acquiesced. She was an adept and enthusiastic partner, her greatest gift as a wife.

"Let's put that kite together," said Deedee, getting up from her little table, with such adult decision that her parents chuckled. "Come on," she said, going to the sofa and bouncing up and down.

Naomi put a tear in the fabric right away, on account of the ambiguity of the directions. There should have been two holes in the kite, through which a lugging-string passed; but the holes hadn't been provided and when she put them there with the point of an icepick they immediately began to grow.

"Scotch tape," she said, like a surgeon asking for sutures.

"There's a picture on the front," said Fred, secretly cross but ostensibly helpful.

"I see it," she said.

"Mummy put holes in the kite," said Deedee with alarm. "Is she going to break it?"

196

"No," said Fred. The directions were certainly ambiguous.

Naomi tied the struts at right-angles, using so much string that Fred was sure the kite would be too heavy. Then she strung the fabric on the notched ends of the struts and the thing began to take shape.

"It doesn't look quite right," she said, puzzled and irritated.

"The surface has to be curved so there's a difference of air pressure." He remembered this, rather unfairly, from high-school physics classes.

She bent the cross-piece and tied it in a bowed arc, and the red film pulled taut. "There now," she said.

"You've forgotten the lugging-string on the front," said Fred critically, "that's what you made the holes for, remember?"

"Why is Daddy mad?" said Deedee.

"I'M NOT MAD!"

It had begun to shower, great pear-shaped drops of rain falling with a plop on the sidewalk.

"That's as close as I can come," said Naomi, staring at Fred, "we aren't going to try it tonight, are we?"

"We promised her," he said, "and it's only a light rain."

"Will we all go?"

"I wish you'd take her," he said, "because my stomach feels upset. I should never drink Coca-Cola."

"It always bothers you. You should know that by now."

"I'm not running out on you," he said anxiously, "and if you can't make it work, I'll take her up tomorrow afternoon."

"I know," she said, "come on, Deedee, we're going to take the kite up the hill." They left the house and crossed the street. Fred watched them through the window as they started up the steep path hand in hand. He felt left out, and slightly nauseated.

They were back in half an hour, their spirits not at all dampened, which surprised him.

"No go, eh?"

"Much too wet, and not enough breeze. The rain knocks it flat."

"O.K.!" he exclaimed with fervour. "I'll try tomorrow."

"We'll try again tomorrow," said Deedee with equal determination — her parents mustn't forget their obligations.

Sunday afternoon the weather was nearly perfect, hot, clear, a firm steady breeze but not too much of it, and a cloudless sky. At two o'clock Fred took his daughter by the hand and they started up the mountain together, taking the path through the woods that led up to the University parking lots.

"We won't come down until we make it fly," Fred swore, "that's a promise."

"Good," she said, hanging on to his hand and letting him drag her up the steep path, "there are lots of bugs in here, aren't there?"

"Yes," he said briefly — he was being liberally bitten.

When they came to the end of the path, they saw that the campus was deserted and still, and there was all kinds of running room. Fred gave Deedee careful instructions about where to sit, and what to do if a car should come along, and then he paid out a little string and began to run across the parking lot towards the main building of the University. He felt a tug at the string and throwing a glance over his shoulder he saw the kite bobbing in the air, about twenty feet off the ground. He let out more string, trying to keep it filled with air, but he couldn't run quite fast enough, and in a moment it fell back to the ground.

"Nearly had it!" he shouted to Deedee, whom he'd left fifty yards behind.

"Daddy, Daddy, come back," she hollered apprehensively. Rolling up the string as he went, he retraced his steps and prepared to try again. It was important to catch a gust of wind and run into it. On the second try the kite went higher than before but as he ran past the entrance to the University he felt the air pressure lapse and saw the kite waver and fall. He walked slowly back, realizing that the bulk of the main building was cutting off the air currents.

"We'll go up higher," he told her, and she seized his hand and climbed obediently up the road beside him, around behind the main building, past ash barrels and trash heaps; they climbed a flight of wooden steps, crossed a parking lot next to L'Ecole Polytechnique and a slanting field further up, and at last came to a pebbly dirt road that ran along the top ridge of the mountain beside the cemetery. Fred remembered the priest as he looked across the fence and along the broad stretch of cemetery land rolling away down the slope of the mountain to the west. They were about six hundred feet above the river, he judged. He'd never been up this far before.

"My sturdy little brown legs are tired," Deedee remarked, and he burst out laughing.

"Where did you hear that," he said, "who has sturdy little brown legs?"

She screwed her face up in a grin. "The gingerbread man," she said, beginning to sing, "I can run away from you, I can, 'cause I'm the little gingerbread man."

The air was dry and clear and without a trace of humidity and the sunshine was dazzling. On either side of the dirt road grew great clumps of wild flowers, yellow and blue, buttercups, daisies and goldenrod, and cornflowers and clover. Deedee disappeared into the flowers — picking bouquets was her favourite game. He could see the shrubs and grasses heave and sway as she moved around. The scent of clover and of dry sweet grass was very keen here, and from the east, over the curved top of the mountain, the wind blew in a steady uneddying stream. Five or six miles off to the southwest he spied the wide intensely gray-white stripe of the river. He heard Deedee cry: "Daddy, Daddy, come and look." He pushed through the coarse grasses and found her.

"Berries," she cried rapturously, "look at all the berries! Can I eat them?" She had found a wild raspberry bush, a thing he hadn't seen since he was six years old. He'd never expected to find one growing in the middle of Montreal.

"Wild raspberries," he said wonderingly, "sure you can pick them dear; but be careful of the prickles." They were all shades and degrees of ripeness from black to vermilion.

"Ouch," said Deedee, pricking her fingers as she pulled off the berries. She put a handful in her mouth and looked wry.

"Are they bitter?"

198

"Juicy," she mumbled with her mouth full. A trickle of dark juice ran down her chin.

"Eat some more," he said, "while I try the kite again." She bent absorbedly to the task of hunting them out, and he walked down the road for some distance and then turned to run up towards her. This time he gave the kite plenty of string before he began to move; he ran as hard as he could, panting and handing the string out over his shoulders, burning his fingers as it slid through them. All at once he felt the line pull and pulse as if there were a living thing on the other end and he turned on his heel and watched while the kite danced into the upper air-currents above the treetops and began to soar up and up. He gave it more line and in an instant it pulled high up away from him across the fence, two hundred feet and more above him up over the cemetery where it steadied and hung, bright red in the sunshine. He thought flashingly of the priest saying "It's all a sham," and he knew all at once that the priest was wrong. Deedee came running down to him, laughing with excitement and pleasure and singing joyfully about the gingerbread man, and he knelt in the dusty roadway and put his arms around her, placing her hands on the line between his. They gazed, squinting in the sun, at the flying red thing, and he turned away and saw in the shadow of her cheek and on her lips and chin the dark rich red of the pulp and juice of the crushed raspberries.

Alice Munro

Alice Laidlaw was born in Wingham, Ontario, in 1931. She studied Honours English Language and Literature at the University of Western Ontario and graduated in 1952. She married James Munro in 1951; the Munros later moved to British Columbia, where they now live in Victoria. Her stories have appeared in such Canadian periodicals as Canadian Forum *and* Tamarack Review; *a collection of her short fiction,* Dance of the Happy Shades, *appeared in 1968 and won a Governor-General's Award. "A Trip to the Coast" is included in this volume. In 1971 she published* Lives of Girls and Women, *a collection of closely related stories about a young girl's growing up in the town of Jubilee, Ontario.*

Mrs. Munro frequently makes use of the same settings in southern and southwestern Ontario as does James Reaney. Like Reaney, too, she combines childhood reminiscence with elements of Gothic terror to re-create what Doug Spettigue has called "the desperately, fatalistically ingrown spirit of Western Ontario."[1] The opening paragraph of "A Trip to the Coast" is characteristic of some of her small-town landscapes, though it is rather weedier than most. Black Horse is situated neither in prosperous farmland nor isolated in the bush; therefore it has the worst of both worlds. On the one hand, although people pass through it, it is no one's destination; on the other hand, it is not sufficiently isolated to exist in a meaningful relationship to nature. The landscape and the town function as a reflection of May's sense of an imprisonment which is more dully irritating than painfully oppressive, and from which she is freed only through a bizarre accident and almost against her will.

Footnotes

[1] *Doug Spettigue, "Alice Laidlaw Munro: A Portrait of the Artist,"* Alumni Gazette, U.W.O., *45, No. 3 (July, 1969), 5.*

A Trip to the Coast

The place called Black Horse is marked on the map but there is nothing there except a store and three houses and an old cemetery and a livery shed which belonged to a church that burned down. It is a hot place in summer, with no shade on the road and no creek nearby. The houses and the store are built of red brick of a faded, gingery colour, with a random decoration of grey or white bricks across the chimneys and around the windows. Behind them the fields are full of milkweed and goldenrod and big purple thistles. People who are passing through, on their way to the Lakes of Muskoka and the northern bush, may notice that around here the bountiful landscape thins and flattens, worn elbows of rock appear in the diminishing fields and the deep, harmonious woodlots of elm and maple give way to a denser, less hospitable scrub-forest of birch and poplar, spruce and pine — where in the heat of the afternoon the pointed trees at the end of the road turn blue, transparent, retreating into the distance like a company of ghosts.

May was lying in a big room full of boxes at the back of the store. That was where she slept in the summer, when it got too hot upstairs. Hazel slept in the front room on the chesterfield and played the radio half the night; her grandmother still slept upstairs, in a tight little room full of big furniture and old photographs that smelled of hot oilcloth and old women's woollen stockings. May could not tell what time it was because she hardly ever woke up this early. Most mornings when she woke up there was a patch of hot sun on the floor at her feet and the farmers' milk trucks were rattling past on the highway and her grandmother was scuttling back and forth from the store to the kitchen, where she had put a pot of coffee and a pan of thick bacon on the stove. Passing the old porch couch where May slept (its cushions still smelled faintly of mould and pine) she would twitch automatically at the sheet, saying, "Get up now, *get* up, do you think you're going to sleep till dinner-time? There's a man wants gas."

And if May did not get up but clung to the sheet, muttering angrily, her grandmother would come through next time with a little cold water in a dipper, which she dumped in passing on her granddaughter's feet. Then May would jump up, pushing her long switch of hair back from her face, which was sulky with sleepiness but not resentful; she accepted the rule of her grandmother as she accepted a rain squall or a stomach ache, with a tough, basic certainty that such things would pass. She put on all her clothes under her nightgown, with her arms underneath free of the sleeves; she was eleven years old and had entered a period of furious modesty during which she refused to receive a vaccination on her buttocks and screamed with rage if Hazel or her grandmother came into a room where she was dressing — which they did, she thought, for their own amusement and to ridicule the very idea of her privacy. She would go out and put gas in the car and come back wide awake, hungry; she would eat for breakfast four or five toast sandwiches with marmalade, peanut butter and bacon.

But this morning when she woke up it was just beginning to be light in the back room; she could just make out the printing on the cardboard boxes. Heinz Tomato Soup, she read, Golden Valley Apricots. She went through a private ritual of dividing

201

the letters into threes; if they came out evenly it meant she would be lucky that day. While she was doing this she thought she heard a noise, as if someone was moving in the yard; a marvellous uneasiness took hold of her body at the soles of her feet and made her curl her toes and stretch her legs until she touched the end of the couch. She had a feeling through her whole body like the feeling inside her head when she was going to sneeze. She got up as quietly as she could and walked carefully across the bare boards of the back room, which felt sandy and springy underfoot, to the rough kitchen linoleum. She was wearing an old cotton nightgown of Hazel's, which billowed out in a soft, ghostly way behind her.

The kitchen was empty; the clock ticked watchfully on the shelf above the sink. One of the taps dripped all the time and the dishcloth was folded into a little pad and placed underneath it. The face of the clock was almost hidden by a yellow tomato, ripening, and a can of powder that her grandmother used on her false teeth. Twenty to six. She moved towards the screen door; as she passed the breadbox one hand reached in of its own accord and came out with a couple of cinnamon buns which she began to eat without looking at them; they were a little dry.

The back yard at this time of day was strange, damp and shadowy; the fields were grey and all the cobwebbed, shaggy bushes along the fences thick with birds; the sky was pale, cool, smoothly ribbed with light and flushed at the edges, like the inside of a shell. It pleased her that her grandmother and Hazel were out of this, that they were still asleep. Nobody had spoken for this day yet; its purity astonished her. She had a delicate premonition of freedom and danger, like a streak of dawn across that sky. Around the corner of the house where the woodpile was she heard a small dry clattering sound.

"Who's there?" said May in a loud voice, first swallowing a mouthful of cinnamon bun. "I know you are there," she said.

Her grandmother came around the house carrying a few sticks of kindling wrapped in her apron and making private unintelligible noises of exasperation. May saw her come, not really with surprise but with a queer let-down feeling that seemed to spread thinly from the present moment into all areas of her life, past and future. It seemed to her that any place she went her grandmother would be there beforehand: anything she found out her grandmother would know already, or else could prove to be of no account.

"I thought it was somebody in the yard," she said defensively. Her grandmother looked at her as if she were a stovepipe and came ahead into the kitchen.

"I didn't think you would of got up so early," May said. "What'd you get up so early for?"

Her grandmother didn't answer. She heard everything you said to her but she didn't answer unless she felt like it. She set to work making a fire in the stove. She was dressed for the day in a print dress, a blue apron rubbed and dirty across the stomach, an unbuttoned, ravelling, no-colour sweater that had belonged once to her husband, and a pair of canvas shoes. Things dangled on her in spite of her attempts to be tidy and fastened up; it was because there was no reasonable shape to her body for clothes to cling to; she was all flat and narrow, except for the little mound of her stomach like a four-months' pregnancy that rode preposterously under her skinny chest. She had knobby fleshless legs and her arms were brown and veined and twisted like whips. Her head was rather big for her body and with her hair pulled tightly over her skull she had the look of an under-nourished but maliciously intelligent baby.

"You go on back to bed," she said to May. May went instead to the kitchen mirror and began combing her hair and twisting it around her finger to see if it would go into a page-boy. She had remembered that it was today Eunie Parker's cousin was coming. She would have taken Hazel's curlers and done her hair up, if she thought she could do that without her grandmother knowing.

Her grandmother closed the door of the front room where Hazel was asleep. She emptied out the coffee pot and put in water and fresh coffee. She got a pitcher of milk out of the icebox, sniffed at it to make sure it was still all right and lifted two ants out of the sugar bowl with her spoon. She rolled herself a cigarette on a little machine she had. Then she sat at the table and read yesterday's newspaper. She did not speak another word to May until the coffee had perked and she had dampered the fire and the room was almost as light as day.

"You get your own cup if you want any," she said.

Usually she said May was too young to drink coffee. May got herself a good cup with green birds on it. Her grandmother didn't say anything. They sat at the table drinking coffee, May in her long nightgown feeling privileged and ill at ease. Her grandmother was looking around the kitchen with its stained walls and calendars as if she had to keep it all in sight; she had a rather sly abstracted look.

May said conversationally, "Eunie Parker has her cousin coming today. Her name is Heather Sue Murray."

Her grandmother did not pay any attention. Presently she said, "Do you know how old I am?"

May said, "No."

"Well take a guess."

May thought and said, "Seventy?"

Her grandmother did not speak for so long that May thought this was only another of her conversational blind alleys. She said, informatively, "This Heather Sue Murray has been a Highland dancer ever since she was three years old. She dances in competitions and all."

"Seventy-eight," her grandmother said. "Nobody knows that, I never told. No birth certificate. Never took the pension. Never took relief." She thought a while and said, "Never was in a hospital. I got enough in the bank to cover burial. Any headstone will have to come out of charity or bad conscience of my relatives."

"What do you want a headstone for?" May said sullenly, picking at the oilcloth at a spot where it was worn through. She did not like this conversation; it reminded her of a rather mean trick her grandmother had played on her about three years ago. She had come home from school and found her grandmother lying on that same couch in the back room where she slept now. Her grandmother lay with her hands dropped at her sides, her face the colour of curdled milk, her eyes closed; she wore an expression of pure and unassailable indifference. May had tried saying "Hello" first and then "Grandma" more or less in her everyday voice; her grandmother did not flick a muscle in her usually live and agitated face. May said again, more respectfully, "Grandma"

203

and bending over did not hear the shallowest breath. She put out her hand to touch her grandmother's cheek, but was checked by something remote and not reassuring in that cold shabby hollow. Then she started to cry, in the anxious, bitten-off way of someone who is crying with no one to hear them. She was afraid to say her grandmother's name again; she was afraid to touch her, and at the same time afraid to take her eyes off her. However, her grandmother opened her eyes. Without lifting her arms or moving her head she looked up at May with a contrived, outrageous innocence and a curious spark of triumph. "Can't a person lay down around here?" she said. "Shame to be such a baby."

"I never said I *wanted* one," her grandmother said. "Go and get some clothes on," she said coldly, as May experimentally stuck one shoulder up through the loose neck of her nightgown. "Unless you think you are one of them Queens of Egypt."

"What?" said May looking at her shoulder splotched unpleasantly with peeling sunburn.

"Oh, one of them Queens of Egypt I understand they got at the Kinkaid Fair."

When May came back to the kitchen her grandmother was still drinking coffee and looking at the want-ad section of the city paper, as if she had no store to open or breakfast to cook or anything to do all day. Hazel had got up and was ironing a dress to wear to work. She worked in a store in Kinkaid which was thirty miles away and she had to leave for work early. She tried to persuade her mother to sell the store and go and live in Kinkaid which had two movie theatres, plenty of stores and restaurants and a Royal Dance Pavilion; but the old woman would not budge. She told Hazel to go and live where she liked but Hazel for some reason did not go. She was a tall drooping girl of thirty-three, with bleached hair, a long wary face and an oblique resentful expression emphasized by a slight cast, a wilful straying of one eye. She had a trunk full of embroidered pillowcases and towels and silverware. She bought a set of dishes and a set of copper-bottomed pots and put them away in her trunk; she and the old woman and May continued to eat off chipped plates and cook in pots so battered they rocked on the stove.

"Hazel's got everything she needs to get married but she just lacks one thing," the old woman would say.

Hazel drove all over the country to dances with other girls who worked in Kinkaid or taught school. On Sunday morning she got up with a hangover and took coffee with aspirin and put on her silk print dress and drove off down the road to sing in the choir. Her mother, who said she had no religion, opened up the store and sold gas and ice cream to tourists.

Hazel hung over the ironing-board yawning and tenderly rubbing her blurred face and the old woman read out loud, "Tall industrious man, thirty-five years old, desires make acquaintance woman of good habits, non-smoker or drinker, fond of home life, no triflers please."

"Aw, Mom," Hazel said.

"What's triflers?" May said.

"Man in prime of life," the old woman read relentlessly, "desires friendship of healthy woman without encumbrances, send photograph first letter."

"Aw cut it out, Mom," Hazel said.

"What's encumbrances?" May said.

"Where would you be if I did get married?" Hazel said gloomily with a look on her face of irritable satisfaction.

"Any time you want to get married you can get."

"I got you and May."

"Oh, go on."

"Well I have."

"Oh, go on," the old woman said with disgust. "I look after my ownself. I always have." She was going to say a lot more, for this speech was indeed a signpost in her life, but the moment after she had energetically summoned up that landscape which was coloured vividly and artlessly like a child's crayon drawing, and presented just such magical distortions, she shut her eyes as if oppressed by a feeling of unreality, a reasonable doubt that any of this had ever existed. She tapped with her spoon on the table and said to Hazel, "Well you never had such a dream as I had last night."

"I never do dream anyway," Hazel said.

The old woman sat tapping her spoon and looking with concentration at nothing but the front of the stove.

"Dreamt I was walking down the road," she said. "I was walking down the road past Simmonses' gate and I felt like a cloud was passing over the sun, felt cold, like. So I looked up and I seen a big bird, oh, the biggest bird you ever saw, black as that stove top there, it was right over me between me and the sun. Did you ever dream a thing like that?"

"I never dream anything," Hazel said rather proudly.

"Remember that nightmare I had when I was sleeping in the front room after I had the red measles?" May said. "Remember that nightmare?"

"I'm not talking about any nightmare," the old woman said.

"I thought there was people in coloured hats going round and round in that room. Faster and faster so all their hats was blurred together. All the rest of them was invisible except they had on these coloured hats."

Her grandmother put her tongue out to lick off some specks of dry tobacco that were stuck to her lips, then got up and lifted the stove lid and spat into the fire. "I might as well talk to a barn wall," she said. "May, put a coupla sticks in that fire I'll fry us some bacon. I don't want to keep the stove on today any longer'n I can help."

"It's going to be hotter today than it was yesterday," Hazel said placidly. "Me and Lois have a bargain on not to wear any stockings. Mr. Peebles says a word to us we're going to say what do you think they hired you for, going around looking at everybody's legs? He gets *embarrassed*," she said. Her bleached head disappeared into the skirt of her dress with a lonesome giggle like the sound of a bell rung once by accident, then caught.

"Huh," the old woman said.

May and Eunie Parker and Heather Sue Murray sat in the afternoon on the front step of the store. The sun had clouded over about noon but it seemed the day got even hotter then. You could not hear a cricket or a bird, but there was a low wind; a hot,

205

creeping wind came through the country grass. Because it was Saturday hardly anyone stopped at the store; the local cars drove on past, heading for town.

Heather Sue said, "Don't you kids ever hitch a ride?"

"No," May said.

Eunie Parker her best friend for two years said, "Oh, May wouldn't even be allowed. You don't know her grandmother. She can't do anything."

May scuffed her feet in the dirt and ground her heel into an ant hill. "Neither can you," she said.

"I can so," Eunie said. "I can do what I like." Heather Sue looked at them in her puzzled company way and said, "Well what is there to do here? I mean what do you kids *do*?"

Her hair was cut short all around her head; it was coarse, black, and curly. She had that Candy Apples lipstick on and it looked as if she shaved her legs.

"We go to the cemetery," May said flatly. They did, too. She and Eunie went and sat in the cemetery almost every afternoon because there was a shady corner there and no younger children bothered them and they could talk speculatively without any danger of being overheard.

"You go *where*?" Heather Sue said, and Eunie scowling into the dirt at their feet said, "Oh, we do not. I hate that stupid cemetery," she said. Sometimes she and May had spent a whole afternoon looking at the tombstones and picking out names that interested them and making up stories about the people who were buried there.

"Gee, don't give me the creeps like that," Heather Sue said. "It's awfully hot, isn't it? If I was at home this afternoon, I guess me and my girl friend would be going to the pool."

"We can go and swim at Third Bridge," Eunie said.

"Where is that?"

"Down the road, it's not far. Half a mile."

"In this heat?" Heather Sue said.

Eunie said, "I'll ride you on my bike." She said to May in an overly gay and hospitable voice, "You get your bike too, come on."

May considered a moment and then got up and went into the store, which was always dark in the daytime, hot too, with a big wooden clock on the wall and bins full of little sweet crumbling cookies, soft oranges, onions. She went to the back where her grandmother was sitting on a stool beside the ice-cream freezer, under a big baking-powder sign that had a background of glittering foil, like a Christmas card.

May said, "Can I go swimming with Eunie and Heather Sue?"

"Where you going to go swimming?" her grandmother said, almost neutrally. She knew there was only one place you could go.

"Third Bridge."

Eunie and Heather Sue had come in and were standing by the door. Heather Sue smiled with delicacy and politeness in the direction of the old woman.

"No, no you can't."

"It's not deep there," May said.

Her grandmother grunted enigmatically. She sat bent over, her elbow on her knee and her chin pressed down on her thumb. She would not bother looking up.

206

"Why can't I?" May said stubbornly.

Her grandmother did not answer. Eunie and Heather Sue watched from the door.

"Why can't I?" she said again. "*Grandma, why can't I?*"

"You know why."

"Why?"

"Because that's where all the boys go. I told you before. You're getting too big for that." Her mouth shut down hard; her face set in the lines of ugly and satisfied secrecy; now she looked up at May and looked at her until she brought up a flush of shame and anger. Some animation came into her own face. "Let the rest of them chase after the boys, see what it gets them." She never once looked at Eunie and Heather Sue but when she said this they turned and fled out of the store. You could hear them running past the gas pumps and breaking into wild, somewhat desperate, whoops of laughter. The old woman did not let on she heard.

May did not say anything. She was exploring in the dark a new dimension of bitterness. She had a feeling that her grandmother did not *believe* in her own reasons any more, that she did not care, but would go on pulling these same reasons out of the bag, flourishing them nastily, only to see what damage they could do. Her grandmother said, "Heather-miss-what's-her-name. I *seen* her, stepping out of the bus this morning."

May walked out of the store straight through the back room and through the kitchen to the back yard. She went and sat down by the pump. And old wooden trough, green with decay, ran down from the spout of the pump to an island of cool mud in the dry clumps of grass. She sat there and after a while she saw a big toad, rather an old and tired one she thought, flopping around in the grass; she trapped it in her hands.

She heard the screen door shut; she did not look. She saw her grandmother's shoes, her incredible ankles moving towards her across the grass. She held the toad in one hand and with the other she picked up a little stick; methodically she began to prod it in the belly.

"You quit that," her grandmother said. May dropped the stick. "Let that miserable thing go," she said, and very slowly May opened her fingers. In the close afternoon she could smell the peculiar flesh smell of her grandmother who stood over her; it was sweetish and corrupt like the smell of old apple peel going soft, and it penetrated and prevailed over the more commonplace odours of strong soap and dry ironed cotton and tobacco which she always carried around with her.

"I bet you don't know," her grandmother said loudly. "I bet you don't know what's been going through my head in there in the store." May did not answer but bent down and began to pick with interest at a scab on her leg.

"I been thinking I might sell the store," her grandmother said in this same loud monotonous voice as if she were talking to a deaf person or some larger power. Standing looking at the ragged pine-blue horizon, holding her apron down in an old woman's gesture with her flat hands, she said, "You and me could get on the train and go out and see Lewis." It was her son in California, whom she had not seen for about twenty years.

Then May had to look up to see if her grandmother was playing some kind of trick. The old woman had always said that the tourists were fools to think one place was any better than another and that they would have been better off at home.

"You and me could take a trip to the coast," her grandmother said. "Wouldn't cost so much, we could sit up nights and pack some food along. It's better to pack your own food, you know what you're getting."

"You're too old," May said cruelly. "You're seventy-eight."

"People my age are travelling to the Old Country and all over, you look in the papers."

"You might have a heart attack," May said.

"They could put me in that car with the lettuce and tomatoes," the old woman said, "and ship me home cold." Meanwhile May could see the coast; she saw a long curve of sand like the beach at the lake only longer and brighter; the very words, *The Coast*, produced a feeling of coolness and delight in her. But she did not trust them, she could not understand; when in her life had her grandmother promised her any fine thing before?

There was a man standing at the front of the store drinking a lemon-lime. He was a small middle-aged man with a puffy, heat-shiny face; he wore a white shirt, not clean, a pale silk tie. The old woman had moved her stool up to the front counter and she sat there talking to him. May stood with her back to both of them looking out the front door. The clouds were dingy; the world was filled with an old, dusty unfriendly light that seemed to come not from the sky alone but from the flat brick walls, the white roads, the grey bush-leaves rustling and the metal signs flapping in the hot, monotonous wind. Ever since her grandmother had followed her into the back yard she had felt as if something had changed, something had cracked; yes, it was that new light she saw in the world. And she felt something about herself — like power, like the unsuspected still unexplored power of her own hostility, and she meant to hold it for a while and turn it like a cold coin in her hand.

"What company are you travelling for?" her grandmother said. The man said, "Rug Company."

"Don't they let a man go home to his family on the weekend?"

"I'm not travelling on business right now," the man said. "At least I'm not travelling on rug business. You might say I'm travelling on private business."

"Oh well," the old woman said, in the tone of one who does not meddle with anybody's private business. "Does it look to you like we're going to have a rain?"

"Could be," the man said. He took a big drink of lemon-lime and put the bottle down and wiped his mouth neatly with his handkerchief. He was the sort who would talk about his private business anyway; indeed he would not talk about anything else. "I'm on my way to see an acquaintance of mine, he's staying at his summer cottage," he said. "He has insomnia so bad he hasn't had a good night's rest in seven years."

"Oh well," the old woman said.

"I'm going to see if I can cure him of it. I've had pretty good success with some insomnia cases. Not one hundred per cent. Pretty good."

"Are you a medical man too?"

"No, I'm not," the little man said agreeably. "I'm a hypnotist. An amateur. I don't think of myself as anything but an amateur."

The old woman looked at him for several moments without saying anything. This did not displease him; he moved around the front of the store picking things up and looking at them in a lively and self-satisfied way. "I'll bet you never saw anybody that said he was a hypnotist before in your life," he said in a joking way to the old woman. "I look just like anybody else, don't I? I look pretty tame."

"I don't believe in any of that kind of thing," she said.

He just laughed. "What do you mean you don't *believe* in it?"

"I don't believe in any superstitious kind of thing."

"It's not superstition, lady, it's a living fact."

"I know what it is."

"Well now a lot of people are of your opinion, a surprising lot of people. Maybe you didn't happen to read an article that was published about two years ago in the *Digest* on this same subject? I wish I had it with me," he said. "All I know is I cured a man of drinking. I cured people of all sorts of itches and rashes and bad habits. Nerves. I don't claim I can cure everybody of their nervous habits but some people I can tell you have been very grateful to me. Very grateful."

The old woman put her hands up to her head and did not answer.

"What's the matter, lady, aren't you feeling well. You got a headache?"

"I feel all right."

"How did you cure those people?" May said boldly, though her grandmother had always told her: don't let me catch you talking to strangers in the store.

The little man swung round attentively. "Why I hypnotize them, young lady. I hypnotize them. Are you asking me to explain to you what hypnotism is?"

May who did not know what she was asking flushed red and had no idea what to say. She saw her grandmother looking straight at her. The old woman looked out of her head at May and the whole world as if they had caught fire and she could do nothing about it, she could not even communicate the fact to them.

"She don't know what she's talking about," her grandmother said.

"Well it's very simple," the man said directly to May, in a luxuriantly gentle voice he must think suitable for children. "It's just like you put a person to sleep. Only they're not really asleep, do you follow me honey? You can talk to them. And listen — listen to this — you can go way deep into their minds and find out things they wouldn't even remember when they were awake. Find out their hidden worries and anxieties that's causing them the trouble. Now isn't that an amazing thing?"

"You couldn't do that with me," the old woman said. "I would know what was going on. You couldn't do that with me."

"I bet he could," May said, and was so startled at herself her mouth stayed open. She did not know why she had said that. Time and again she had watched her grandmother's encounters with the outside world, not with pride so much as a solid, fundamental conviction that the old woman would get the better of it. Now for the first time it seemed to her she saw the possibility of her grandmother's defeat; in her grandmother's face she saw it and not in the little man who must be crazy, she

209

thought, and who made her want to laugh. The idea filled her with dismay and with a painful, irresistible excitement.

"Well you never can tell till you give it a try," the man said, as if it were a joke. He looked at May. The old woman made up her mind. She said scornfully, "It don't matter to me." She put her elbows on the counter and held her head between her two hands, as if she were pressing something in. "Pity to take your time," she said.

"You really ought to lay down so you can relax better."

"Sitting down — " she said, and seemed to lose her breath a moment — "sitting down's good enough for me."

Then the man took a bottle-opener off a card of knick-knacks they had in the store and he walked over to stand in front of the counter. He was not in any hurry. When he spoke it was in a natural voice but it had changed a little; it had grown mild and unconcerned. "Now I know you're resisting this idea," he said softly. "I know you're resisting it and I know why. It's because you're afraid." The old woman made a noise of protest or alarm and he held up his hand, but gently. "You're afraid," he said, "and all I want to show you, all I mean to show you, is that there is nothing to be afraid of. Nothing to be afraid of. Nothing. Nothing to be afraid of, I just want you to keep your eyes on this shiny metal object I'm holding in my hand. That's right, just keep your eyes on it. Don't think. Don't worry. Just say to yourself, there's nothing to be afraid of, nothing to be afraid of, nothing to be afraid of — " His voice sank; May could not make out the words. She stayed pressed against the soft-drink cooler. She wanted to laugh, she could not help it, watching the somehow disreputable back of this man's head and his white, rounded, twitching shoulders. But she did not laugh because she had to wait to see what her grandmother would do. If her grandmother capitulated it would be as unsettling an event as an earthquake or a flood; it would crack the foundations of her life and set her terrifyingly free. The old woman stared with furious unblinking obedience at the bottle-opener in the man's hand.

"Now I just want you to tell me," he said, "if you can still see — if you can still see — " He bent forward to look into her face. "I just want you to tell me if you can still see — " The old woman's face with its enormous cold eyes and its hard ferocious expression was on a level with his own. He stopped; he drew back.

"Hey what's the matter?" he said, not in his hypnotizing but his ordinary voice — in fact a sharper voice than ordinary, which made May jump. "What's the matter, lady, come on, wake up. Wake up," he said, and touched her shoulder to give her a little shake. The old woman with a look of intemperate scorn still on her face fell forwards across the counter with a loud noise, scattering several packages of Kleenex, bubble gum, and cake decorations over the floor. The man dropped the bottle-opener and giving May an outraged look and crying, "I'm not responsible — it never happened before," he ran out of the store to his car. May heard his car start and then she ran out after him, as if she wanted to call something, as if she wanted to call "Help" or "Stay." But she did not call anything, she stood with her mouth open in the dust in front of the gas pumps, and he would not have heard her anyway; he gave one wildly negative wave out the window of his car and roared away to the north.

May stood outside the store and no other cars went by on the highway, no one came. The yards were empty in Black Horse. It had begun to rain a little while before

210

and the drops of rain fell separately around her, sputtering in the dust. Finally she went back and sat on the step of the store where the rain fell too. It was quite warm and she did not mind. She sat with her legs folded under her looking out at the road where she might walk now in any direction she liked, and the world which lay flat and accessible and full of silence in front of her. She sat and waited for that moment to come when she could not wait any longer, when she would have to get up and go into the store where it was darker than ever now on account of the rain and where her grandmother lay fallen across the counter dead, and what was more, victorious.

Mordecai Richler

Mordecai Richler's family were Jewish immigrants from Galicia who settled in the St. Urbain area of Montreal, where Richler was born in 1931. He attended Baron Byng High School (later immortalized as Fletcher's Field High School in The Apprenticeship of Duddy Kravitz) *and then went on to Sir George Williams College. He withdrew without graduating and went to Paris in 1951. The following year he returned to Montreal where he did manual work and also did work for the CBC. Since 1954 he has lived mainly in England, where he supports himself by writing scripts for film and television, as well as by journalism. He has published several important novels, including* The Apprenticeship of Duddy Kravitz *(1959), and a number of short stories. His most recent novel is* Saint Urbain's Horseman *(1971). In 1968 he was Writer-in-Residence at Sir George Williams University.*

Much of Richler's best fiction has a strongly regional flavour; its roots are in the working-class Jewish section of Montreal where he grew up. However, although he has lived abroad for many years, Richler has remained interested in the Canadian scene. This interest is reflected in his journalism as well as in his fiction. He sees the Jewish and Canadian situations as parallel in many ways. "To be a Jew and a Canadian," he claims, "is to emerge from the ghetto twice, for self-conscious Canadians, like some touchy Jews, tend to look at the world through a wrong-ended telescope. . . . Like Jews again, Canadians are inclined to regard with a mixture of envy and suspicion those who have forsaken the homestead (or shtetl) *for the assimilationist fleshpots of New York and London."[1] He maintains a sharp eye for Canadian, as for Jewish, pretensions, and his expatriate status helps him to regard them with a certain objectivity. The following essay on the growth of separatist feeling in Quebec in the early nineteen-sixties, written for an English audience and published in* Encounter *in 1964, reflects the combination of detachment and involvement which makes for much of the comedy in his fiction. Though he grew up in the middle of the area most affected by Anglo-French hostilities and prejudices, his Jewishness and his expatriation enable him to view the claims of both sides with irony.*

Footnotes

[1] *Mordecai Richler,* Hunting Tigers Under Glass *(Toronto: 1968), p. 8.*

212

"Quebec Oui, Ottawa Non!"

I returned to Montreal recently on Queen Victoria's birthday, a national holiday in Canada. A thousand policemen were required to put down a French-Canadian Separatist demonstration. Flags were burnt, a defective bomb was planted on Victoria Bridge, and a wreath was laid at the *Monument aux Patriots* which marks the spot where twelve men were executed after the 1837-8 rebellion.

The last time I remember such excitement in Montreal was when Maurice Richard, the greatest ice-hockey player of our time, was suspended and could not play in the first three games of the all-important Stanley Cup Series. Richard, a French-Canadian hero, was disciplined by the President of the National League, a Scot named Campbell, and that didn't help. On the contrary: it illustrated yet again that in Canada it is almost without exception the Scots who are the managers and officers and the French who are the clerks and enlisted men. The French, though they make up something less than a third of Canada's total population of more than nineteen million, hold something less than fifteen per cent of all responsible federal jobs. Furthermore, a recent study showed that while four-fifths of the directors of 183 major companies in Canada were Canadian-born, ninety per cent of them were of British origin. Less than seven per cent of these positions were held by French Canadians. Commenting on this already inflammatory situation in 1962, Donald Gordon, president of Canadian National Railways, said that he had never appointed any French-Canadian vice-presidents because they lacked the necessary university training. French-Canadian students replied by burning Gordon's effigy in Montreal's Place Ville Marie. Then an enterprising Toronto reporter discovered that of the thirty vice-presidents employed by Canada's two railway systems, only seven had actually been to university. The arrogant Mr. Gordon wasn't among them.

Now QUEBEC LIBRE is painted on many a Montreal wall, students fix stickers that read QUEBEC OUI OTTAWA NON to cars, and there have been bombing outrages. After one of the most recent and successful dawn lootings of an armoury (62nd Field Regiment in Shawinigan), John Diefenbaker, leader of the Opposition, asked in parliament what was being done 'to protect the armed forces'. *Parti Pris*, an intellectual Separatist monthly with a circulation of 3,500, is frankly for revolution now: 'we are colonised and exploited . . . Quebec society has entered a revolutionary phase. It is ready to take all means, not excluding violence. . . . ' Since then the Queen has come and gone, and the temperature has risen still higher.

All this should be disturbing, but as a returning native I must confess that what I felt was a certain childish glee. W. H. Auden has written in *Encounter* (Jan. 1963), 'The dominions . . . are for me *tiefste Provinz*, places which have produced no art and are inhabited by the kind of person with whom I have least in common.' When I was in

213

New York an editor told me that he and his associates had recently compiled a list of twelve books with which to start a new publishing firm that was bound to fail. Leading the list of unreadables was *Canada: Our Good Neighbor to the North.* Well, now something was happening. At last something was happening in what our most notable gossip columnist still calls 'Our-Town-With-A-Heart.'

Montreal, incidentally, has a total population going on 1,200,000. Of these nearly 800,000 are of French origin and another 150,000 are of British origin. There are also some 50,000 Jews living in this city that was, in 1878, the victim of a poem, 'A Psalm of Montreal', by Samuel Butler.

> Stowed away in a Montreal lumber room
> The Discobolus standeth and turneth his face to the wall;
> Dusty, cobweb-covered, maimed and set at naught,
> Beauty crieth in an attic, and no man regardeth:
> > O God! O Montreal!

> 'The Discobolus is put here because he is vulgar —
> He has neither vest nor pants with which to cover his limbs;
> I, Sir, am a person of most respectable connections —
> My brother-in-law is haberdasher to Mr. Spurgeon:
> > O God! O Montreal!

In all fairness, I should add that Butler in Montreal today would be all but overwhelmed by the arts industry. There is a *Place des Arts* bang in the middle of town and the National Film Board of Canada turning out documentaries, some of them highly imaginative, just outside. French-Canadian feature films of festival quality are being made for the first time. One of the most successful of these, Claude Jutra's jerky, self-indulgent, but adventurous *A Tout Prendre*, had what I suppose you might call a mood shot added to it a year after completion. It shows the hero (who also happens to be the director, star, *and* subject of the film) strolling past a wall on which QUEBEC LIBRE has been painted, and of course nothing could be more topical.

One night an old schoolmate told me, 'I was going to buy a place in the Laurentians this year, but the truth is now I'm thinking of looking for something in Vermont. I hate to say this, but if I was going to buy a place in Montreal I'd get myself the biggest possible mortgage. Let somebody else get stuck if there's trouble.'

One of the most responsible journalists in town said, 'The men on the fringe are dangerous. Honestly, the next step could be an assassination and don't think the RCMP isn't worried. It could be Vanier, the French-Canadian Governor-General. That would certainly provoke Ottawa. They might have to send in troops and then the whole thing would blow up.'

Again and again I was asked, 'What are people saying in London? What do they think?,' and I had to tell them the truth: nobody was saying anything.

'If this was happening in Africa,' a friend said, 'or South America, everybody would be excited. Another Cuba, they'd say. But Canada — hell, we're always taken for granted.'

Another journalist, an old Montrealer not generally given to hyperbole, told me, 'You know what I'd like more than anything? To be twenty and French Canadian. My

God, it must be exciting.' He went on to say, 'All my sympathies are with the French in this. They're the best people in the country, aren't they? I mean the Protestants are so guilt-ridden and joyless. The French have such a damn good case too, but it's emotional, not rational. I mean you can't get them to sit down at a table and say I want this and I want that, you can't bargain. . . . '

Off to visit an old friend the next morning, I spied a lonely and defiant Red Ensign, our semi-official flag *manqué*, fluttering in a garden in Westmount, a district where only a year ago FLQ *(Front de Libération Québecois)* terrorists were planting bombs in mailboxes. Happy birthday, Queen Victoria, I thought, and good luck to you too, Charlie. Not yet a Separatist, I already felt pleased to think of the WASPS of Montreal in trouble. Maybe your time is coming soon, I thought, and we'll see how good you are at being a minority. A touchy minority.

To begin with, I'd recommend that all White Anglo-Saxon Protestant kids begin their school day by being roughed up by other kids who would then dance around them, chanting, 'You killed Joan of Arc.' If the WASP kids insisted on observing holidays as archaic as Victoria Day, they would have to bring a note to school from their parents, which note would be read aloud to the amusement of the rest of the class. Come Christmas, the WASP kids would all have to rise and stand silently with the rest to listen to de Gaulle's message from Paris.

Maybe the process has already begun. For when I was downtown the following day and went to my old college, Sir George Williams, to see a faculty member, I was told, 'Sorry he can't be disturbed now. He's having his French lesson.'

In English-speaking board rooms all over Montreal it was the same. The Berlitz school now runs company programs, and I got a picture of lots of big boys doing penance. Why, there was even a French column in the *Canadian Jewish Chronicle*. The next step was difficult to predict. It could be a Pantagruel Festival in Rabelais, Quebec, if there was such a place, or frogs' legs replacing Super 'K' on the breakfast tables of Westmount. We already have, as *The New Yorker* once noted, a Notre Dame de Grace Kosher Meat Market.

Then only last autumn, André Malraux came to town to open a *'France in Canada'* exhibition. 'France needs you,' he told the sapient aldermen of the Montreal City Council. 'We will build the next civilization together.' Malraux added that he brought a personal message from General de Gaulle. It was that 'Montreal was France's second city. He wanted this message to reach you. . . . You are not aware of the meaning you have for France. There is nowhere in the world where the spirit of France works so movingly as it does in the Province of Quebec.'

Opening the exhibition the next day, Malraux said, 'For France, Canada is not the past. It is not Jacques Cartier. . . . It is what we will do together.'

Four days later the Montreal *Star* replied with THE MALRAUX STORY: IF QUEBEC BELONGED TO FRANCE. 'If Quebec still belonged to France,' the story began, the big policy decisions would be made by a super-president three thousand miles away in Paris. Every man would have to spend at least 18 months in the nuclear army. There would be better schools — but fewer universities — and education would be in the hands of the State, not the Church. All television and radio operations would be a part of the state propaganda machine. All citizens would enjoy liberal welfare benefits because Quebec — like the motherland — would be a welfare state. Businessmen would have to accept a higher degree of planning. In the courts, an accused would be presumed guilty until proven innocent. . . .

At a press conference the next day, Malraux said, 'The mere thought that French Canada could become politically or otherwise dependent on France is a dangerous and even a ridiculous one.' He added that his 'utterances never implied anything beyond the historical and the artistic, even though as a cabinet minister I might have been thought to be somehow politically involved.'

But even as M. Malraux explained himself in Montreal, General de Gaulle sent a warm letter of congratulation to a Frenchman, Jean Cathelin, who had visited Canada twice and written a book called *Révolution au Canada*. De Gaulle wrote that he'd 'draw a profit' from the book and Cathelin, a member of the *Comité International de l'Indépendance de Québec*, a Paris lobbying agency for Separatists, claimed official blessing. The Elysée Palace insisted that de Gaulle's letter was a formality and that he was not a Separatist. Meanwhile the two French Canadians who started the *Comité* — and who, incidentally, have been compared by one Paris newspaper to 'Tom Paine and Benjamin Franklin' — claim that both Algeria and Senégal have promised diplomatic support for a free state of Quebec. *Carrefour*, a French Catholic weekly, has run a headline that reads FORTY-FOUR INDEPENDENT NATIONS SINCE THE WAR. WHY NOT FRENCH CANADA?, and Jacques Berque, a professor at the Collège de France and a member of the *Comité*, has written in *France Observateur* that Ottawa's imperialism 'has not exercised the same rigours and crudeness as [imperialism] elsewhere but takes the more insidious form of fake bilingualism, economic pressure, and financial exploitation.'

French intellectuals have not always been so enamoured of Quebec, a province which was largely pro-Vichy in sentiment during the war and whose flag is still the *fleur-de-lis*. When Gomez, the Spanish republican in Jean-Paul Sartre's novel, *Iron in the Soul*, finds himself in New York on the day that Paris has fallen, he sees only grins and indifference on Seventh Avenue. Then, on 55th Street, he spots a French restaurant, *A La Petite Coquette*, and enters, hoping to find solace. 'Paris has fallen,' Gomez says to the bartender, but only gets a melancholy grunt for a reply. Gomez tries again, 'Afraid France is a goner.' Finally the barman says, 'France is going to learn what it costs to abandon her natural allies.' Gomez is confused until the barman adds, 'In the reign of Louis-the-Well-Beloved, sir, France had already committed every fault there is to commit.'

> 'Ah,' said Gomez, 'you're a Canadian.'
> 'I'm from Montreal,' said the barman.
> 'Are you now?''

And Gomez goes off in search of a *real* Frenchman.

Marcel Chaput, a leading French-Canadian Separatist, has said, 'If Quebec still belonged to France I should preach Separatism just as hard as I do today.' In his book *Why I am a Separatist*, Dr. Chaput wrote, 'The French Canadians form a nation. . . . There is no Canadian nation. . . . There is a Canadian state [which is] a purely political and artificial entity [while] the French-Canadian nation is a natural entity whose bonds are those of culture, flesh, and blood.'

The English-Canadian response has not always been strikingly intelligent. An editorial first printed in the *Orillia Packet and Times* and then widely reprinted by Thompson Newspapers Limited is titled, THE CANADA I LOVE: AN UNFASHIONABLE TESTAMENT.

> I love Canada . . . a thousand critics inform me that there is no such thing as a Canadian, no separate and distinct Canadian identity. I am one. Politicians and pundits assure me that there is no Canadian flag, no national anthem, but I am content with our flag, a sort of red ensign . . . and I am always moved when a good band plays 'the Queen' but I could learn to stand up for 'O Canada' too. I love Canada. There are people like . . . Marcel Chaput who . . . assail me for oppressing my French-Canadian brothers and threaten me with a promise to pull Quebec out of confederation, but I have been . . . drunk with the Van Doos and kissed Ghislaine Gagnon . . . and saluted Georges Vanier . . . and I know they're Canadians too. . . . I love Canada. Our politics are dull and our sports bush league, but you can't beat the beer or the air . . . I am a Canadian. Are there any more like me?

Unfortunately, yes. Lots. But there are others too. In a seminar on French Canada held in Montreal recently, Eric Kierans, President of the Montreal Stock Exchange, said, 'This feeling not of revolt but of assertion in Quebec is deep, all-pervasive, and it's not going to go away, and I for one don't think it should go away.' He added that it was plain there had been a lack of any real direction on a federal level in Canada for the past ten years. 'The Liberals,' he said, 'were used to running this country like a clock. . . . This country is too diverse to ever let it run like that. . . . So we have a vacuum, and in a vacuum all of the inherent differences in the country emerge.' A European refugee I know in Montreal told me, 'The Separatists are right when they say Canada isn't a nation, it's a state, but if only they knew how lucky they were! They haven't seen our European-style of nationalism and what it does. This isn't a country — but that's what I like best about it here!'

The last time I was in Montreal for a lengthy stay, in 1960, the *Union Nationale* was defeated in the Quebec provincial election. A year earlier Premier Maurice Duplessis, leader of the *Union Nationale* and virtually Quebec's dictator for fifteen years, died of a stroke. Duplessis' successor, Paul Sauvé, died four months later; and in 1960 the Liberals, led by silky Jean Lesage and prodded by a brilliant newcomer to politics, René Lévesque, toppled one of the most corrupt and deeply rooted political machines in North America. It was more than a heartening political upset. What amounts to a French-Canadian revolution had begun.

Today there is a sense of liberation everywhere in Quebec — a province that is, incidentally, twice the size of Texas. Stalin, so to speak, is dead. All manner of hitherto suppressed energies have been released. Anything can happen. And 'anything' includes the possibility that Quebec will separate to form an independent state. If

Quebec secedes, it is generally assumed that British Columbia would follow quickly. Confederation, as we know it, could collapse. Then it is not unfeasible that a number of provinces (there are ten) would sue for entry into the U.S.A. In fact, should Quebec secede the structure of North American politics could be drastically shaken up.

Mind you, I'm not saying it's likely, but it is possible. A survey undertaken by *Maclean's* magazine in June 1964 showed that twenty-nine per cent of all Canadians, almost one voter in three, were in favour of political union with the U.S.A.; forty-two per cent wanted economic union only. A. M. Lower, a Canadian historian worried about the many young people who quit Canada for the U.S.A. (an estimated 50,000 in 1963), has written, 'It has tended to be the more able and especially the spontaneous who have gone. . . . Canada has retained the withdrawn, the sedate, and those with the least energy and ability.' One of those with ability who *has* stayed behind is Professor Frank Underhill, who, in his book, *In Search of Canadian Liberalism,* wrote, ' . . . if we allow ourselves to be obsessed by the danger of American cultural annexation, so that the thought preys on us day and night, we shall only become a slightly bigger Ulster. . . . If we will only be natural . . . we shall discover that we are very like the Americans, both in our good qualities and our bad qualities.' An earlier *Maclean's* survey, conducted in 1963 when the Separatist movement was barely two years old, revealed that thirteen per cent of French Canadians were already convinced Separatists. This group, the survey showed, was largely urban, young, and well educated; it included a number of influential journalists and many professional people and senior civil servants.

The French, the first to colonize Canada, are a conquered people. Jacques Cartier explored the St. Lawrence Gulf in 1534 and brought the Indian chief Donnacona back to France with him, where Donnacona spun the French court tales about 'immense quantities of gold, rubies, and other rich things'. In 1608 Samuel de Champlain founded the city of Quebec in New France and opened up the fur trade with the Indians. Maisonneuve founded Montreal in 1642.

> He sprang ashore [Francis Parkman wrote in *The Jesuits in North America*] and fell on his knees. His followers imitated his example, and all joined their voices in enthusiastic songs of thanksgiving. Tents, baggage, arms, and stores were landed. An altar was raised on a pleasant spot near at hand, and Mademoiselle Mance, with Madame de la Peltrie . . . decorated it with a taste which was the admiration of beholders. Now all the company gathered before the shrine. . . . They knelt in reverent silence as the Host was raised aloft, and when the rite was over the priest turned and addressed them:
> 'You are a grain of mustard seed that shall rise and grow until its branches overshadow the earth. You are few, but your work is the work of God. His smile is on you, and your children shall fill the land.'

A century passed. More. Then, in 1759, Wolfe defeated Montcalm on the Plains of Abraham, Quebec City fell to the British, and the cry of a people was to become *'Je me souviens.'* Montreal was taken a year later and in 1763 France ceded its North American territories east of the Mississippi to Britain. New France — a few arpents of snow, as Voltaire wrote so contemptuously in *Candide* — was no more. But according to the Quebec Act of 1774 the boundaries of Quebec Province were enlarged and freedom of religion for Catholics was confirmed under a combination of British and French law. Lord Durham, in his famous report on Canada in 1839, wrote,

> There can hardly be conceived a nationality more destitute of all that can invigorate and elevate a people than that which is exhibited by the descendants of the French in Lower Canada, owing to their retaining their peculiar language and manners. They are a people with no history and no literature.

Twenty-eight years later, in 1867, the British North America Act was passed and the Dominion of Canada was created.

Quebec, from the beginning, put graft-ridden governments into office. Maurice Duplessis, who was first elected to the legislature in 1937, did not introduce corruption to the province, but under the *Union Nationale*, from 1944 to 1960, 'the pay-off' just about defined the régime. A royal commission investigating the *Union Nationale* government in 1961 estimated that the graft paid out by companies doing business with the provincial government over a sixteen-year span came to about 100 million dollars. (Liquor licences for night-clubs in Montreal, for example, sold for as much as $30,000, whereas now, under a 'clean' Liberal government, they can be had for a hundred.) Duplessis himself, it's worth noting, did not acquire a private fortune. He ran Quebec as his private manor, and short of ordering his ministers to dance the Gopak, he made sure that their public humiliation was complete. He contradicted and ridiculed them almost sadistically in the legislature and mocked them before journalists. Duplessis, a hysterical antibolshie, time and again employed brutal strike-breaking tactics in the province and threatened townships blatantly when he needed the vote. From the platform, he would say, 'Do you want a new hospital? A new bridge? A new school? Then vote *Union Nationale*. I would hate to force gifts on you that wouldn't be appreciated.'

Miriam Chapin, author of *Quebec Now*, writes that when she asked a farmer in one county why he voted *Union Nationale*, he replied, 'We've got to have roads. Look at Verchères. They sent a Liberal to Quebec six years ago and they haven't laid eyes on a bulldozer since. A woman down there, they tell me, died in childbirth last spring; the doctor couldn't get to her through the mud. We *got* to have roads. See?'

Throughout Duplessis's reign the rich and powerful English-speaking community in Montreal — the bankers and brokers and industrialists who live in Westmount, where they have their own police force, postal and street cleaning systems — remained aloof. The English-language newspapers never criticized. In exchange for silence, the English-speaking community won contracts and tax concessions. They were, in effect, allowed to run the province's economy.

Though Montreal is the second-largest French city in the world, as recently as 1956 only three per cent of the English-speaking population was bilingual. The French, on the other hand, have always had to speak English or moulder in second-rate jobs.

Montreal is a sequence of ghettos. Even though I was born and brought up there, my experience of the French was a pathetically limited and distorted one. Our street was called St. Urbain, after Pope Urban I. It led ultimately to routes 11 and 18, and all day and night big refrigeration trucks and peddlers in Chevvies and sometimes tourists used to pass, going to and from northern Quebec, Ontario, and New York State. Occasionally the truckers, usually French-Canadian, would pull up at Tansky's Cigars & Soda for a breather. Some of the truckers had tattoos on their arms, others chewed tobacco. Tansky's regulars would whisper about them in Yiddish.

'I wonder how long that one's been out of prison?'

'But you don't understand. Statistics prove they're happier than we are. They care their kids should go to college? They have one every nine months regular as clock-work for the family allowance cheque.'

The French-Canadian truckers struck matches against the seat of their trousers or by flicking them with a thumbnail. They could spit on the floor with such a splash of assurance that it was the regulars who ended up feeling like intruders in Tansky's store.

If the French Canadians were our enemies, then it must also be said that they were not entirely unloved. In fact it was the English we truly hated and feared. 'Among them,' I heard it said, 'with their porridge faces, who can tell what they're thinking?' It was, we felt, *their* country, and who knew when, released by booze, they'd make trouble. The French, like us, were poor and rough and spoke English badly.

During the war years St. Urbain Street families used to club together to rent clapboard cottages from the French Canadians in the Laurentian mountains. Every week the farmers came to market with fruit and vegetables, and once a summer a French-Canadian strongman came to town and we all went out to watch him bend an iron bar between his teeth and swallow razor blades. Then things went sour between the French Canadians and us. One day the kids fished and stole apples together and the next there were signs painted on the highway, *A bas les Juifs*. Adrian Arcand, the fascist leader, alarmed us. Laurent Barré, a minister in the Duplessis cabinet, told the legislature that his son, on entering the army, had been exposed to the insult of a medical examination by a Jewish doctor. 'Infamous Jewish examiners,' he said, 'are regaling themselves on naked Canadian flesh.' The Liberal government in Ottawa called for a plebiscite on conscription for military service overseas and on a sleazy beach outside Montreal, French Canadians and Jews fought with clubs. A popular Jewish sportsman lost an eye. French Canadians and Jews met to fight again outside the YMHA. Duplessis published a pamphlet showing a Jew, with an elongated nose and skullcap, raking in gold, and the caption underneath invited Abie to return to Palestine. Swastikas were painted on sidewalks here and there.

Looking back, I can see that the real trouble was there was no dialogue between us. We went to one set of schools and the French Canadians to another. I'm sure many of them believed that there was such an order as The Elders of Zion and that the St. Urbain Street Jews were secretly rich. On my side, I was convinced all French Canadians were abysmally stupid. 'Frenchies', as I recall it, were for turning the lights on and off on the sabbath and running elevators and cleaning chimneys and furnaces. They were stinky, ridden with TB and rickets. Their older women were for washing windows and waxing floors and the younger ones were for maids in the higher reaches of Outremont, working in factories, and making time with, if you had the chance. Zabitsky, the most feared of Tansky's regulars, said, 'It's not very well known, but there's a tunnel that runs from the nunnery to the priest-house — and it isn't there in case of an air-raid either.' He told us how an altar boy could become a bishop's favourite, that a nun's habit could easily conceal pregnancy, and suggested a new definition for bishopric.

We fought them stereotype for stereotype. If the French Canadians felt the Jews were running the black market, then my typical French Canadian (we called them 'frogs' or 'pea soups') was a gum-chewer. He wore the greasy black hair parted down the middle and also affected an eyebrow moustache. His zoot trousers were belted just under the breastbone and ended in a peg hugging his ankles. He was a dolt who held you up endlessly at the liquor commission while he tried unsuccessfully to add three figures, or, if he was employed at the customs office, he never knew which form to give you. Furthermore, he only held this or any other government job because he was the second cousin of some backwoods notary who had delivered the family vote to the *Union Nationale* for a generation. Other French Canadians were speed cops, and if any of these ever stopped you on the highway, you made sure to hand him a folded two-dollar bill with your licence.

Wartime shortages, the admirable Protestant spirit of making-do, benefitted both Jews and French Canadians. Jews with clean fingernails were allowed to teach within the Protestant school system and French Canadians off the sandlots broke into the International Baseball League. Jean-Pierre Roy won twenty-five games for the Montreal Royals one year and a young man named Stan Breard enjoyed a season as a stylish but no-hit shortstop. Come to think of it, the only French Canadians I knew of were athletes. Of course there was Maurice Richard, the incomparable hockey player, but there was also Dave Castiloux, a clever welterweight, and, above all, the wrestler-hero, Yvon Robert, who week after week gave the blond Anglo-Saxon wrestlers what for at the Forum.

I believed that Montreal was the largest inland seaport and the second-biggest French city in the world, *but only because my geography books said so.* Aside from boyhood street fights and what I read on the sports pages, all I knew of French Canadians was that they were clearly hilarious. Our Scots schoolmaster could always raise a laugh in class by reading us the atrocious Uncle Tom-like dialect verse of William Henry Drummond:

> On wan dark night on Lac St. Pierre,
> De win' she blow, blow, blow,
> An' de crew of de wood scow 'Julie Plante'
> Got scar't an' run below —
> For de win' she blow lak' hurricane,
> Bimeby she blow some more,
> An' de scow bus' up on Lac St. Pierre
> Wan arpent from de shore.

St. Jean Baptiste is still the patron saint of Quebec, but in this summer's annual parade he was no longer played by a boy. He was, for the first time, represented by an adult, and the sheep that accompanied him in former years was tossed out. A few days before the parade, the extremely influential *Société Saint Jean Baptiste de Montréal*, with a membership of more than 300,000 throughout the province, presented a 125-page brief to the Quebec Parliamentary Committee on the Constitution. The *Société* said that Canada must consist of two equal partners — the Ottawa government leading the nine 'English' provinces and a fully self-determined Quebec. The brief recommended, among other things, sovereign status for Quebec, including Quebec citizenship, for all its residents, and recognition of two nations in Canada. 'This,' Professor Michel Brunet of the University of Montreal told reporters, 'is the answer to outright separatism'. He added that French-Canadian nationalism was not a fad.

The 'contract' which was made in 1867 was one between an adult and a minor, but the French partner in the contract feels very much that he has come of age and he thinks strongly that he has been 'had'.

Another indication, if it's needed, of how much times have changed in Quebec was the recall from Swiss exile this summer of the Marist Brother Pierre-Jerome. Brother Pierre-Jerome, now a legend in the province, is the author of a witty and engaging book, *Les Insolences du Frère Untel*, that was published anonymously in 1960 and sold an astonishing 127,000 copies in Quebec, making it the best-selling book in the history of the province. *Les Insolences* is not merely a good book: it is one of those rare and timely volumes that has become a factor in the making of a social revolution. It was the first book with a wide circulation outspokenly to criticize the church-run educational system, the sloppy French spoken by the young *(joual)*, and the corruption of Quebec's political autocracy. 'The whole of French-Canadian society is foundering,' Brother Pierre-Jerome wrote in 1960. 'We are a servile race; our loins were broken two hundred years ago, and it shows.'

Shortly after *Les Insolences* became a *succès de scandale*, Brother Pierre-Jerome was sent off to the Mother House in Rome by his Marist superiors. He lived there under strict discipline for a year before going on to teach at the University of Fribourg from where he was finally recalled to Quebec.

Les Insolences was first published as a series of letters by André Laurendeau, then editor of *Le Devoir* and a long-standing enemy of Duplessis. Laurendeau is now serving on the Royal Commission on Bilingualism and Biculturalism with Davidson Dunton, the president of Carleton University in Ottawa, and F. R. Scott, the brilliant dean of the McGill law school and a poet with a sharp satirical eye. It was Laurendeau who developed the theory of the *'Roi Nègre'* — that is to say that the real rulers of Quebec (the English) used a French-Canadian chieftain (Duplessis) to govern the province, just as colonial powers used African puppets to keep their tribes in order.

Laurendeau is not alone among French Canadian intellectuals who would like to see Quebec's revolution develop quietly within confederation.

On May 14th, 1964, the Montreal *Star* reprinted a 'Canadian Manifesto' that first appeared in *Cité Libre* and was signed by seven distinguished French-Canadian intellectuals who called themselves 'The Committee For Political Realism'. The Committee called for social justice, a fairer distribution of wealth, and a revised penal code, rather than more nationalistic heat.

222

To use nationalism as a yardstick for deciding policies and priorities is both sterile and retrograde. Overflowing nationalism distorts one's vision of reality, prevents one from seeing problems in their true perspective, falsifies solutions, and constitutes a classic diversionary tactic for politicians caught by facts.

Our comments in this regard apply equally to Canadian or French-Canadian nationalism. . . . We are not any more impressed by the cries in some English circles when American financiers buy Canadian enterprises, than we are by the adoption in the Province of Quebec of economic policies based upon the slogan 'maîtres chez nous'.

Separatism in Quebec appears to us not only a waste of time but as a step backwards. . . . We refuse to let ourselves be locked into a constitutional frame smaller than Canada. . . . We do not attach to its existence any sacred or eternal meaning, but it is an historical fact. To take it apart would require an enormous expenditure of energy and gain no proven advantage. . . .

Among the authors of the Manifesto is Pierre-Elliott Trudeau, a founder and editor of *Cité Libre*, a magazine that was once considered the most radical in Quebec, but that is now arrogantly dismissed by Separatists. For the Separatists have gone beyond abandoning the traditional sheep on St. Jean Baptiste Day. The symbol of the RIN *(Le Parti Republicain du Québec)* is the ram's head. Young Separatists smoke made-in-the-province Québecois cigarettes and are scornful of anyone over thirty — anyone who belonged to that generation that tolerated Duplessis. Governor-General Vanier, a French Canadian, is their Pétain-figure ('he speaks French with an English accent'), and even Jean Lesage, who brought decent government to the province, is considered a transitional figure.

'Duplessis isn't our problem,' a Separatist told me. 'Lesage and the others pushed open the door and for that they deserve credit, but they were totally unprepared for the new release of energy.'

Neither do the Separatists take the many conciliatory gestures of English-speaking Canada, including the Royal Commission on Bilingualism, very seriously.

'I never heard of anything so silly as bilingualism,' and RIN member said. 'Why should they speak French in Vancouver? It's stupid!'

I spent an afternoon in Montreal with two RIN members, both students at the University of Montreal, both articulate and middle-class. Jacques, referring to one of Montreal's largest department stores, said: 'Now they advertise that nine out of ten people who work there speak French. Sure, only the tenth one is the president of the company.'

André said: 'We have nothing against English Canada, you know. We don't hate them. We want to run our own affairs, that's all. And if you ask me they'd be better off without us too.'

I asked Jacques if he felt the standard of living in Quebec would decline if the province was to separate.

'English Canada,' he said, 'puts up with a lower standard of living in order to remain independent of the United States. Why don't they credit us with the same sort of pride.'

'Anyway, the standard of living would not go down,' André said. 'The Belgians would invest. So would the French and the Americans.'

André and Jacques both said they were opposed to violence. They claimed that they were often followed by the RCMP and photographed at demonstrations. I spoke to them about English-Canadian anxieties. Quebec, I said, has an unfortunate history of corrupt politicians and right-wing demagogues. There was Duplessis and even more recently Réal Caouette, a backwoods car-salesman whose *Le Ralliement des Créditistes* won an astonishing twenty-six seats in the 1962 federal elections. Caouette, a bigot and a self-confessed admirer of Hitler and Mussolini, told his simple followers, 'You don't have to understand Social Credit to vote for it.' English Canadians, then, fear a right-wing coup should Quebec become an independent state. And several French-Canadian trade unionists I spoke to, men with a long and honourable history of fighting Duplessis, were also unhappy about the Separatists. They feared that an independent nationalist government would necessarily support reactionary but indigenous capitalists, such as Jean-Louis Lévesque, against the unions. I also pointed out to the two students that the authors of a 'Canadian Manifesto' had written: 'Nationalistic policies in Canada or in Quebec are generally advantageous to the middle class, though they run counter to the interests of the majority of the population in general, of the economically weak in particular. . . . '

André and Jacques dismissed the Manifesto as the work of Anglicized French Canadians and claimed a broadening trade union support. As for English-Canadian criticism, 'Well,' André said, 'sure we had Duplessis, but he was backed and kept in power by English-Canadian financial interests.'

This, of course, is an extension of André Laurendeau's theory of *Le Roi Nègre*. Many French-Canadian intellectuals tend to identify with resurgent Africans and the American Negro. They see themselves as Canada's white Negroes.

A well-known literary critic told me, 'It was when I first saw on TV all those Africans in their flowing robes at the UN that I thought: why not us too?'

Looking back on my own boyhood in Montreal, I must say, unfortunately, that we didn't see the French Canadians as down-trodden Negroes; in fact *within that particular context* we saw them more clearly as rednecks ready to fall in behind the first demagogue to come along and spread violence in our own community. Sorry, but that's how it was. *Je me souviens aussi.* And today Montreal's large Jewish community is alarmed about the Separatists. 'They've as much as told us,' I heard again and again, 'that we've got to get off the fence. We're supposed to come down with the French or against them.' Anxiety, I should add, is smeared with a patina of condescension that is shared with the larger and most poorly informed sector of the English-speaking community, which group feels that the French Canadians could no more manage a country than, say, the Egyptians could run the Suez Canal.

Many Jews I spoke to felt the Separatist movement was potentially rich in anti-semitic content. 'If anything starts, who'll get it in the neck? Us. . . . ' But as far as I could make out, from my limited and necessarily stilted conversations with Separatist leaders and students, there is no anti-semitic content to the movement; in fact again and again Separatists ingratiatingly quoted the Zionist analogy to the demand for their own state. All the same, I understand the apprehensions.

Intellectually I can see little to fear, but when I drove out to Ste. Agathe in the Laurentians one day I felt what must be the standard Jewish response to the trouble. The French Canadians are writing on the highway again — true, this time out it was *Québec Libre* and not *A bas les Juifs* — but when the French Canadians are writing on the highway I don't feel so good.

I have other reservations about the *Roi Nègre* theory. While I agree that the role of the English-language press in Montreal during the Duplessis era was, to say the least, disgraceful, the French Canadians, unlike the southern Negro, had the vote; they were not kept from the polls; and so if I was brought up in a notoriously backward and corrupt province it was, no matter how artfully you slice it, a French-Canadian electoral majority that put the government in office and kept it there and kept it there. The English-speaking community may have been more than pleased about it; there is no doubt that they behaved slyly, shabbily, even dishonestly; but the shame, such as it is, is largely French-Canadian. And pride and shame, not economics, is what the French-Canadian problem is about.

André d'Allemagne, one of the leaders of the RIN, told me, 'As a French Canadian, I have no country.' D'Allemagne, who is 34 years old, is a University of Montreal graduate and used to work in the House of Commons in Ottawa as a translator. Like so many other French-Canadian civil servants, some of them in the most senior positions, he has now returned to Quebec Province. Ottawa, for them, is foreign. Today d'Allemagne lives in Montreal, where he works as an advertising copywriter. He told me that the RIN was opposed to violence and would try to get its policies accepted by direct appeal to the electorate. If, however, the RIN were outlawed, they would have to turn to violence. 'Like the *maquis*,' he said.

Quebec, d'Allemagne is convinced, will ultimately opt for independence. If English Canada resists, he told a reporter a month earlier, 'two sunken ships would block the Seaway. We don't want to do it. The Seaway is international. But we will if we have to.'

The RIN, d'Allemagne said, was not precisely socialist, 'but somewhat to the left of centre.' It was for secular control of the schools and one official language in the new state: French. D'Allemagne looks to the next Quebec provincial elections in 1966 as the big test — and he isn't the only one.

Between now and 1966 there will undoubtedly be more and uglier outbreaks of violence in the province. More armouries will be looted and more banks raided. If it is doubtful, given its present level of popular support, that Quebec will actually sue for separation, then it is largely because the movement still lacks a leader of real stature. But there is just such a *potential* leader now active in the province — René Lévesque. For the present, Lévesque is the Minister of Natural Resources in Jean Lesage's cabinet. He is also, as far as most French-Canadian intellectuals are concerned, the conscience and the most advanced thinker in that cabinet and, to the English-speaking community, anathema, the likely wild man. Lévesque, a man of style and brilliance, did not enter politics until 1960. Once elected and in the cabinet his first act was to prod the government into nationalizing all hydro-electric power in Quebec, a measure

225

for which he was abused in English-Canadian newspapers. 'Why attack us now,' he said, 'for doing what a Conservative government of Ontario did in 1905?'

Before standing as a Liberal candidate, Lévesque was widely known and respected throughout Quebec as a television commentator who was outspokenly critical of Duplessis. 'I am not a Separatist,' he says, 'but I admit my thoughts are running in that direction.' He has been described as 'a last-resort Separatist' — i.e., if English Canada stands in the way of Quebec's social and economic development then, but only then, would he bolt the Liberals. He gives Ottawa, it is said, two more years, until 1966, and meanwhile English Canada makes no pretence about despising and fearing him. He is to my mind the most refreshing figure in Canadian politics. Speaking at something called the Empire Club in Toronto recently, Lévesque said, 'Actually, I am a forty-year-old moderate. There are guys behind me who make me feel nervous.' A pity English Canada doesn't realize how badly it needs him.

Alden Nowlan

Alden Nowlan was born in 1933 in Hants County, Nova Scotia. Leaving school in Grade 5, he held various manual jobs such as cutting pulpwood and working for the Nova Scotia Department of Highways. In 1952 he went to Hartland, New Brunswick, to work on the town's weekly newspaper, the Observer; *he later became its editor. In 1967 he went to St. John to work for the* Telegraph-Journal, *and in 1968 he became Writer-in-Residence at the University of New Brunswick.*

Nowlan has published six volumes of poetry; his first was The Rose and the Puritan *(1958).* Bread, Wine, and Salt *(1967) won a Governor-General's Award. He has also published a volume of short stories,* Miracle at Indian River *(1968). His early verse tends to be somewhat conventional in form, but he now uses more conversational rhythms and the idioms of local speech. His poetry is markedly regional, but in a manner quite unlike that of his predecessor, Sir Charles G. D. Roberts, for he characteristically examines the effects of chronic economic deprivation and the lack of spiritual resources on individuals.*

The best regional art, however, suggests universals as well. One way of approaching Nowlan's poetry is as a quest for God, for some principle of permanence; underlying the shabby surface of ordinary life, and sometimes in conflict with its life-denying values, is a strong sense of mythical and supernatural forces. Louis Dudek has pointed out how "The Bull Moose" can be interpreted in archetypal terms; the alder switches and the purple cap of thistles associate the moose with the sacrificial figure of Christ.[1] The divine energy of the moose, however, has its origins in the forest. Thus, when this energy is brought up against the pasture fences which mark the edge of civilization, the townspeople trivialize and eventually destroy it, though not before the moose has, at the last, managed to terrify them out of their wits. The poem suggests some of the main concerns of Nowlan's poetry, and in the opposition which it sets up between society and the life of nature, it invites comparison with a poem like Layton's "The Bull Calf." Another way of interpreting the poem is to see it as a classic example from recent Canadian poetry of Northrop Frye's belief that Canadian culture is a "garrison" culture dedicated to keeping the wilderness at bay.[2]

Footnotes

[1.] Louis Dudek, "A Reading of Two Poems by Alden Nowlan," Fiddlehead, 81 (1969), 55-59.
[2.] Northrop Frye, "Conclusion" to Literary History of Canada, ed., C. F. Klinck, (Toronto: 1965), p. 830; see also D. G. Jones, Butterfly on Rock (Toronto: 1970), p. 34; passim.

God Sour the Milk of the Knacking Wench

God sour the milk of the knacking wench
with razor and twine she comes
to stanchion our blond and bucking bull,
pluck out his lovely plumbs.

God shiver the prunes on her bark of chest,
who capons the prancing young.
Let maggots befoul her alive in bed,
and dibble thorns in her tongue.

The Bull Moose

Down from the purple mist of trees on the mountain,
lurching through forests of white spruce and cedar,
stumbling through tamarack swamps,
came the bull moose
to be stopped at last by a pole-fenced pasture.

Too tired to turn or, perhaps, aware
there was no place left to go, he stood with the cattle.
They, scenting the musk of death, seeing his great head
like the ritual mask of a blood god, moved to the other end
of the field, and waited.

The neighbours heard of it, and by afternoon
cars lined the road. The children teased him
with alder switches and he gazed at them
like an old, tolerant collie. The women asked
if he could have escaped from a Fair.

The oldest man in the parish remembered seeing
a gelded moose yoked with an ox for plowing.
The young men snickered and tried to pour beer
down his throat, while their girl friends took their pictures.

And the bull moose let them stroke his tick-ravaged flanks,
let them pry open his jaws with bottles, let a giggling girl
plant a little purple cap
of thistles on his head.

When the wardens came, everyone agreed it was a shame
to shoot anything so shaggy and cuddlesome.
He looked like the kind of pet
women put to bed with their sons.

So they held their fire. But just as the sun dropped in the river
the bull moose gathered his strength
like a scaffolded king, straightened and lifted his horns
so that even the wardens backed away as they raised their rifles.
When he roared, people ran to their cars. All the young men
leaned on their automobile horns as he toppled.

Canadian Love Song

Your body's a small word with many meanings.
Love. If. Yes. But. Death.
Surely I will love you a little while,
perhaps as long as I have breath.

December is thirteen months long,
July's one afternoon; therefore,
lovers must outwit wool,
learn how to puncture fur.

To my love's bed, to keep her warm,
I'll carry wrapped and heated stones.
That which is comfort to the flesh
is sometimes torture to the bones.

And He Wept Aloud,
so that the Egyptians Heard it

In my grandfather's house
for the first time in years,
houseflies big as bumblebees
playing crazy football
in the skim-milk-coloured windows,

leap-frogging from
the cracked butter saucer
to our tin plates of
rainbow trout and potatoes, catching the bread
on its way to our mouths,
        mounting one another
        on the rough deal table.

It was not so much their filth
as their numbers and persistence and —
oh, admit this, man, there's no point in poetry
if you withhold the truth
once you've come by it —
        their symbolism:
        Baal-Zebub,
        god of the poor and outcast,

that enraged me, made me snatch the old man's
Family Herald, attack them like a maniac,
lay to left and right until the window sills
overflowed with their smashed corpses,
until bits of their wings
stuck to my fingers,
until the room buzzed with their terror. . .

And my grandfather, bewildered and afraid,
came to help me:
        "Never seen a year
          when the flies were so thick"
as though he'd seen them at all before I came!

His voice so old and baffled and pitiful
that I threw my club into the wood box and sat down
        and wanted to beg his forgiveness
as we ate on in silence broken only
by the almost inaudible humming
of the flies rebuilding their world.

Daughter of Zion

Seeing the bloodless lips, the ugly knot of salt-coloured hair,
the shapeless housedress with its grotesque flowers
like those printed on the wallpaper in cheap rooming houses,
sadder than if she wore black,

observing how she tries to avoid the sun,
crossing the street with eyes cast down
as though such a fierce light were an indecent spectacle:
if darkness could be bought like yard goods
she would stuff her shopping bag with shadows,

noting all this and more,
who would look at her twice?
What stranger would suspect that only last night
in a tent by the river
in the aisles between the rows
of rough planks laid on kitchen chairs,
before an altar of orange crates,
in the light of a kerosene lantern,

God Himself, the Old One, seized her in his arms and lifted her up
        and danced with her,
and Christ, with the sawdust clinging to his garments and
        the sweat of the carpenter's shop
on his body and the smell of wine and garlic on his breath,
drew her to his breast and kissed her,

and the Holy Ghost
went into her body and spoke through her mouth
the language that they speak in heaven!

For Jean Vincent D'Abbadie, Baron St. Castin

Take heart, monsieur, four-fifths of this province
is still much as you left it: forest, swamp and barren.
Even now, after three hundred years, your enemies
        fear ambush, huddle by coasts and rivers,
the dark woods at their backs.

        Oh, you'd laugh to see
how old Increase Mather and his ghastly Calvinists
patrol the palisades, how they bury their money
under the floors of their hideous churches
lest you come again in the night
with the red ochre mark of the sun god
on your forehead, you exile from the Pyrenees,
        you baron of France and Navarre,
you squaw man, you Latin poet,
        you war chief of Penobscot
and of Kennebec and of Maliseet!

        At the winter solstice
your enemies cry out in their sleep
and the great trees throw back their heads and shout
        nabujcol!
Take heart, monsieur,
even the premier, even the archbishop,
even the poor gnome-like slaves
at the all-night diner and the service station
will hear you chant
        The Song of Roland
as you cross yourself
and reach for your scalping knife.

Greatness

I would be the greatest poet the world has ever known
if only I could make you see
here on the page
sunlight
a sparrow
three kernels of popcorn
spilled on the snow.

The Mysterious Naked Man

A mysterious naked man has been reported
on Cranston Avenue. The police are performing
the usual ceremonies with coloured lights and sirens.
Almost everyone is outdoors and strangers are conversing
    excitedly
as they do during disasters when their involvement is
    peripheral.
"What did he look like?" the lieutenant is asking.
"I don't know," says the witness. "He was naked."
There is talk of dogs — this is no ordinary case
of indecent exposure, the man has been seen
a dozen times since the milkman spotted him and now
the sky is turning purple and voices
carry a long way and the children
have gone a little crazy as they often do at dusk
and cars are arriving
from other sections of the city.
And the mysterious naked man
is kneeling behind a garbage can or lying on his belly
in somebody's garden
or maybe even hiding in the branches of a tree,
where the wind from the harbour
whips at his naked body,
and by now he's probably done
whatever it was he wanted to do
and wishes he could go to sleep
or die
or take to the air like Superman.

233

The People Who Are Gone

In the days of the people who are gone — that was the way
the old people began their stories, Peter Little Bear says,
and now, well, those story tellers they've gone too.
Until the white man came we had no history
and now we have nothing else.
        But in the old days,
in the days of the people who are gone (he grins because
even though we're friends he still needs
that grin to escape through
should I suddenly betray him
and it's a weapon too that he can use
if I ask more than he's able to give.)
        In the old days, then,
every one of our boys when he came to a certain age
was sent into the woods to talk alone with God.
They fasted, I guess, and I don't think they were allowed
to take any weapons. The men may even have done
things to them before they went. I don't know. But every one
when he got to be, oh, thirteen or fourteen, had to go
into the woods and wait for God to come
down from the sun or out of the trees. So every man
had spoken with God, face to face.
        — And what did he say, I ask, their God I mean?
I don't know, Peter says. Maybe they never told,
maybe he only said hello
in Maliseet. My gosh, if God himself
spoke to you would you remember what he said
and would it matter if you did?
And, gently this time,
Peter grins again.

Leonard Cohen

Leonard Cohen was born in Westmount in 1934. He graduated from McGill University in 1956, and studied briefly at Columbia University's Graduate School. Since then he has lived for various periods in Greece, England, Norway, and the United States, as well as in Montreal. In 1961 he visited Cuba for two months; however, he found himself "the only tourist in Havana," and was not made very welcome by the new regime there.

Since 1956, when Cohen's first volume of poems, Let Us Compare Mythologies, *appeared, he has written three more books of poems and two novels. The second of these,* Beautiful Losers *(1966), one of the most difficult and controversial novels to have been written by a Canadian, reflects Cohen's interest in the magical and mythical qualities of language. This interest is present in his poetry as well. One of his major themes is the death of worn-out mythologies and a quest for something with which to replace them. One of the results of this quest is a fascination with evil which, as Sandra Djwa has observed, allies him with the world of Baudelaire and Genet.[1] Another is a heavy dependence on the language of ritual. These aspects of his poetry are clearly exemplified by his best-known poem, "Suzanne," in which the "half crazy" Suzanne becomes a figure of redemption, complementing Jesus who has been "forsaken"; drowned by conventional wisdom. "She shows you where to look/among the garbage and the flowers"; for Cohen, all experience, ugly as well as beautiful, is worth investigating.*

Many of the poems in his third volume of poetry, Flowers for Hitler *(1964), demonstrate a capacity for satire and a more "public" voice in poetry. But after 1966 Cohen turned much of his attention to the world of popular music and returned to a very private and personal idiom in many of his songs. He has produced three record albums; one result of their success has been that his reputation as a Canadian literary figure has been overshadowed by his growing fame as a hero of the international pop music culture. Whether this turn of his career has been good for the quality of his poetry is open to dispute. Of his songs, he has said that "I don't think too much about the words, because I know that the words are completely empty and any emotion can be poured into them."[2] A poet who does not "think too much about the words" is, after all, not a poet. However, a writer on popular music recently insisted that "Leonard Cohen's fans are word people. . . . For most of them, words have become the first aid station in the preventive detention camp of the feelings.*"[3] *It is, finally, on the words rather than the singing style that analysis of the poetry of his songs must stand or fall.*

Footnotes

[1]. *Sandra Djwa, "Leonard Cohen: Black Romantic,"* Canadian Literature, *34 (Autumn, 1967), 33.*
[2]. *Interview with Leonard Cohen by Michael Harris,* Saturday Night, *84 (June, 1969), 26; see also George Woodcock,* Odysseus Ever Returning *(Toronto: 1970), pp. 109-110.*
[3]. *Jack Hafferkamp, "Ladies and Gents, Leonard Cohen,"* Rolling Stone, *76 (February 4, 1971), 26.*

For Wilf and his House

When young the Christians told me
how we pinned Jesus
like a lovely butterfly against the wood,
and I wept beside paintings of Calvary
at velvet wounds
and delicate twisted feet.

But he could not hang softly long,
your fighters so proud with bugles,
bending flowers with their silver stain,
and when I faced the Ark for counting,
trembling underneath the burning oil,
the meadow of running flesh turned sour
and I kissed away my gentle teachers,
warned my younger brothers.

Among the young and turning-great
of the large nations, innocent
of the spiked wish and the bright crusade,
there I could sing my heathen tears
between the summersaults and chestnut battles,
love the distant saint
who fed his arm to flies,
mourn the crushed ant
and despise the reason of the heel.

Raging and weeping are left on the early road.
Now each in his holy hill
the glittering and hurting days are almost done.
        Then let us compare mythologies.
I have learned my elaborate lie
of soaring crosses and poisoned thorns
and how my fathers nailed him
like a bat against a barn
to greet the autumn and late hungry ravens
as a hollow yellow sign.

Warning

If your neighbour disappears
O if your neighbour disappears
The quiet man who raked his lawn
The girl who always took the sun

Never mention it to your wife
Never say at dinner time
Whatever happened to that man
Who used to rake his lawn

Never say to your daughter
As you're walking home from church
Funny thing about that girl
I haven't seen her for a month

And if your son says to you
Nobody lives next door
They've all gone away
Send him to bed with no supper

Because it can spread, it can spread
And one fine evening coming home
Your wife and daughter and son
They'll have caught the idea and will be gone.

A Kite is a Victim

A kite is a victim you are sure of.
You love it because it pulls
gentle enough to call you master,
strong enough to call you fool;
because it lives
like a desperate trained falcon
in the high sweet air,
and you can always haul it down
to tame it in your drawer.

A kite is a fish you have already caught
in a pool where no fish come,
so you play him carefully and long,
and hope he won't give up,
or the wind die down.

A kite is the last poem you've written,
so you give it to the wind,
but you don't let it go
until someone finds you
something else to do.

A kite is a contract of glory
that must be made with the sun,
so you make friends with the field
the river and the wind,
then you pray the whole cold night before,
under the travelling cordless moon,
to make you worthy and lyric and pure.

You Have the Lovers

You have the lovers,
they are nameless, their histories only for each other,
and you have the room, the bed and the windows.
Pretend it is a ritual.
Unfurl the bed, bury the lovers, blacken the windows,
let them live in that house for a generation or two.
No one dares disturb them.
Visitors in the corridor tip-toe past the long closed door,
they listen for sounds, for a moan, for a song:
nothing is heard, not even breathing.
You know they are not dead,
you can feel the presence of their intense love.
Your children grow up, they leave you,
they have become soldiers and riders.
Your mate dies after a life of service.
Who knows you? Who remembers you?
But in your house a ritual is in progress:
it is not finished: it needs more people.
One day the door is opened to the lover's chamber.
The room has become a dense garden,
full of colours, smells, sounds you have never known.
The bed is smooth as a wafer of sunlight,
in the midst of the garden it stands alone.
In the bed the lovers, slowly and deliberately and silently,
perform the act of love.
Their eyes are closed,
as tightly as if heavy coins of flesh lay on them.
Their lips are bruised with new and old bruises.
Her hair and his beard are hopelessly tangled.
When he puts his mouth against her shoulder
she is uncertain whether her shoulder
has given or received the kiss.
All her flesh is like a mouth.
He carries his fingers along her waist
and feels his own waist caressed.
She holds him closer and his own arms tighten around her.
She kisses the hand beside her mouth.
It is his hand or her hand, it hardly matters,
there are so many more kisses.
You stand beside the bed, weeping with happiness,
you carefully peel away the sheets

239

from the slow-moving bodies.
Your eyes are filled with tears, you barely make out the lovers.
As you undress you sing out, and your voice is magnificent
because now you believe it is the first human voice
heard in that room.
The garments you let fall grow into vines.
You climb into bed and recover the flesh.
You close your eyes and allow them to be sewn shut.
You create an embrace and fall into it.
There is only one moment of pain or doubt
as you wonder how many multitudes are lying beside your body,
but a mouth kisses and a hand soothes the moment away.

For Anne

With Annie gone,
whose eyes to compare
With the morning sun?

Not that I did compare,
But I do compare
Now that she's gone.

The Only Tourist in Havana
Turns his Thoughts Homeward

Come, my brothers,
let us govern Canada,
let us find our serious heads,
let us dump asbestos on the White House,
let us make the French talk English,
    not only here but everywhere,

let us torture the Senate individually
    until they confess,
let us purge the New Party,
let us encourage the dark races
    so they'll be lenient
    when they take over,
let us make the CBC talk English,
let us all lean in one direction
    and float down
    to the coast of Florida,
let us have tourism,
let us flirt with the enemy,
let us smelt pig-iron in our backyards,
let us sell snow
    to under-developed nations,
(Is it true one of our national leaders
    was a Roman Catholic?)
let us terrorize Alaska,
let us unite
    Church and State,
let us not take it lying down,
let us have two Governor Generals
    at the same time,
let us have another official language,
let us determine what it will be,
let us give a Canada Council Fellowship
    to the most original suggestion,
let us teach sex in the home
    to parents,
let us threaten to join the U.S.A.
    and pull out at the last moment,
my brothers, come,
our serious heads are waiting for us somewhere
    like Gladstone bags abandoned
    after a coup d'état,
let us put them on very quickly,
let us maintain a stony silence
    on the St. Lawrence Seaway.

All There is to Know About Adolph Eichmann

```
EYES:. . . . . . . . . . . . . . . . . . . . . . . . . . . . . . . . . . . . Medium
HAIR:. . . . . . . . . . . . . . . . . . . . . . . . . . . . . . . . . . . . Medium
WEIGHT: . . . . . . . . . . . . . . . . . . . . . . . . . . . . . . . . Medium
HEIGHT: . . . . . . . . . . . . . . . . . . . . . . . . . . . . . . . . . Medium
DISTINGUISHING FEATURES:. . . . . . . . . . . . . . . . . . None
NUMBER OF FINGERS: . . . . . . . . . . . . . . . . . . . . . . . Ten
NUMBER OF TOES: . . . . . . . . . . . . . . . . . . . . . . . . Ten
INTELLIGENCE: . . . . . . . . . . . . . . . . . . . . . . . . . . . . Medium
```

What did you expect?

Talons?

Oversize incisors?

Green saliva?

Madness?

Suzanne Takes You Down

Suzanne takes you down
to her place near the river,
you can hear the boats go by
you can stay the night beside her.
And you know that she's half crazy
but that's why you want to be there
and she feeds you tea and oranges
that come all the way from China.
Just when you mean to tell her
that you have no gifts to give her,
she gets you on her wave-length
and she lets the river answer
that you've always been her lover.

242

And you want to travel with her,
you want to travel blind
and you know that she can trust you
because you've touched her perfect body
with your mind

Jesus was a sailor
when he walked upon the water
and he spent a long time watching
from a lonely wooden tower
and when he knew for certain
only drowning men could see him
he said All men will be sailors then
until the sea shall free them,
but he himself was broken
long before the sky would open,
forsaken, almost human,
he sank beneath your wisdom like a stone.
 And you want to travel with him,
 you want to travel blind
 and you think maybe you'll trust him
 because he touched your perfect body
 with his mind.

Suzanne takes your hand
and she leads you to the river,
she is wearing rags and feathers
from Salvation Army counters.
The sun pours down like honey
on our lady of the harbour
as she shows you where to look
among the garbage and the flowers,
there are heroes in the seaweed
there are children in the morning,
they are leaning out for love
they will lean that way forever
while Suzanne she holds the mirror.
 And you want to travel with her
 and you want to travel blind
 and you're sure that she can find you
 because she's touched her perfect body
 with her mind.

The Stranger Song

It's true that all the men you knew were dealers
who said they were through with dealing
Every time you gave them shelter
I know that kind of man
It's hard to hold the hand of anyone
who is reaching for the sky just to surrender.

And then sweeping up the jokers that he left behind
you find he did not leave you very much
not even laughter
Like any dealer he was watching for the card
that is so high and wild
he'll never need to deal another
He was just some Joseph looking for a manger
He was just some Joseph looking for a manger.

And then leaning on your window sill
he'll say one day you caused his will
to weaken with your love and warmth and shelter
And then taking from his wallet
an old schedule of trains, he'll say
I told you when I came I was a stranger
I told you when I came I was a stranger.

But now another stranger seems
to want you to ignore his dreams
as though they were the burden of some other
O you've seen that man before
his golden arm dispatching cards
but now it's rusted from the elbow to the finger
And he wants to trade the game he plays for shelter
Yes he wants to trade the game he plays for shelter.

You hate to watch another tired man
lay down his hand
like he was giving up the holy game of poker
And while he talks his dreams to sleep
you notice there's a highway
that is curling up like smoke above his shoulder
Its curling just like smoke above his shoulder.

244

You tell him to come in sit down
but something makes you turn around
The door is open you can't close your shelter
You try the handle of the road
It opens do not be afraid
It's you my love, you who are the stranger
It is you my love, you who are the stranger.

Well I've been waiting, I was sure
We'd meet between the trains we're waiting for
I think it's time to board another
Please understand, I never had a secret chart
to get me to the heart of this
or any other matter
Well he talks like this
you don't know what he's after
When he speaks like this
you don't know what he's after.

Let's meet tomorrow if you choose
upon the shore, beneath the bridge
that they are building on some endless river
Then he leaves the platform
for the sleeping car that's warm
You realize, he's only advertising one more shelter
And it comes to you, he never was a stranger
And you say, ok the bridge or someplace later.

And then sweeping up the jokers
that he left behind
you find he did not leave you very much
not even laughter
Like any dealer he was watching for the card
that is so high and wild he'll never need
to deal another
He was just some Joseph looking for a manger.
He was just some Joseph looking for a manger.

And leaning on your window sill
he'll say one day you caused his will
to weaken with your love and warmth and shelter
And then taking from his wallet
an old schedule of trains
he'll say, I told you when I came I was a stranger
I told you when I came I was a stranger.

Story of Isaac

The door it opened slowly
My father he came in;
I was nine years old
And he stood so tall above me
His blue eyes they were shining
And his voice was very cold.
He said, I've had a vision
And you know I'm strong and holy,
I must do what I've been told.
So we started up the mountain,
I was running, he was walking,
And his axe was made of gold.

The trees they got much smaller,
The lake a lady's mirror
We stopped to drink some wine;
Then he threw the bottle over
It broke a minute later
And he put his hand on mine.
I thought I saw an eagle
But it might have been a vulture
I never could decide.
Then my father built an altar
He looked once behind his shoulder,
He knew I would not hide.

You who build these altars now
To sacrifice these children,
You must not do it any more.
A scheme is not a vision
And you never have been tempted
By a demon or a god.
You who stand above them now
Your hatchets blunt and bloody,
You were not there before
When I lay upon a mountain
and my father's hand was trembling
With the beauty of the Word.

And if you call me brother now
Forgive me if I inquire
Just according to whose plan?
When it all comes down to dust,
I will kill you if I must
I will help you if I can.
When it all comes down to dust,
I will help you if I must,
I will kill you if I can;
Have mercy on our uniform,
Man of peace or man of war.
The peacock spreads his fan.

John Newlove

John Newlove was born in Regina in 1938. He grew up in various small towns in eastern Saskatchewan, and briefly attended the University of Saskatchewan, Saskatoon. He has worked in diverse occupations, as a teacher, social worker, news editor, and casual labourer. In 1960 he moved to Vancouver, a city which was then becoming an important poetry centre. He now works for a publishing company in Toronto.

Newlove's style exhibits a strong distrust of rhetoric and conventional form. "His is a poetry," Desmond Pacey remarks, "so restrained, so low-keyed, so apparently artless as to make Raymond Souster seem a veritable show-off."[1] This restraint is apparent sometimes in stark Imagist poems, and sometimes in longer poems where the tone is more conversational. "I am too tense,/decline to dance/verbally," he says in "The Flower," a poem which is important for what it suggests about his poetic practice.

A characteristic persona in his poetry is the hitchhiker, uprooted, unencumbered by baggage, without a clearly defined destination or any assurance that he will arrive at one. The Prairies remain an important influence in his work; he often conveys a sense of the individual's isolation in a bleak and incomprehensible environment. But the "desolate country/a long way between fires" is internal as well as external. Nothing is certain for Newlove; personal relationships, even personality itself, are impermanent.

Newlove, however, is not one of Birney's Canadians, haunted only by a lack of ghosts. In "By the Church Wall" the fear is only partly that of knowing he is alone; he is also haunted by an ancient dread arising from the necessity of confronting his own past. In the long poem, "The Pride," this sense of a personal past is linked with an almost forgotten aboriginal past, violent and mysterious, yet waiting only to be repossessed. "They become our true forbears," he concludes of the Indians, and until we understand this we will all be hitchhikers, haunted by a sense of not really belonging to the land.

Footnotes

[1]. *Desmond Pacey, Review of "The Cave," Canadian Forum, 50 (November-December, 1970), 309.*

Kamsack

Plump eastern saskatchewan river town,
where even in depression it's said the wheat
went thirty bushels and was full-bodied,
the river laying good black dirt each year:
but I found it arid, as young men will.

Vancouver

Give me back the green fat
fields of the place where I learned
to be human, and the flooding rivers —
take away these dolorous mountains,
this ever-watching, garbage-soaked ocean.

By the Church Wall

The mocking faces appear in the churchyard,
appear as I curl on the hard ground
trying to sleep — trying to sleep
as the voices call me, asking why
must I always be frightened and dreaming?

I have travelled this road many times,
though not in this place, tired
in the bones and the long blistered feet,
beneath a black mass of flat clouds,
dry in a damned and useless land.

Frogs croak hollowly, the loons cry
their thin bewildered song on a far-off lake,
the wind rises and the wet grass waves;
by the wall of the white rural church
I count a thousand to go to sleep.

But it will not happen. The faces
float before me, bloated and grinning,
succubus and incubus, a child
screams in a house across the road;
I turn and turn in my fear.

There is nothing to hurt me here,
and I know it, but an ancient dread
clenches my belly and fluttering heart,
and in the cold wet grass I count
what may happen and what has.

All the mistakes and desires are here,
old nameless shame for my lies,
and the boy's terrible wish to be good and
not to be alone, not to be alone,
to be loved, and to love.

I remember a letter a friend sent,
trivial and gossiping, quite plain,
of no consequence to him, casually typed
and then signed easily by hand,
All our love, and wish I could say that.

But I lie alone in the shadowed grass,
fond only, incapable of love or truth,
caught in all I have done, afraid
and unable to escape, formulating
one more ruinous way to safety.

The Hitchhiker

On that black highway,
where are you going? —

It is in Alberta
among the trees

where the road sweeps
left and right

in great concrete arcs
at the famous resort —

there you stood on
the road in the wind

the cold wind going
through you and you

going through the country
to no end, only

to turn again at one sea
and begin it again,

feeling safe with strangers
in a moving car.

The Pride

I

The image/the pawnees
in their earth-lodge villages,
the clear image
of teton sioux, wild
fickle people the chronicler says,

the crazy dogs, men
tethered with leather dog-thongs
to a stake, fighting until dead,

image: arikaras
with traded spanish sabre-blades
mounted on the long
heavy buffalo lances,
riding the sioux
down, the centaurs, the horsemen
scouring the level plains
in war or hunt
until smallpox got them,
4,000 warriors.

image — of a desolate country,
a long way between fires,
unfound lakes, mirages, cold rocks,
and lone men going through it,
cree with good guns
creating terror in athabaska
among the inhabitants, frightened
stone-age people, "so that
they fled at the mere sight
of a strange smoke miles away."

II

This western country crammed
with the ghosts of indians,
haunting the coastal stones and shores,
the forested pacific islands,
mountains, hills and plains:

beside the ocean ethlinga,
man in the moon, empties
his bucket, on
a sigh from Spirit
of the Wind ethlinga
empties his bucket, refreshing
the earth, and it rains
on the white cities;

that black joker, broken-
jawed raven, most prominent
among haida and tsimshyan tribes,
is in the kwakiutl
dance masks too —
it was he who brought fire,
food and water to man,
the trickster;

and thunderbird hilunga,
little thought of
by haida for lack of thunderstorms
in their district, goes
by many names, exquisite disguises
carved in the painted wood,

he is nootka tootooch, the wings
causing thunder and the tongue
or flashing eyes engendering
rabid white lightning,
whose food was whales,

called kwunusela by the kwakiutl,
it was he who laid down the house-logs
for the people at Place
Where Kwunusela Alighted:

in full force and virtue
and terror of the law, eagle —
he is authority, the sun
assumed his form once,
the sun which used to be
a flicker's egg, success-
fully transformed;

and malevolence comes to the land,
the wild woman of the woods;
grinning, she wears
a hummingbird in her hair,
d'sonoqua, the furious one —

they are all ready
to be found, the legends
and the people, or
all their ghosts and memories,
whatever is strong enough
to be remembered.

III

But what image, bewildered
son of all men
under the hot sun,
do you worship,
what completeness
do you hope to have
from these tales,
a half-understood massiveness, mirage,
in men's minds — what
is your purpose;

254

with what force
will you proceed
along a line
neither straight nor short,
whose future
you cannot know
or result foretell,
whose meaning is still
obscured as the incidents
occur and accumulate?

IV

The country moves on:
there are orchards in the interior,
the mountain passes
are broken, the foothills
covered with cattle and fences,
and the fading hills covered;
but the plains are bare,
not barren, easy
for me to love their people
for me to love their people
without selection.

V

In 1787, the old cree saukemappee,
aged 75 or thereabout, speaking then
of things that had happened when he was 16,
just a man, told david thompson,
of the raid the shoshonis,
the snakes, had made on the westward-
reaching piegan, of their war-parties
sometimes sent 10 days journey to enemy camps,
the men all afoot in battle array for
the encounter, crouching
behind their giant shields;

the piegan armed with guns
drove these snakes out of the plains,
where they had been settled since living
memory (though nothing is remembered
beyond a grandfather's time),
to the west of the rockies;

these people moved without rest,
backward and forward with the wind,
the seasons, the game, great herds,
in hunger and abundance —

in summer and in the bloody fall
they gathered on the killing grounds,
fat and shining with fat, amused
with the luxuries of war and death,

relieved from the steam of knowledge,
consoled by the stream of blood
and steam rising from the fresh hides
and tired horses, wheeling in their pride
on the sweating horses, their pride.

VI

Those are all stories;
the pride, the grand poem
of our land, of the earth itself,
will come, welcome, and
sought for, and found,
in a line of running verse,
sweating, our pride;

we seize on
what has happened before,
one line only
will be enough,

a single line and
then the sunlit brilliant image suddenly floods us

256

with understanding, shocks our
attentions, and all desire
stops, stands alone;

we stand alone,
we are no longer lonely
but have roots,
and the rooted words
recur in the mind, mirror, so that
we dwell on nothing else, in nothing else,
touched, repeating them,
at home freely
at last, in amazement;

"the unyielding phrase
in tune with the epoch,"
the thing made up
of our desires,
not of its words, not only
of them, but of something else,
as well, that which we desire
so ardently, that which
will not come when
it is summoned alone,
but grows in us
and idles about and hides
until the moment is due —

the knowledge of
our origins, and where
we are in truth,
whose land this is
and is to be.

VII

The unyielding phrase:
when the moment is due, then
it springs upon us
out of our own mouths,
unconsidered, overwhelming
in its knowledge, complete —

not this handful
of fragments, as the indians
are not composed of
the romantic stories
about them, or of the stories
they tell only, but
still ride the soil
in us, dry bones a part
of the dust in our eyes,
needed and troubling
in the glare, in
our breath, in our
ears, in our mouths,
in our bodies entire, in our minds, until at
last we become them

in our desires, our desires,
mirages, mirrors, that are theirs, hard-
riding desires, and they
become our true forbears, moulded
by the same wind or rain,
and in this land we
are their people, come
back to life.

The Flower

I am too tense,
decline to danse
verbally. The flower
is not in its colour,
but in the seed.

Margaret Atwood

Margaret Atwood was born in Ottawa in 1939, and grew up in towns in northern Quebec and Ontario. She graduated from Victoria College, University of Toronto, in 1961 with a degree in Honours English; subsequently she did graduate work at Radcliffe College in Cambridge, Massachusetts. She has taught at the University of British Columbia, and at Sir George Williams University; she recently visited England with her husband, James Polk, where she wrote full-time, and is at present Writer-in-Residence at York University, Toronto. She published several small pamphlets of poetry in the early nineteen-sixties; since 1966 she has produced five volumes of poetry and one novel, The Edible Woman *(1969), which is being made into a film. This novel and her volume of poems* The Circle Game *(1966) both won Governor-General's Awards.*

The poems "Further Arrivals," "The Two Fires," and "Thoughts from Underground" are from The Journals of Susanna Moodie *(1970), a collection of poems inspired by the writings of Mrs. Moodie about pioneer life in Canada. In an afterword to this collection, Miss Atwood makes this comment:*

> *If the national mental illness of the United States is megalomania, that of Canada is paranoid schizophrenia. Mrs. Moodie is divided down the middle: she praises the landscape but accuses it of destroying her; she dislikes the people already in Canada but finds in the people her only refuge from the land itself; she preaches progress and the march of civilization while brooding elegiacally upon the destruction of the wilderness. . . . Perhaps that is the way we still live. We are all immigrants to this place even if we were born here: the country is too big for anyone to inhabit completely, and in the parts unknown to us we move in fear, exiles and invaders.*[1]

This tells us something about Miss Atwood's view of Mrs. Moodie and of Canada, and about the origin of these poems. It also suggests something about her poetry as a whole. The imaginative landscape of her poems is a violent, frightening, and irrational one where conventional guides and compasses are useless. The best that agents of order and civilization such as Mrs. Moodie or "The City Planners" can do is to "neatly/sidestep hysteria." The refusal to sidestep hysteria, the willingness to confront it head-on, involves her in questions of perception; the individual, in a world where nothing is fixed, is faced with the issue of deciding "whether the wilderness is/real or not" and what its relationship is to himself. The rejection of conventional formulations of reality and the attempt to render the difficulties of perception lead to an imagery which is often startling and surrealistic. Her poetic lines, usually short, seem to be divided quite arbitrarily, and this arbitrariness extends to her use of punctuation. The effect, however, is constantly to remind the reader that this is a world where all his expectations have to be redirected.

Footnotes

[1.] *Margaret Atwood*, The Journals of Susanna Moodie *(Toronto: 1970), p. 62.*

This is a Photograph of Me

It was taken some time ago.
At first it seems to be
a smeared
print: blurred lines and grey flecks
blended with the paper;

then, as you scan
it, you see in the left-hand corner
a thing that is like a branch: part of a tree
(balsam or spruce) emerging
and, to the right, halfway up
what ought to be a gentle
slope, a small frame house.

In the background there is a lake,
and beyond that, some low hills.

(The photograph was taken
the day after I drowned.

I am in the lake, in the centre
of the picture, just under the surface.

It is difficult to say where
precisely, or to say
how large or small I am:
the effect of water
on light is a distortion

but if you look long enough,
eventually
you will be able to see me.)

The City Planners

Cruising these residential Sunday
streets in dry August sunlight:
what offends us is
the sanities:
the houses in pedantic rows, the planted
sanitary trees, assert
levelness of surface like a rebuke
to the dent in our car door.
No shouting here, or
shatter of glass; nothing more abrupt
than the rational whine of a power mower
cutting a straight swath in the discouraged grass.

But though the driveways neatly
sidestep hysteria
by being even, the roofs all display
the same slant of avoidance to the hot sky,
certain things;
the smell of spilled oil a faint
sickness lingering in the garages,
a splash of paint on brick surprising as a bruise,
a plastic hose poised in a vicious
coil; even the too-fixed stare of the wide windows

give momentary access to
the landscape behind or under
the future cracks in the plaster

when the houses, capsized, will slide
obliquely into the clay seas, gradual as glaciers
that right now nobody notices.

That is where the City Planners
with the insane faces of political conspirators
are scattered over unsurveyed
territories, concealed from each other,
each in his own private blizzard;

guessing directions, they sketch
transitory lines rigid as wooden borders
on a wall in the white vanishing air

tracing the panic of suburb
order in a bland madness of snows.

Provisions

What should we have taken
with us? We never could decide
on that; or what to wear,
or at what time of
year we should make this journey

so here we are, in thin
raincoats and rubber boots

on the disastrous ice, the wind rising,

nothing in our pockets

but a pencil stub, two oranges
four toronto streetcar tickets

and an elastic band, holding a bundle
of small white filing-cards
printed with important facts.

The Animals in that Country

In that country the animals
have the faces of people:

the ceremonial
cats possessing the streets

the fox run
politely to earth, the huntsmen
standing around him, fixed
in their tapestry of manners

the bull, embroidered
with blood and given
an elegant death, trumpets, his name
stamped on him, heraldic brand
because

(when he rolled
on the sand, sword in his heart, the teeth
in his blue mouth were human)

he is really a man

even the wolves, holding resonant
conversations in their
forests thickened with legend.

> In this country the animals
> have the faces of
> animals.
>
> Their eyes
> flash once in car headlights
> and are gone.
>
> Their deaths are not elegant.
>
> They have the faces of
> no-one.

Backdrop Addresses Cowboy

Starspangled cowboy
sauntering out of the almost-
silly West, on your face
a porcelain grin,
tugging a papier-mâché cactus
on wheels behind you with a string,

you are innocent as a bathtub
full of bullets.

Your righteous eyes, your laconic
trigger-fingers
people the streets with villains:
as you move, the air in front of you
blossoms with targets

and you leave behind you a heroic
trail of desolation:
beer bottles
slaughtered by the side
of the road, bird-
skulls bleaching in the sunset.

I ought to be watching
from behind a cliff or a cardboard storefront
when the shooting starts, hands clasped
in admiration,

but I am elsewhere.

Then what about me

what about the I
confronting you on that border
you are always trying to cross?

I am the horizon
you ride towards, the thing you can never lasso

I am also what surrounds you:
my brain
scattered with your
tincans, bones, empty shells,
the litter of your invasions.

I am the space you desecrate
as you pass through.

Further Arrivals

After we had crossed the long illness
that was the ocean, we sailed up-river

On the first island
the immigrants threw off their clothes
and danced like sandflies

We left behind one by one
the cities rotting with cholera,
one by one our civilized
distinctions

and entered a large darkness.

It was our own
ignorance we entered.

I have not come out yet

My brain gropes nervous
tentacles in the night, sends out
fears hairy as bears,
demands lamps; or waiting

for my shadowy husband, hears
malice in the trees' whispers.

I need wolf's eyes to see
the truth.

I refuse to look in a mirror.

Whether the wilderness is
real or not
depends on who lives there.

The Two Fires

One, the summer fire
outside: the trees melting, returning
to their first red elements
on all sides, cutting me off
from escape or the saving
lake

I sat in the house, raised up
between that shapeless raging
and my sleeping children
a charm: concentrate on
form, geometry, the human
architecture of the house, square
closed doors, proved roofbeams,
the logic of windows

(the children could not be wakened:
in their calm dreaming
the trees were straight and still
had branches and were green)

The other, the winter
fire inside: the protective roof
shrivelling overhead, the rafters
incandescent, all those corners

and straight lines flaming, the carefully-
made structure
prisoning us in a cage of blazing
bars
    the children
were awake and crying;

I wrapped them, carried them
outside into the snow.
Then I tried to rescue
what was left of their scorched dream
about the house: blankets,
warm clothes, the singed furniture
of safety cast away with them
in a white chaos

Two fires in-
formed me,

(each refuge fails
us; each danger
becomes a haven)

left charred marks
now around which I
try to grow

Thoughts from Underground

When I first reached this country
I hated it
and I hated it more each year:

in summer the light a
violent blur, the heat
thick as a swamp,
the green things fiercely
shoving themselves upwards, the
eyelids bitten by insects

In winter our teeth were brittle
with cold. We fed on squirrels.
At night the house cracked.
In the mornings, we thawed
the bad bread over the stove.

Then we were made successful
and I felt I ought to love
this country.
            I said I loved it
and my mind saw double.

I began to forget myself
in the middle
of sentences. Events
were split apart

I fought. I constructed
desperate paragraphs of praise, everyone
ought to love it because

and set them up at intervals

        due to natural resources, native industry, superior
        penitentiaries
        we will all be rich and powerful

268

flat as highway billboards

who can doubt it, look how
fast Belleville is growing

(though it is still no place for an english gentleman)

Two Gardens

What stands in this garden
is there because I measured, placed, reached
down into the soil and pulled out
stems, leaves, gradually:
                          fabric-
textured zinnias; asters
the colours of chintz; thick
pot-shaped marigolds, the
sunflowers brilliant as
imitations

but outside the string borders

other things raise
themselves, brief
motions at the path's edge

                    the bonewhite
plants that grow
without sunlight, flickering
in the evening forest

certain ferns: fungi
like buried feet
                the blue-
flags, ice flames
reflected in the bay
that melt when the
sun hits noon

these have their roots
in another land

they are mist

if you touch them, your
eyes go through them.

you fit into me
like a hook into an eye

a fish hook
an open eye

b p Nichol

Barry Philip Nichol was born in Vancouver in 1944; he spent his youth in various cities in Western Canada and attended the University of British Columbia. Since then he has worked at various jobs, including that of a library assistant at the University of Toronto.

"1335 Comox Avenue" suggests that he is capable of working in the area of conventional verse, but it is as an experimental "concrete" poet that he has achieved his reputation and a distinctive voice in Canadian poetry. His closest rival in the area of experimental poetry is Vancouver's Bill Bissett. Nichol co-edits Ganglia *and* Gronk, *little magazines devoted to concrete poetry, and has published several volumes of his own. One of the most interesting of these is* Journeyings and the Returns *(1967), a box containing a conventionally bound book of poems, a plastic record of sounds, coloured cardboard cutouts, cards, and little booklets containing concrete poems. The box therefore contains a whole range of sense experience and demands the reader's involvement. Grasping the contents of the box is not only a mental activity; it is also an immediate auditory, tactile, and visual experience.*

In 1970 Nichol won a Governor-General's Award and was the subject of a short film by Michael Ondaatje, Sons of Captain Poetry. *In the same year he edited* The Cosmic Chef: An Evening of Concrete, *an anthology of Canadian concrete poems. He says of this that "everything presented here comes from that point where language and/or the image blur together into the inbetween & become concrete objects to be understood as such."[1] While the variety of concrete poetry makes a single definition of the term difficult, this statement of Nichol's provides an approach to it; concrete poetry seeks a new relationship between the poetic image and language by exploiting the sensory and spatial qualities of print. Thus, "love" offers an example of a poem which, as Mike Doyle points out, rejects the linearity of print and can be read from many different directions toward a common centre.[2] The untitled arrangement of n's is an even purer example of a concentration on the visual rather than on the mentally apprehensible meaning of language. On the other hand, "Inquiry of Ministry/ Demande de Renseignements au Gouvernement," which was originally published in a book about the Canadian economy,* Gordon to Watkins to You *(1970), indicates that concrete poetry may also be turned to commentary on a public issue — the takeover of Canadian companies by foreign-dominated concerns — without losing its playful quality.*

Footnotes

[1]. *b p Nichol, "some afterwords,"* The Cosmic Chef *(Ottawa: 1970), p. 78.*
[2]. *Mike Doyle, "Notes on Concrete Poetry,"* Canadian Literature, *46 (Autumn, 1970), 92.*

turnips are
inturps are
urnspit are
rustpin are
stunrip are
piturns are
ritpuns are
punstir are
nutrips are
suntrip are
untrips are
spinrut are
runspit are
pitnurs are
runtsip are
puntsir are
turnsip are
tipruns are
turpsin are

dear deanna

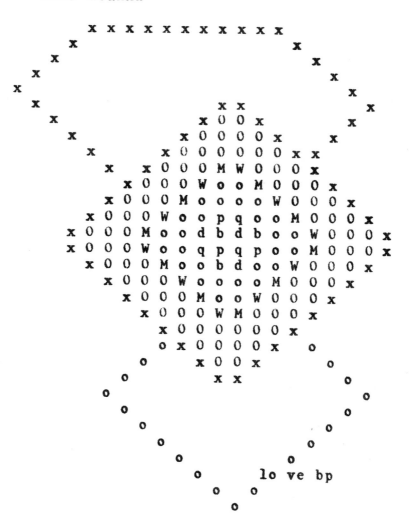

lo ve bp

1335 Comox Avenue (for dave & barb)

in fall
we lose ourselves
in new rooms, gaze
from windows grown old
in this season

we choose
new beds
to love in, cover our bodies
in confusions
of tears and memories
of all
that should be left
behind

bury our faces in each other
tasting flesh in mouth
gathering warmth
possessing each other
as a way of loving

we are too near the sea
we hear the gulls cry
cars pass
the horns of ships
and cry
to see the moss grown

throw windows open
to night   to kneel   to pray
hands on each other
pressing body into body
— some sort of liturgy

hear the sea   the bells
the sound of people passing
voices drifting up
and cold winds come
to chill our naked hearts

love is some sort of fire
come to warm us
to fill our aching bodies
all eternity in these motions
flowing into each other
in despair — the room —
one narrow world
that might be anywhere

INQUIRY OF MINISTRY
DEMANDE DE RENSEIGNEMENTS AU GOUVERNEMENT

prepare 10 copies in english and french marked "text" and "translation"
preparer 10 copies an englais et francais inscrivant "texte" et "traduc
tion"

QUESTION NO 468

by - de Mr Saltsman

ORDER OF THE DAY NO 16

november 13 1969

page viii

SUBJECT -SUJET

FOREIGN TAKEOVER OF CANADIAN BUSINESSES RECORDED BY THE COMBINES INVES
TIGATION BRANCH

              reply by the ministe of consumer and corporate affai
rs   reponse par le ministre de la consommation et des corporations
signature   minister or parliamentary secretary   ministre ou secretai
re parlementaire

275

QUESTION   FOR THE YEARS 1963 1964 1965 1966 1967 1968 AND 1969
WHAT AND HOW MANY FOREIGN TAKEOVERS OF CANADIAN BUSINESSES HAVE
BEEN RECORDED BY THE COMBINES INVESTIGATION BRANCH OF THE DEPARTMENT
OF CONSUMER AND CORPORATE AFFAIRS   REPLY-REPONSE   FOREIGN
ACQUISITIONS OF CANADIAN BUSINESSES   RECORDED ANNUALLY BY THE OFFICE
OF THE DIRECTOR OF INVESTIGATION AND RESEARCH UNDER THE COMBINES
INVESTIGATION ACT FROM PRESS AND OTHER PUBLIC REPORTS CONCERNING
ONLY INDUSTRIES UNDER THE JURISDICTION OF THE ACT (AND EXCLUDING
FIRMS WHOSE ACTIVITIES DO NOT FALL WITHIN THE SCOPE OF THE ACT)
WERE AS FOLLOWS   1963 - 35   1964 - 87   1965 - 74   1966 - 74
1967 - 79   1968 - 155   1969 - 102   THE FOREIGN OWNED OR
CONTROLLED ACQUIRING COMPANY AND THE CANADIAN OWNED ACQUIRED
COMPANY RECORDED IN EACH INSTANCE ARE IDENTIFIED ON ATTACHED
SCHEDULES A TO G INCLUSIVE

SCHEDULE A 1963

foreign owned or controlled acquiring   CANADIAN OWNED ACQUIRED

british petroleum co ltd
                                            PARIS PETROLEUM LTD
  canada crushed and cut stone ltd (steetley co ltd)
                                   MILLS STEEL PRODUCTS LTD

   canadian chemical co
                                   CANADIAN CELANESE LTD

    anlage bank zurich
                                   CHARTER OIL CO LTD

     chrysler corporation
                             THERM-O-RITE PRODUCTS LTD

      w k davidson & co
                                   ADANAC SUPPLIES LTD

       dow chemical of canada ltd
                             RICHMOND PLASTICS LTD

        eddy match co ltd
                             GRANT INDUSTRIES LTD

         eddy industrial products co
                                   EDDY MATCH CO LTD

          charles e frosst & co
                             MOWATT & MOORE LTD

           hickok electrical instrument co
                        STARK ELECTRONIC INSTRUMENTS LTD
            kinnear manufacturing co of canada
                        PRESTON STEEL PRODUCTS LTD
             montreal locomotive works ltd
                        W K DAVIDSON AND CO LTD
              national dairy products corp
                        LAUREL DAIRY PRODUCTS CO LTD
               occidental petroleum corp
           JEFFERSON LAKE PETROCHEMICALS OF CANADA LTD
                the odeon theatres (canada) limited
                        DON MILLS THEATRE
                   ODEON DUFFERIN DRIVE-IN
                        NORTH BAY DRIVE-IN
                   NEW WESTMINSTER DRIVE-IN

                              276

```
                    pacific petroleums ltd (phillips petroleum u s)
                         BAILEY SELBURN OIL & GAS LTD
                      paramount international films inc
                      ASSOCIATED BROADCASTING CORPORATION
                      $paramount international films inc$
                      $$HAMILTON CO-AXIAL (1958) LTD3$
                    $$$paramount international films inc$$$
                      $$$$TWIN CITY BROADCASTING LTD$$$$
                 $$$$$rio algom mines limited (rio tinto co ltd$$$$$
                      $$$$$$ATLAS STEELS LTD$$$$$$
                      $$$$$$$rockwell-standard corp$$$$$$$
                 $$$$$$$$$ONTARIO STEEL PRODUCTS LTD$$$$$$$$$
                 $$$$$$$$$sir isaac pitman (canada) ltd$$$$$$$$$
              $$$$$$$$$$COPP-CLARK PUBLISHING CO LTD$$$$$$$$$$
                 $$$$$$$$$$$w h smith and son ltd$$$$$$$$$$$
                    $$$$$$$$$$$$BURNILL'S LTD$$$$$$$$$$$$$
           $societe routiere colas (societe parisienne raveau cartier and etc$
                      $$$$$$$$$$$$$$FABI LTD$$$$$$$$$$$$$$
            $$$$$$$$$$$$$$$$$spartan air services ltd$$$$$$$$$$$$$$$$$
             $$$$$$$$$$$$$$$$$$MERIDIAN AIRMAPS LTD$$$$$$$$$$$$$$$$$$
           $$$$$$$$$$$$$$$$$$$$tinnerman products inc$$$$$$$$$$$$$$$$$$$$
           $$$$$$$$$$$$$$$$$$$$$DOMINION FASTENERS LTD$$$$$$$$$$$$$$$$$$$$$
           $$$$$$$$$$$$$$$$$$$$$union carbide canada ltd$$$$$$$$$$$$$$$$$$$$$$
           $$$$$$$$$$$$$$$$$$$$$$POLYETHELENE BAG MFG CO LTD$$$$$$$$$$$$$$$$$$$$$$$
           $$$$$$$$$$$$$$$$$$$$$$$western decalta petroleum ltd$$$$$$$$$$$$$$$$$$$$$$
           $$$$$$$$$$$$$$$$$$$$$$$NEW BRUNSWICK OILFIELDS LTD$$$$$$$$$$$$$$$$$$$$$$
           $$$$$$$$$$$$$$$$$$$$$$$western decalta petroleum ltd$$$$$$$$$$$$$$$$$$$$$
           $$$$$$$$$$$$$$$$$$$$$$$$SOUTH BRAZEAU PETROLEUMS LTD$$$$$$$$$$$$$$$$$$$
           $$$$$$$$$$$$$$$$$$$$$$$$$witco chemical co$$$$$$$$$$$$$$$$$$$$$$$$$
           $$$$$$$$$$$$$$$$$$$$$$$$$$DELTA CHEMICALS LTD$$$$$$$$$$$$$$$$$$$$$$$$$$
           $$$$$$$$$$$$$$$$$$$$$$$$$$$$$$$$$$$$$$$$$$$$$$$$$$$$$$$$$$$$$$$$$$$$$$$
           $$$$$$$$$$$$$$$$$$$$$$$$$$$$$$$$$SCHEDULE B 1964$$$$$$$$$$$$$$$$$$$$$$$$
           $$$$$$$$$$$$$$$$$$$$$$$$$$$$$$$$$$$$$$$$$$$$$$$$$$$$$$$$$$$$$$$$$$$$$$$$
           $$$$$$$$$$$$$$$$$$$$$$$$$$$$$$$$$$ametek inc$$$$$$$$$$$$$$$$$$$$$$$$$$$$
           $$$$$$$$$$$$$$$$$$$$$$$$$$$$$$$$$$$$PANTEX MFG CO (CANADA) LTD$$$$$$$$$$$
           $$$$$$$$$$$$$$$$$$$$$$$$$$$$$$$$$$$$$amphenol-borg electronics corp$$$$
           $$$$$$$$$$$$$$$$$$$$$$$$$$$$$$$$$$$$$$AMPHENOL CANADA LTD$$$$$$$$$$$$$$$$$
           $$$$$$$$$$$$$$$$$$$$$$$$$$$$$$$$$$$$$$anglo-canadian pulp &paper mills
           $$$$$$$$$$$$$$$$$$$$$$$$$$$$$$$$$$$$$$$ACME-MOLSON GROUP$$$$$$$$$$$$$$$
           $$$$$$$$$$$$$$$$$$$$$$$$$$$$$$$$$$$$$$$ACME PAPER PRODUCTS CO LTD$$$$
           $$$$$$$$$$$$$$$$$$$$$$$$$$$$$$$$$$$$$$$$ACME PAPER PRODUCTS INC$$$$$$$
           $$$$$$$$$$$$$$$$$$$$$$$$$$$$$$$$$$$$$$$$$INTER PROVINCIAL BAG LTD$$$$$
           $$$$$$$$$$$$$$$$$$$$$$$$$$$$$$$$$$$$$$$$$$MOLSON BAG & PAPER CO LTD$$
           $$$$$$$$$$$$$$$$$$$$$$$$$$$$$$$$$$$$$$$$$$$SUPERIOR GUMMED & WAXED PA
           $$$$$$$$$$$$$$$$$$$$$$$$$$$$$$$$$$$$$$$$$$$$SEABROOK-HARRIS PAPER PRO
           3$$$$$$$$$$$$$$$$$$$$$$$$$$$$$$$$$$$$$$$$$$$$STERLING PAPER PRODUCTS
           $$$$$$$$$$$$$$$$$$$$$$$$$$$$$$$$$$$$$$$$$$$$$anglo-canadian pulp & p
           $$$$$$$$$$$$$$$$$$$$$$$$$$$$$$$$$$$$$$$$$$$$$TEXTILE & PAPER WASTE
           $$$$$$$$$$$$$$$$$$$$$$$$$$$$$$$$$$$$$$$$$$$$$appleton wire works i
           $$$$$$$$$$$$$$$$$$$$$$$$$$$$$$$$$$$$$$$$$$$$$$CAPITAL WIRE CLOTH L
           $$$$$$$$$$$$$$$$$$$$$$$$$$$$$$$$$$$$$$$$$$$$$$august-thyssen huet
           $$$$$$$$$$$$$$$$$$$$$$$$$$$$$$$$$$$$$$$$$$$$$$$GREENING INDUSTRIE
           $$$$$$$$$$$$$$$$$$$$$$$$$$$$$$$$$$$$$$$$$$$$$$$avco corporation$
```

$$$DELTA ACCEPTANCE
$$$british aeroplan
$$$ASHTON MFG CO L
$$$british petrol
$$$GOBLES GAS &
$$$british petr
$$$TIDEWATER C
$$$b p canada
$$$CITY SERV
$$$californ
$$$BOESE F
$$$cameri
$$$McALE
$$$cana
$$$DRU
$$$ca
$$$N
$$$

$$$$$$$$$$$$$$$$$$$$$ $$$$$$$$$$$$$$$$$$$$$
$$$$$$$$$$$$$$$$$$$$$ $$$$$$$$$$$$$$$$$$$$$
$$$$$$$$$$$$$$$$$$$$$ $$$$$$$$$$$$$$$$$$$$$
$$$$$$$$$$$$$$$$$$$$$ $$ $$$$$$$$$$$$$$$$$$$$$
$$$$$$$$$$$$$$$$$$$$$ $$$$$$$$ $$$$$$$$$$$$$$$$$$$$$
$$$$$$$$$$$$$$$$$$$$$ $$$$$$$ $$$$$$$$$$$$$$$$$$$$$
$$$$$$$$$$$$$$$$$$$$$ $$ $$$$$$$$ $$$ $$$$$$$$$$$$$$$$$$$$$
$$$$$$$$$$$$$$$$$$$$$ $$$$$$$$$$$$$$$$$$$$ $$$$$$$$$$$$$$$$$$$$$
$$$$$$$$$$$$$$$$$$$$$ $$$$$$$$$$$$$$$$$$$$$ $$$$$$$$$$$$$$$$$$$$$
$$$$$$$$$$$$$$$$$$$$$ $$$$$ $$ $$$$$$ $$$$$$$$$$$$$$$$$$$$$
$$$$$$$$$$$$$$$$$$$$$ $$ $$$$$$$$$$$$$$$$$$$$$
$$$$$$$$$$$$$$$$$$$$$ $ $$$$$$$$$$$$$$$$$$$$$
$$$$$$$$$$$$$$$$$$$$$ $$$$$$$$$$$$$$$$$$$$$
$$$$$$$$$$$$$$$$$$$$$? $$$$$$$$$$$$$$$$$$$$$
$$$$$$$$$$$$$$$$$$$$$ $$$$$$$$$$$$$$$$$$$$$
$$$$$$$$$$$$$$$$$$$$$ $$$$$$$$$$$$$$$$$$$$$
$$$
$$$
$$$
$$$
$$$
$$$
$$$
$$$
$$$
$$$
$$$
$$$

SCHEDULE C 1965   acme visible records inc   STEELEY SYSTEMS
LTD   american hospital supply corp   TEXPACK LTD   ameroc
k   HAHN BRASS LTD   'mor ele   co   A HORN ELEVATOR CO
LTD   barringham   cs ltd   3-HERSEY TUBES LTD (PLAST
IC PIPE MILLS ONLY   .iss & l   in industries inc   FRANK
DOERNER & SONS LTD   .orp   MINNESOTA AND ONTA
RIO PAPER CO   .ON STATIONERS & ENV
ELOPES LTD   .rk)   LONDON PUR
E MILK CO   .an   :ted and bathur
st paper li   .x VALLE   .P   .R LIMITED
burlington   anada) l   urlin.   industries inc
us)   TRIC(nada vin   ltd (cerebos ltd)   GEOR
GIAN BAY F.   TD   SMA   OTHERS LTD   canadian a
cceptance c   t financ   orp us)   HOLT RENFREW AN
D CO LTD   dustries   CAMPBELL MANUFACTURING
CO   canac   es ltd   ISH AMERICAN PAINT CO LTD
charter   ltd   I   RK WIRE WORKS LTD   con
trol data can   'rol da   rp usa)   (COMPUTER SYSTE
MS DIVISION OF   VICI   crown zellerbach canada
ltd (crown zelle   .   als ltd   S M SIMPSON LTD
cynamid of ca   cynamid co)   RAINBOW CHE
MICALS LTD   dan   .IAN TRACTION LTD   de
nver chemical manu   .F CANADA LTD   domi
nion dairies limit   N..   .CTS CORP   domini
on dairies limited   iona.   .orp)   WHITFIELD-
MORRISON DAIRY   sharp in   N CHEMICALS INDU
STRIES INC   exq   e form b   ) ltd   PARADIS
E CRINOLINES LTD   quisite   .nada) ltd   L
AWSONIT PRODUCTS I   f m c :   .e.   als lts (f m
c corporation (of   sa))   H   L.   .tkote compan
y of canada ltd   X COMPA.   )   coach of can
ada ltd (divco-way   .p)   ES   INDU   D   genera
l plastics co (wal   silversm   .canac   f toronto in
turn a sub of hami   vatch co   .CON I   LTD   gene
ral signal corp   .N INDUS   LTD   -national ba
tteries inc   MARV   .DUCTS   eat pl   elopment co
of canada   WESTB(IL DEVEL   T LTD   .t western ga
rment   ltd (levi   ass & co   ITCHF   Y GARMENTS LT
D   en giant   CLARK FO   TD   .und lines of
can   (greyh(f the un   st.   .NSTER TRANSPOR
T CO   'EWST.   KY MOUNT   )   imperial
tobac   ..   CANADA F   .erial tobacco c
o of c   .rial tobacco co
of canac   .nemical corporatio
n   RINSh.   international util
ities corp   .amloops pulp and pape
r co ltd (weye..   .T DIAMOND MILLS LTD
kitchen installat   .u   ...   RODUCTS LTD   the kiwi p
olish company (ca   limited (polish co - pty melbourne
australia   TILLEY   ITED   r brothers ltd (unilever)
     WOODBRIDGE MOULDED PRODUCTS LTD   lightolier inc   MODULI
E INC   lockwood kessler & bartlett inc   HUNTING SURVEY CO
RP LTD   lunkeheimer-morrison canada ltd   JAMES MORRISON BR

279

SCHEDULE D 1966

```
          O SEE CAN A DA
          BY THE DOOM'S EARLY LIGHT
          HOW SO LOUDLY WE FAILED
          AT THE TWILIGHT'S FIRST DAWNING
          WHOSE BLOOD STARS BLIGHTED STRIPES
          THROUGH THE PERILOUS NIGHT
          O'ER THE RAMPARTS WE WATCHED
          CAME SO ENDLESSLY SCREAMING

          AND THE ROCKETS RED GLARE
          THE BOMBS BURSTING IN AIR
          GIVE PROOF THRU THE NIGHT THAT
          THE DEATH COMES FROM THERE

          O SAY
                DOES    THAT
          STAR — SPANGLED
                            BANNER
                                      NOW
          WAVE
          O'ER THE LAND OF THE CREE
          THE HOME OF THE BRAVE
```

```
                                    deaths
                                    eathss
                                    athsss
                                    thssss
                                    hsssss
                                    ssssss
                                    ssssss$
                                    ssss$$
                                    sss$$$
                                    ss$$$$
                                    s$$$$$
                                    $$$$$$
                                    $$$$$d
                                    $$$$de
                                    $$$dea
                                    $$deat
                                    $death
                                    deaths
                                    eathss
                                    athsss
                                    thssss
                                    hsssss
                                    ssssss
                                    sssss$
                                    ssss$$
                                    sss$$$
                                    ss$$$$
                                    s$$$$$
                                    $$$$$$
                                    $$$$$d
                                    $$$$de
                                    $$$dea
                                    $$deat
                                    $death
                                    deaths
                                    eathss
                                    athsss
                                    thssss
                                    hsssss
                                    ssssss
                                    sssss$
                                    ssss$$
                                    sss$$$
                                    ss$$$$
                                    s$$$$$
                                    $$$$$$
                                    $$$$$d
                                    $$$$de
                                    $$$dea
                                    $$deat
                                    $death
```

Bibliography

I. Primary Sources

Acorn, Milton. *I've Tasted My Blood*, ed. Al Purdy. Toronto: Ryerson, 1969.

Atwood, Margaret. *The Animals in that Country*. Toronto: Oxford University Press, 1968.

————. *The Circle Game*. Toronto: Contact Press, 1966; House of Anansi, 1967.

————. *The Journals of Susanna Moodie*. Toronto: Oxford University Press, 1970.

————. *Power Politics*. Toronto: House of Anansi, 1971.

————. *Procedures for Underground*. Toronto: Oxford University Press, 1970.

Avison, Margaret. *The Dumbfounding*. New York: Norton, 1966.

————. Thirteen Poems. *Origin*, No. 4 (January , 1962), pp. 1-21.

————. *Winter Sun*. Toronto: University of Toronto Press, 1960.

Birney, Earle. *The Creative Writer*. Toronto: CBC Publications, 1966.

————. *Rag and Bone Shop*. Toronto: McClelland and Stewart, 1971.

————. *Selected Poems*. Toronto: McClelland and Stewart, 1966.

Bowering, George. *Rocky Mountain Foot*. Toronto: McClelland and Stewart, 1969.

Cohen, Leonard. *Let Us Compare Mythologies*. Toronto: Contact Press, 1956; McClelland and Stewart, 1966.

————. *Flowers for Hitler*. Toronto: McClelland and Stewart, 1964.

————. *Parasites of Heaven*. Toronto: McClelland and Stewart, 1966.

————. *Songs from a Room*. Columbia Records, 1969.

————. *Songs of Leonard Cohen*. Columbia Records, 1967.

————. *The Spice-Box of Earth*. Toronto: McClelland and Stewart, 1961.

Gallant, Mavis. *My Heart is Broken*. New York: Random House, 1964.

Garner, Hugh. *Hugh Garner's Best Stories*. Toronto: Ryerson, 1963.

Grant, George. *Technology and Empire: Perspectives on North America*. Toronto: House of Anansi, 1967.

Godfrey, Dave, and Mel Watkins, eds., *Gordon to Watkins to You: A Documentary: the Battle for Control of our Economy*. Toronto: new press, 1970.

Hood, Hugh. *Flying a Red Kite.* Toronto: Ryerson, 1962.

Layton, Irving. *Balls for a One-Armed Juggler.* Toronto: McClelland and Stewart, 1963.

—————. *Collected Poems.* Toronto: McClelland and Stewart, 1965.

—————. *Periods of the Moon.* Toronto: McClelland and Stewart, 1967.

—————. *A Red Carpet for the Sun.* Toronto: McClelland and Stewart, 1959.

Laurence, Margaret. *The Tomorrow-Tamer.* London: Macmillan, 1964.

Macpherson, Jay. *The Boatman and other Poems.* Toronto: Oxford University Press, 1968.

Mandel, Eli. *Black and Secret Man.* Toronto: Ryerson, 1964.

—————. *Fuseli Poems.* Toronto: Contact Press, 1960.

—————. *An Idiot Joy.* Edmonton: Hurtig, 1967.

—————. Gael Turnbull, and Phyllis Webb. *Trio.* Toronto: Contact Press, 1954.

Mathews, Robin, and James Steele, eds. *The Struggle for Canadian Universities.* Toronto: new press, 1969.

Mitchell, W.O. *Jake and the Kid.* Toronto: Macmillan, 1961.

Munro, Alice. *Dance of the Happy Shades.* Toronto: Ryerson, 1968.

Newlove, John. *Black Night Window.* Toronto: McClelland and Stewart, 1968.

—————. *The Cave.* Toronto: McClelland and Stewart, 1970.

—————. *Moving in Alone.* Toronto: Contact Press, 1965.

Nichol, b p. *Journeyings and the Returns.* Toronto: Coach House Press, 1967.

—————, ed. *The Cosmic Chef: an Evening of Concrete.* Ottawa: Oberon Press, 1970.

Nowlan, Alden. *Bread, Wine, and Salt.* Toronto: Clarke Irwin, 1967.

—————. *The Mysterious Naked Man.* Toronto: Clarke Irwin, 1969.

—————. *The Things which Are.* Toronto: Contact Press, 1962.

—————. *Wind in a Rocky Country.* Toronto: Emblem Books, 1960.

Page, P. K. *Cry Ararat! Poems New and Selected.* Toronto: McClelland and Stewart, 1967.

Purdy, Alfred. *The Cariboo Horses.* Toronto: McClelland and Stewart, 1966.

—————. *North of Summer.* Toronto: McClelland and Stewart, 1967.

—————. *Poems for All the Annettes.* Toronto: House of Anansi, 1968.

—————. *Wild Grape Wine.* Toronto: McClelland and Stewart, 1968.

Reaney, James. "Editorial," *Alphabet,* No. 4 (June, 1962), p. 3.

—————. *The Killdeer and Other Plays.* Toronto: Macmillan, 1962.

—————. *Twelve Letters to a Small Town.* Toronto: Ryerson, 1962.

Richler, Mordecai. "Quebec Oui, Ottawa Non," *Tamarack Review,* No. 34 (Winter, 1965), pp. 15-35.

Smith, A.J.M., ed., *The Book of Canadian Poetry,* 3rd. ed. Toronto: Gage, 1957.

Solt, Mary Ellen, ed. *Concrete Poetry: A World View.* Bloomington, Indiana: Indiana University Press, 1968.

Souster, Raymond. *As Is.* Toronto: Oxford University Press, 1967.

————————. *The Colour of the Times: Collected Poems.* Toronto: Ryerson, 1964.

————————. *Lost and Found.* Toronto: Clarke Irwin, 1968.

————————. *So Far So Good.* Ottawa: Oberon Press, 1969.

————————. *Ten Elephants on Yonge Street.* Toronto: Ryerson, 1965.

————————, ed. *New Wave Canada: The New Explosion in Canadian Poetry.* Toronto: Contact Press, 1966.

Wilson, Ethel. *Mrs. Golightly and Other Stories.* Toronto: Macmillan, 1961.

II. Secondary Sources

In this section are listed those works to which direct reference is made in the introductory material to this volume.

Bann, Stephen, ed. *Concrete Poetry: An International Anthology.* London: London Magazine Editions, 1967.

Bowering, George. "Acorn Blood," *Canadian Literature,* No. 42 (Autumn, 1969), pp. 84-86.

Creighton, Donald G. *Canada's First Century, 1867-1967.* Toronto: Macmillan, 1970.

Davey, Frank. "Leonard Cohen and Bob Dylan: Poetry and the Popular Song," *Alphabet,* No. 17 (December, 1969), pp. 12-29.

Djwa, Sandra. "Leonard Cohen, Black Romantic," *Canadian Literature,* No. 34 (Autumn, 1967), pp. 32-42.

Doyle, Mike. "Notes on Concrete Poetry," *Canadian Literature,* No. 46 (Autumn, 1970), pp. 91-95.

Dudek, Louis. "Poetry in English," *Canadian Literature,* No. 41 (Summer, 1969), pp. 110-120.

————————. "A Reading of Two Poems by Alden Nowlan," *Fiddlehead,* No. 81 (1969), pp. 51-59.

Francis, Wynne. "Montreal Poets of the Forties," *Canadian Literature,* No. 14 (Autumn, 1962), pp. 21-34.

Gabree, John. *The World of Rock.* Greenwich, Conn.: Fawcett Publications, 1968.

Godfrey, Dave, David Lewis Stein, and Clark Blaise. *New Canadian Writing 1968.* Toronto: Clarke Irwin, 1968.

Grant, George. *Lament for a Nation: the Defeat of Canadian Nationalism.* Toronto: McClelland and Stewart, 1965.

Gustafson, Ralph. "New Wave in Canadian Poetry," *Canadian Literature,* No. 32 (Spring, 1967), pp. 6-14.

Hafferkamp, Jack. "Ladies and Gents, Leonard Cohen," *Rolling Stone,* No. 76 (February 4, 1971), pp. 26, 28.

Harris, Michael. Interview with Leonard Cohen, *Saturday Night,* LXXXIV (June, 1969), pp. 26-30.

Jones, D. G. *Butterfly on Rock: a Study of Themes and Images in Canadian Literature.* Toronto: University of Toronto Press, 1970.

Klinck, Carl F., ed. *Literary History of Canada: Canadian Literature in English.* Toronto: University of Toronto Press, 1965.

Livesay, Dorothy. "Search for a Style: the Poetry of Milton Acorn," *Canadian Literature*, No. 40 (Spring, 1969), pp. 33-42.

McNaught, Kenneth. *The Pelican History of Canada*. London: Penguin, 1969.

Mandel, Eli. *Irving Layton*. Toronto: Forum House, 1969.

Olson, Charles. "Against Wisdom as Such," *Black Mountain Review*, No. 1 (Spring, 1954), pp. 35-39.

Ower, John. "Black and Secret Poet: Notes on Eli Mandel," *Canadian Literature*, No. 42 (Autumn, 1969), pp. 14-25.

Pacey, Desmond. *Creative Writing in Canada*, rev. ed. Toronto: Ryerson, 1961.

————————. Review of *The Cave. Canadian Forum*, L (November-December, 1970), pp. 309-310.

Reaney, James. "The Third Eye: Jay Macpherson's *The Boatman*," *Canadian Literature*, No. 3 (Winter, 1960), pp. 23-34.

Redekop, Ernest. *Margaret Avison*. Toronto: Copp Clarke, 1970.

Spettigue, D. O. "Alice Laidlaw Munro: A Portrait of the Artist," *Alumni Gazette*, U.W.O. XLV, No. 3 (July, 1969), p. 5.

Stephens, Donald. "The Short Story in English," *Canadian Literature*, No. 41 (Summer, 1969), pp. 126-130.

Tallman, Warren. "Poet in Progress: Notes on Frank Davey," *Canadian Literature*, No. 24 (Spring, 1965), pp. 23-27.

Wilson, Edmund. *O Canada: An American's Notes on Canadian Culture*. New York: Farrar, Straus, and Giroux, 1964.

Wilson, Milton. "The Poetry of Margaret Avison," *Canadian Literature*, No. 2 (Autumn, 1959), pp. 47-58.

Woodcock, George. *Odysseus Ever Returning: Essays on Canadian Writers and Writings*. Toronto: McClelland and Stewart, 1970.